Management and Regulation of Pension Schemes

Perhaps the greatest long-term challenge facing modern economies is how to pay for the living expenses and care costs of the elderly. Following policy decisions made in Australia in the 1990s, a substantial part of the pension requirements of the next cohort of retirees will be met from savings accumulated during working years. The effective management of these savings is crucial. If they are invested wisely, the assets available to fund pensions and care will grow; if not, available funds may turn out to be insufficient. Unfortunately, there is considerable evidence worldwide that the management of funds attracts rent-seeking behaviour by the financial services industry which erodes much of the potential return.

Australia introduced compulsory superannuation contributions for its working population in 1991, leading to a proliferation of funded schemes that are largely run by the private sector. Complexity, and many degrees of separation between fund members and those who manage their funds, have emerged as serious problems. Combined with weak competitive pressures and governance systems, and insufficient legal and regulatory constraints, the result is a system that does not serve its members well.

This book provides a detailed evaluation of the Australian experience, highlights the extent to which the financial services industry has extracted rents from Australian pensioners, and how and why this occurred. Based on original empirical research, and on examination of industry reviews and relevant literature, the book demonstrates the numerous principal–agent, conflict of interest and rent extraction problems that have emerged in Australia. As a result, it is estimated that Australian superannuation funds underperformed a passively-managed benchmark by up to A$900 billion during the past 20 years. The book makes suggestions for how these problems can be addressed in Australia, and also provides lessons for other countries wishing to enact pension reform.

Nicholas Morris is an Adjunct Professor in the Faculty of Law, University of New South Wales, Sydney, Australia, He has also served as an economist in the UK Government Economic Service, was Deputy Director of the influential UK policy think-tank, the Institute for Fiscal Studies (IFS), founder and CEO of London Economics, and Senior Research Associate and Academic Visitor at Balliol College, University of Oxford, UK.

Routledge Research in Finance and Banking Law

Available:

Microfinance and Financial Inclusion
The Challenge of Regulating Alternative Forms of Finance
Eugenia Macchiavello

Law and Regulation of Mobile Payment Systems
Issues Arising 'Post' Financial Inclusion in Kenya
Joy Malala

Management and Regulation of Pension Scheme
Australia: A Cautionary Tale
Nicholas Morris

The Regulation and Supervision of Banks
The Post Crisis Regulatory Responses of the EU
Chen Chen Hu

Forthcoming:

Competition Law and Financial Services
David Harrison

Institutional Structure of Financial Regulation
Theories and International Experiences
Robin Hui Huang and Dirk Schoenmaker

Banking and Society
Mapping Financial Regulation and Social Justice for the 21st Century
Gary Wilson and Sarah Wilson

Value Added Tax Fraud
Marius-Cristian Frunza

Management and Regulation of Pension Schemes

Australia – a Cautionary Tale

Nicholas Morris

Routledge
Taylor & Francis Group
LONDON AND NEW YORK

First published 2018 by Routledge

2 Park Square, Milton Park, Abingdon, Oxfordshire OX14 4RN
52 Vanderbilt Avenue, New York, NY 10017

Routledge is an imprint of the Taylor & Francis Group, an informa business

First issued in paperback 2020

British Library Cataloguing in Publication Data
A catalogue record for this book is available from the British Library

Library of Congress Cataloging in Publication Data
Names: Morris, Nicholas (Economist), author.
Title: Management and regulation of pension schemes : Australia–a cautionary tale / Nicholas Morris.
Description: Abingdon, Oxon ; New York, NY : Routledge, 2018. | Series: Routledge research in finance and banking law
Identifiers: LCCN 2017053653| ISBN 9781138287792 (hardback) | ISBN 9781351975155 (epub) | ISBN 9781351975162 (web pdf) | ISBN 9781351975148 (mobipocket)
Subjects: LCSH: Pensions—Australia. | Pensions—Government policy—Australia. | Pension trusts—Australia—Management.
Classification: LCC HD7250 .M67 2018 | DDC 331.25/20994—dc23
LC record available at https://lccn.loc.gov/2017053653

ISBN: 978-1-138-28779-2 (hbk)
ISBN: 978-0-367-59183-0 (pbk)

Typeset in Galliard
by Swales & Willis Ltd, Exeter, Devon, UK

They answered, as they took their fees, “There is no cure for this disease.”
Hilaire Belloc, *Cautionary Verses*

Contents

Acknowledgements and thanks

This book is the result of work carried out between 2012 and 2017 at the Faculty of Law, University of New South Wales, Sydney, Australia.

I would like to thank Professors Hazel Bateman, Ross Buckley, Justin O'Brien and David Vines for their support and encouragement, and particularly for their guidance, which helped to focus a large subject down to something manageable. I would also like to thank my colleagues in the Faculty of Law at UNSW for numerous helpful comments, especially Mark Aronson, John Chellew, Scott Donald, Jonathan Greenacre, Joshua Getzler, Colin Picker, Theunis Roux, Lisa Toohey, Dimity Kingsford Smith and Leon Trakman. Also thanks go to the attendees at various internal UNSW seminars, and at annual CEPAR Colloquia of Superannuation Researchers at which we discussed aspects of my work.

Thank you, too, to Ron Bird, James Cummings, Kevin Liu, Jason Qu, Aaron Skinner, Sue Jaffer and Roy Wilson for suggestions about the empirical work and data, and to Anthony Asher, Michael Ansell, Ron Bird, Jeremy Cooper, Paul Davies and Rob Nicholls for insights into the Australian financial services industry. Thanks also go to Bernard Casey, Leslie Hannah, Stephen King, Robert Marks, Avner Offer, Paul Secunda, Lynn Stout, Susan Thorp and Noel Whiteside for recommendations about appropriate literature.

I am also grateful to Rotman ICPM, Toronto, for permission to use the CEM dataset of international comparator funds, and to APRA for making available data on superannuation funds which had been withdrawn from circulation.

Finally, I would like to thank my family for their tolerance and encouragement, and especially my wife, Sue.

Nicholas Morris
October 2017

Table of statutes

(arranged by date order)

Australian Constitution 1901

Invalid and Old-age Pensions Act 1908

Income Tax (Assessment) Act 1915

Financial Relief Acts 1932, 1934, 1935 and 1937

US Securities Act 1933 (Glass Steagal)

Income Tax (Assessment) Act 1936

Superannuation and Family Benefits Act 1938

US Investment Company Act 1940

Commonwealth Bank Act 1945

Life Insurance Act 1945

Social Services Consolidation Act 1947

Stevedoring Industry Act 1949

Income Tax and Social Services Contribution Assessment Act 1961

Insurance Act 1973

UK Fair Trading Act 1973

Family Law Act 1975

Insurance (Agents and Brokers) Act 1984

UCITS Directive and the Directive on Markets in Financial Instruments, Council Directive of 20 December 1985

UK Financial Services Act 1986

Occupational Superannuation Standards Act 1987 (OSSA)

National Corporations Act 1991

Corporations (Unlisted Property Trusts) Act 1991

Superannuation Guarantee (Administration) Act 1992

Superannuation Guarantee Charge Act 1992

Income Tax (Assessment) Act 1993

Superannuation Industry (Supervision) Act 1993 (SIS Act)

Superannuation Industry (Supervision) Regulations 1994

Life Insurance Act 1995

Income Tax Assessment Act 1997

Payment Systems (Regulation) Act 1998

Payment Systems and Netting Act 1998

Managed Investment Act 1998 (MIA)

Australian Prudential Authority Act 1998

Competition Act 1998 (UK)

UK Competition Act 1998

Superannuation Legislation Amendment Act (No. 3) 1999 (SLAA3)

Corporate Law Economic Reform Program Act 1999 (CLERPA)

Gramm-Leach-Bliley Act of 1999 (Act of 12 November 1999, Pub L 106–102), which set aside the protections of the Glass-Steagal Act of 1933 (Act of 16 June 1933, ch 89, 48 Stat 162).

US Gramm-Leach-Bliley Act 1999

Corporations Act 2001

Corporations Regulations 2001

Financial Services Reform Act 2001 (FSRA)

Corporations (Financial Services Reform Amendments) Act 2002

Superannuation Legislation Amendment (Choice of Superannuation Funds) Bill 2002

Enterprise Act 2002 (UK)

UK Enterprise Act 2002

US Global Legal Settlement 2002

US Sarbanes-Oxley Act 2002

Superannuation Safety Amendment Act 2004

Directive 2004/39/EC of the European Parliament and of the Council of 21 April 2004 on markets in financial instruments

Tax Laws Amendment (Simplified Superannuation) Act 2007

Tax Laws Amendment (2008 Measures No. 1) Bill 2008

Same-Sex Relationships (Equal Treatment in Commonwealth Laws – Superannuation) Act 2008

Temporary Residents' Superannuation Legislation Amendment Act 2008

Pensions Act 2008 (UK)

Tax Laws Amendment (2009 Budget Measures No. 1) Act 2009

Corporations Amendment Regulations 2012, Nos 4, 8, 10

Corporations Amendment (Future of Financial Advice) Act 2012

Corporations Amendment (Further Future of Financial Advice Measures) Act 2012 (FOFA Acts)

Superannuation Legislation Amendment (Trustee Obligations and Prudential Standards) Act 2012

Corporations Amendment (Intra-fund Advice Fees) Regulation 2013

Corporations Amendment Regulations 2013, Nos 2, 3, 4, 5

Corporations Amendment (Intra-fund Advice Fees) Regulation 2013

Table of cases

Aronson v Lewis, 473 A 2d 805, 812 (Del, 1984)

Australian Securities and Investments Commission (ASIC) v ABC Fund Managers Ltd (2001) 39 ACSR 443, 125 (Warren J)

Beach Petroleum v Kennedy (1999) 48 NSWLR 1, 188

Bray v Ford [1896] AC 44, 51

Dillon v Burns Philp Finance Ltd (Unreported, Supreme Court of New South Wales, Bryson J, 20 July 1988)

Fairfax v Federal Commissioner of Taxation (1965) 114 CLR 1

National Wage Case – June 1986 (1986) 301 CAR 611

Phipps v Boardman [1967] 2 AC 46, 123

Sayseng v Kellogg Superannuation Pty Ltd [2007] NSWSC 1009 (12 September 2007)

Smith v Van Gorkom, 488 A 2d 858 (Del, 1985)

Vidovic v Email Superannuation (Unreported, Supreme Court of New South Wales, Bryson J, 3 March 1995)

Wingecarribee Shire Council v Lehman Brothers Australia Ltd (in liq) [2012] FCA 1028

Abbreviations

AAA	American Arbitration Association
AASB	Australian Accounting Standards Board
ABI	Association of British Insurers
ABS	Australian Bureau of Statistics
ACCC	Australian Competition and Consumer Commission
ACF	Australian Capital Fund
ACSI	Australian Council of Superannuation Investors
ACTU	Australian Council of Trade Unions
ADIs	authorised deposit-taking institutions
AE	allocative efficiency
AFA	Association of Financial Advisers
AFT	Australian Fixed Trusts
AFP	Administradoras de Fondos de Pensiones (Chile)
AGSM	Australian Graduate School of Management
AHV	Alters und Hinterlassen Enversicherung (Switzerland)
AIPA	Australian Investment Planner's Association
AIST	Australian Institute of Superannuation Trustees
ALP	Australian Labor Party
ALRC	Australian Law Reform Commission
AMP	Australian Mutual Provident
ANZ	Australia and New Zealand Banking Group Ltd
AOW	Algemeene Onderdomswet (Netherlands)
APRA	Australian Prudential Regulatory Authority
APRC	Australian Prudential Regulation Commission
ARF	Australian Retirement Fund
ASFA	Association of Superannuation Funds of Australia
ASIC	Australian Securities and Investment Commission
ASX	Australian Stock Exchange
ATO	Australian Taxation Office
ATP	Arbejdsmarkedets Tillaegspension (Denmark)
AUST	Allied Unions Superannuation Trust
BCA	Business Council of Australia

BHS	British Home Stores
BIS	Bank for International Settlements
BT	Bankers Trust
BUS	Building Unions Superannuation Scheme
CAI	Confederation of Australian Industry
CAP	Committee of Advertising Practice
CASAC	Companies and Securities Advisory Committee
CBC	Commercial Banking Company
CBUSS	Construction and Building Unions Superannuation Scheme (later CBUS)
CEM	CEM Benchmarking, Inc., Toronto
CEO	Chief Executive Officer
CFR	Council of Financial Regulators
CFSC	Corporations and Financial Services Commission
CFTC	Commodities and Futures Trading Commission
CIPR	comprehensive income product for retirement
CLERPA	Corporate Law Economic Reform Program Act 1999
CMSF	Conference of Major Superannuation Funds
CMT	cash management trust
CRS	constant returns to scale
Cth	Commonwealth
D&P	Dyck and Pomorsky
DB	defined benefit
DC	defined contribution
DEA	data envelopment analysis
DMFs	discretionary mutual funds
EE	economic efficiency
ER	expense ratio
ERF	eligible rollover fund
ESOP	employee stock ownership plan
FAUT	First Australian Unit Trust
FCA	Financial Conduct Authority (UK)
FICA	Finance Industry Council of Australia
FINRA	Financial Industry Regulatory Authority
FOFA	Future of Financial Advice
FPA	Financial Planning Association
FRM	fractional response model
FSI	Financial System Inquiry 2014
FSA	Financial Services Authority (UK)
FSCS	Financial Services Compensation Scheme (UK)
FSPU	Federated Storemen and Packers Union
FSRA	Financial Services Reform Act 2001
FST	First State Superannuation
FTSE	Financial Times and Stock Exchange
FUM	funds under management

G&S	Galagedera and Silvapulle
GDP	gross domestic product
GFC	global financial crisis
Govt.	government
GPIF	Nenkin Tsumitate-kin Kanri Un'yō Dokuritsu-gyōsei-Hōjin (Japan)
GRV	Gesetzliche Rentenversicherung (Germany)
HM	Her Majesty's
HOCOLEA	Heads of Commonwealth Operational Law Enforcement Agencies
HSBC	Hong Kong and Shanghai Banking Corporation
ICB	Independent Commission on Banking (UK)
ICPM	(Rotman) International Centre for Pension Management
IDPS	Investor-Directed Portfolio Service
IFA	Investment Funds Association
IFM	Industry Funds Management
IFPP	Industry Fund Financial Planning
IFS	Industry Fund Services
IFSA	Investment and Financial Services Association
IIM	Integrity Investment Management
IRA	individual retirement arrangements (US)
IRC	Industrial Relations Commission
IRR	internal rate of return
ISC	Insurance and Superannuation Commission
ISE	International Securities Exchange
KPIs	key performance indicators
LISTO	low income superannuation tax offset
LP	linear programming
LPT	listed property trust
LSE	London Stock Exchange
LUCRF	Labour Union Co-operative Retirement Fund
M&A	mergers and acquisitions
MER	management expense ratio
MIA	Managed Investment Act 1998
MLC	Mutual Life Company (National Australia Bank)
MRSB	Municipal Securities Regulatory Board
MSCI	MSCI Inc. (US)
NAB	National Australia Bank
NASD	National Association of Securities Dealers
NBER	National Bureau for Economic Research (US)
NBFI	non-bank financial institution
NCC	National Consumer Council (UK)
NCSC	National Companies and Securities Commission
NCSI	National Superannuation Committee of Inquiry
NEST	National Employment Savings Trust (UK)
NGC	National Guarantee Fund
NZ	New Zealand

NYSE	New York Stock Exchange
OASDI	Old Age, Survivors, and Disability Insurance (US)
OECD	Organisation for Economic Cooperation and Development
OEIC	Open Ended Investment Company
OFT	Office of Fair Trading (UK)
OSSA	Occupational Superannuation Standards Act
PAIRS	probability and impact rating system
PAS	productivity award superannuation
PAYG	pay-as-you-go
PCAOB	Public Company Accounting Oversight Board (US)
PDS	Product Disclosure Statement
PFAC	Phillips Fox Actuaries and Consultants
PIG	public interest group
PJCCFS	Parliamentary Joint Committee on Corporations and Financial Services
PPG	Prudential Practice Guide
PPI	payment protection insurance
RBA	Reserve Bank of Australia
RBL	Reasonable Benefit Limit
RBS	Royal Bank of Scotland
RE	responsible entity
REIT	Real Estate Investment Trust
REST	Retail Employees Superannuation Trust
RFCs	registered financial corporations
ROA	return on assets
RPP	registered pension plan (Canada)
RRSP	registered retirement savings plan (Canada)
RSE	registrable superannuation entity
S&P	Standard and Poors
SAF	small APRA fund
SEC	Securities and Exchange Commission
SEGC	Securities Exchanges Guarantee Corporation Limited
SERF	Stevedoring Employees Retirement Fund
SERPS	State Earnings Related Pension Scheme (UK)
SGC	superannuation guarantee charge
SIH	Survey of Income and Housing
SIPC	Securities Investor Protection Corporation (US)
SIPF	Securities Investor Protection Fund (China)
SIS Act	Superannuation Industry (Supervision) Act 1993
SMSF	self-managed superannuation fund
SOARS	supervisory oversight and response system
SRF	Seafarers Retirement Fund
STA	Superannuation Trust of Australia
T&G	Temperance and General (Mutual Life Association)
TE	technical efficiency

TEA	Trustees, Executor and Agency Co.
TFT	'tit-for-tat'
UBS	Union Bank of Switzerland
UFT	universal flexible trusts
UNSW	University of New South Wales
UTAA	Unit Trust Association of Australia
VRS	variable returns to scale
WWF	Waterside Workers Federation

1 Introduction and overview

In the early 1990s, Australia took important decisions to require its population to save for retirement, introducing a *Superannuation Guarantee Charge*, which is currently 9.5% of earnings. As a result, superannuation funds today comprise a significant proportion of Australian personal wealth.[1] Their effective management and regulation, the subject of this book, is vital for the well-being of Australian retirees. Unfortunately, the Australian superannuation system exhibits numerous problems including that it currently delivers an income replacement rate for retirees that is among the lowest in the OECD, that it forces fund members to bear risks they are ill-equipped to manage, and that it provides significantly poorer returns on investment than could reasonably have been expected.

In Section 2.1, we consider the design of the Australian system that has led to these outcomes. This begins by evaluating three fundamental policy choices: whether to use a pay-as-you-go (PAYG) or a funded system; whether to allocate pensions on a defined benefit (DB) or a defined contribution (DC) basis; and whether the public or the private sector should manage the funds. For historical and ideological reasons set out in Chapter 3, Australia chose the latter option in each case (funded, DC and privately managed). The outcomes we describe in this book, and much of the relevant literature, suggest that the former would have been a better choice (PAYG, DB and publicly managed).

Empirical estimates presented in Chapter 4 show that, over the last 20 years, the Australian superannuation industry has delivered a return of A$700–900 billion less for its members than it could have if different policy choices had been made.[2] The result is that Australia's superannuation funds, instead of potentially being worth around A$3 trillion, are now only worth around A$2.2 trillion[3]

1 In 2013–2014, superannuation comprised 17% of household assets, figures based on the latest Survey of Income and Housing (SIH). Australian Bureau of Statistics, 'Household Income and Wealth, Australia, 2013–14' (6523.0, 4 September 2015).

2 The calculations leading to these estimates of shortfall are described in detail in Chapter 4.

3 Australian Prudential Regulation Authority (2017) 'Quarterly Superannuation Performance June 2017' (APRA, 22 August 2017) 8, available at www.apra.gov.au/Super/Publications/Documents/2017QSP201706.pdf. Note: A$ = Australian dollar. In all subsequent Sections, '$' refers to the Australian dollar, except where specified otherwise, for example 'US$'.

(a cumulative shortfall equivalent to about 45% of Australia's annual Gross Domestic Product (GDP)).[4] This shortfall is, in large part, a reflection of the high costs of the superannuation industry that has been created to manage the funds.

The industry that has emerged in Australia is complex, to an extent that it is imperfectly understood by policymakers and by most members. As Section 2.2 explores, this facilitates rent extraction and works against policy reform. Complexity strengthens the hand of those who seek to manipulate the system for their own benefit, while making it difficult or impossible for regulators and representatives of fund members to ensure that returns are maximised and costs minimised. The more complex the industry, the less likely are members (and trustees on their behalf) to be able to negotiate an acceptable outcome.

International literature highlights how principal-agent and conflict of interest problems abound in financial services, and demonstrates that a high proportion of the potential return to investors from managed funds is routinely extracted by fund managers (and associated intermediaries) through excessive fees and charges. In Australia competitive pressures, governance systems, and legal and regulatory constraints, appear to have been inadequate to curtail *rent-seeking behaviour* by advisers and managers.[5] Competition and choice do not seem to work well enough in this industry to impose the necessary constraints, partly because of a lack of transparency over costs. The high degree of separation between members and those who manage their funds, a result of extensive outsourcing, both increases costs (because all the intermediaries charge a margin) and reduces focus. In addition, individuals in DC schemes face severe longevity and market risks, the management of which (including the provision of fairly priced products) has so far received insufficient attention. In Section 2.3, the reasons why stronger and more effective regulation is therefore needed are discussed.

Other countries, notably the UK, are now following Australia down the path of introducing more individually funded, defined contribution pensions, and reducing reliance on both publicly funded and defined benefit provision while increasing the proportion of funds outsourced to private sector managers. This book highlights the dangers of these changes, and how such moves impose greater risks and welfare losses on retirees, current and future. Although Australia

4 2015–2016 GDP was A$1.66 trillion, Australian Bureau of Statistics (2017) '1345.0 – Key Economic Indicators, 2017', available at www.abs.gov.au/ausstats/abs@.nsf/Latestproducts/1345.0Main%20Features12017?opendocument&tabname=Summary&prodno=1345.0&issue=2017&num=&view=.

5 Economists use the term 'rent' to capture the idea of excess payments, over and above what would normally be considered necessary, an idea that dates back to the work of Gordon Tullock: Tullock, Gordon (1967) 'The Welfare Costs of Tariffs, Monopolies and Theft' 5 *Western Economic Journal* 3, 224–332. See Congleton, Roger D., Arye L. Hillman and Kai A. Konrad (eds) (2008) *Forty Years of Research on Rent Seeking 1 – Theory of Rent Seeking* (Springer, Heidelberg), 45–53; Hillman, Arye L. and Heinrich W. Ursprung (2015) 'Rent Seeking: The Idea, the Reality, and the Ideological Resistance' (paper presented at the Department of Economics, International Trade and Development Seminar, University of Pittsburgh, 7 October 2015), available at www.econ.pitt.edu/sites/default/files/Hillman.Rent%20seeking.2015.pdf.

is our primary focus, Section 2.4 includes brief summaries of the policy choices made by a number of other countries. This is partly to inform analysis of the Australian situation, and partly to draw out the lessons that can be learned from the Australian case that may be relevant to other countries as they develop their own pension systems.

Section 2.5 summarises the challenges Australia now faces. These include that those about to retire will do so with inadequate pensions; high administration and fund management costs; a lack of trust in the industry and its advisers; and the transfer of risks to individuals who are poorly equipped to manage them. Legal and regulatory constraints and guidance provided by a combination of trust law, the *Superannuation Industry (Supervision) Act* (SIS Act), and the various regulatory agencies in Australia need rationalising and strengthening. Organisation and governance of the system also needs overhaul, and action is required to assist members with the risk management that has been imposed on them. Although large tax concessions have been provided to encourage contributions to superannuation funds, these have been disproportionately available to the rich, while the poorest individuals suffer from paying contributions they cannot afford, while receiving little or no tax benefit. As a result of all these issues, the Australian system can best be described, after 25 years, as still a work-in-progress.

Chapter 3 describes how the Australian system, and the financial industry which supports it, evolved. Australia developed a 'three pillar' system, with a means-tested old-age pension enhanced by charitable giving, occupational and public sector schemes, and voluntary savings encouraged by tax incentives. This history is presented in four epochs, with the final one starting with the introduction of the *Superannuation Guarantee Charge* in 1992. The situation today is that Australia has the highest incidence of poverty, among the old, in the OECD.

Superannuation policy in Australia has suffered from the 'stop-go' effects of a short electoral cycle and the tendency of incoming governments to overturn policies initiated by their predecessors. In the post-war period, the influence of the union movement and its interface with Labor administrations also had a crucial impact. Australian superannuation policy also reflected developments in Europe, the UK and the US, and, in particular, ideological struggles between those who believed in public control and administration, and those who believed in the primacy and efficiency of markets. Section 3.8 describes the reasons why strategy for, and management of, superannuation funds was to a large extent handed over to the private sector, Section 3.9 discusses how the modern legal and regulatory framework evolved, and Section 3.10 sets out how the modern superannuation industry emerged. A timeline of key legislation and events from 1849 to the present is provided in Annex A.

Chapter 4 seeks to benchmark the investment performance of Australian superannuation funds against what might have been possible if different policy choices about the management of the funds had been made. Section 4.3 shows that Australia's retirees will be considerably poorer than they would have been if drafted was less prescriptive than might have been possible in terms of setting out the required conduct of trustees and managers. It would be possible to redress this through new legislation, using precedents from other industries. The Australian telecommunications industry, for example, has developed codes of conduct that are agreed between the industry and its regulators, but which become 'mandatory on breach' and subject to penalties. We explore the extent to which this idea could be adapted to superannuation.

Section 6.4 raises the possibility that competition law could be applied more vigorously to superannuation, in order to reduce cross subsidies and anti-competitive behaviour. This is something that has received considerable attention in other countries since the Global Financial Crisis (GFC), and in other industries, where vertically integrated companies have been unbundled. Attention needs to be paid by the competition authorities both to the incidence of cross subsidy and about preferential access to information. A further problem in the superannuation industry is lack of consumer response to variations in cost and performance. Better disclosure and publication of benchmarks would assist in this process, but the key is to ensure that trustees both understand and take action about these issues.

A major problem with the Australian superannuation industry is lack of disclosure of all costs. Despite this issue being raised in all reviews since the industry was established, so far regulators have not succeeded in forcing the industry to disclose fully the costs of outsourced activities, especially funds management. Section 6.5 explains how the industry has argued successfully that it is sufficient to simply report net-of-costs performance, and that disclosure of the underlying cost structures of various intermediaries is unnecessary. While this might be true if (a) performance was properly measured and presented, and comparison between funds understood by all stakeholders, and (b) competitive pressures did indeed exert discipline on those who sought to overcharge, neither condition holds in the Australian context. We argue, therefore, that attention to better disclosure and publication of relative costs is urgently needed.

In Section 6.6 we conclude by putting forward an innovative idea, that a new, publicly administered, fund be established with a mandate to provide a low cost, passively managed investment vehicle. Migration to this fund, which is likely to easily outperform, after costs, the majority of existing funds, should be encouraged, and the government should provide active and well-publicised support to its development. The new fund would then provide a clear benchmark against which the performance of other funds could be judged. In addition, it would be able to assist its members with risk management, and, in particular, the management of longevity risk.

How to manage pension funds effectively is one of the most important policy questions of our age. All countries, rich and poor, are struggling with questions of how to finance the retirement and healthcare costs of an increasingly long-lived population. Australia responded to this 25 years ago by compelling its population to save throughout their working lives. However, this is only the first part of a three-part story: once the assets have been accumulated, it is also important that they are managed well, and not dissipated in excessive fees and charges or mismanagement. And then it is crucial that individuals are assisted with the risks they face during retirement, not least uncertain longevity. So far, Australia has not done so well with these parts.

This book sets out what has gone wrong, how it happened, and the results of these mistakes. It also suggests a variety of ways of fixing the problem, including improvements to regulatory structure, legislation, market discipline and transparency. Hopefully, these will eventually lead to the development of a well-run, simpler system that meets the needs of Australia's retirees better. I also hope that other countries will take note of Australia's mistakes, and ensure their superannuation systems perform at their best to meet the needs of future retirees.

2 System design and problems

> . . .there are enormous risks in bringing together deep-pocketed investors who are not adequately conscious of prices and risks, and the highly motivated private financial sector.
>
> Raghuram G. Rajan[1]

Migration of the Australian Superannuation system to a funded, defined contribution (DC) system, predominately managed by the private sector, was always likely to generate worse outcomes for Australian retirees than if a pay-as-you-go, defined benefit (DB) system, with appropriate elements of public management and provision, had been chosen.[2] The choice of a PAYG system would have permitted those who are now retiring, or have retired in the last few decades, to be supported better without hurting future generations. The choice of defined benefit schemes would have enabled risks, particularly of individual longevity, to be shared between members of each scheme, and reduced the need, for example, to purchase expensive annuities.

Although the prevailing ethos of the time was that private sector management of superannuation funds would be superior to public provision, with hindsight this has not turned out be the case, and the choice of predominately private sector management has led to many of the problems explored in this book. The legal and governance framework has allowed conflict of interest problems to arise and

1 Rajan, Raghuram G. (2010) *Fault Lines: How Hidden Fractures Still Threaten the World Economy* (Princeton University Press), 132. Rajan was Governor of the Reserve Bank of India until September 2016 and is now the Katherine Dusak Miller Distinguished Service Professor of Finance at the University of Chicago, Booth School of Business.

2 For definition and discussion of these terms, please see Section 2.1 'The structure of pension systems' below. In a PAYG system, the pensions of those who are currently retired are paid for through taxation, or through other contributions made by those who are currently working. In a funded system, the pensions are paid out of funds that have previously been accumulated. 'Defined contribution' (DC) systems limit pension payments to those possible with the funds they have themselves contributed, while 'defined benefit' (DB) systems pay pensions based on a set of rules, which usually include final salary or some other measure of earnings during the individual's working life,

failed to enforce fiduciary duties and duties of care. There are too many regulatory agencies, with inadequate focus on costs and performance. As described in detail below, these failures have led to the creation of a complex and expensive industry which performs poorly by international standards.

Those who were responsible for Australia's policy choices in the 1990s could reasonably have been expected to understand these potential problems. The merits of pay-as-you-go and defined benefit systems were widely discussed in the international literature prior to these decisions being taken. Evidence from the UK and Chile, which had both introduced decentralised systems, was available to show that such systems had surprisingly high costs.[3] The necessary calculations are not difficult: the US Advisory Council of Social Security,[4] for example, has estimated that the costs of such a system, even in a properly competitive environment, could easily amount to 100 basis points or more per year, and hence consume about 20% of the value of accumulated funds over a 40-year work career.[5] In contrast, the Council estimated that a system with centralised management and more limited investment options could be managed for roughly 10 basis points per year, consuming only 2% of the accumulated value.[6]

Australian workers are now required to fund, mostly through contributions made on their behalf by employers, a substantial part of the cost of their retirement, with the majority relying on expensive private sector management of the accumulated funds.[7] In addition, encouraging Australian fund members to move out of defined benefit and into defined contribution regimes has transferred the risk of underperformance from fund sponsors to (less well informed) members, and denied them the advantages of risk pooling. The consequences of both are that the assets available to support retirement for many Australians (despite substantial and growing contributions) are less than they could have been, and the development of an overly complex system with attendant high costs and risks.

3 Diamond, Peter (1998) 'The Economics of Social Security Reform' in R. Douglas, Michael J. Gratz and Alicia H. Munnell (eds) *Framing the Social Security Debate: Values, Politics and Economics* (Brookings Institutional Press); Congressional Budget Office (1999) 'Social Security Privatisation: Experiences Abroad' (Paper, January 1999).

4 USA Social Security Administration (1997) *Report of the 1994–1996 Advisory Council on Social Security* (January 1997), available at www.ssa.gov/history/reports/adcouncil/report/toc.htm.

5 This point has also been emphasised more recently by William Sharpe: "A person saving for retirement who chooses low-cost investments could have a standard of living throughout retirement more than 20% higher than that of a comparable investor in high-cost investments." Sharpe, William F. (2103) 'The Arithmetic of Investment Expenses' 69 *Financial Analysts Journal* 2, 34–41.

6 Figures quoted in Orszag, Peter R. and Joseph E. Stiglitz (2001) 'Rethinking Pension Reform: Ten Myths about Social Security Systems' in Robert Holzman and Joseph E. Stiglitz (eds) *New Ideas about Old Age Security* (World Bank), 35.

7 In some cases, for example *retail funds* managed by the banks, the private sector does this directly. In the case of *industry funds* and *government funds*, much of the management is outsourced to private sector managers.

2.1 The structure of pension systems

The public finance literature often describes pension systems as consisting of two 'tiers' or 'pillars'. The first tier is provision by government, often funded on a pay-as-you-go basis from tax revenue, but sometimes from hypothecated funds. This can take the form of a 'basic' pension, sometimes means-tested or related to contributions made during working life, 'minimum' pensions, or social assistance.[8] The second tier consists of public or private earnings-related schemes, which can take the form of *defined benefit* (DB – where entitlement is determined by rules based on the number of years of contribution and earnings, with variants) or *defined contribution* (DC – where contributions flow into an account for each individual, which is then available to fund their own benefits).[9] All OECD countries except Ireland and New Zealand have some form of mandatory second-tier provision, with mandatory private schemes in Iceland, the Netherlands and Switzerland. Sometimes countries use points (France, Estonia, Germany and Slovakia) or notional-accounts (Italy, Norway, Poland and Sweden) to determine entitlement to benefits.[10]

Pension systems are needed whenever the savings accumulated, or insurance purchases made, by the currently retiring generation are insufficient to maintain an acceptable living standard in retirement.[11] However, the introduction of a pension system has important effects on the economy, especially on the level of the capital stock, especially if forced saving – as in the Australian case – leads to greater incomes in retirement than the population would naturally choose. The interaction between pensions and other sources of income is also likely to affect the retirement decision itself.[12] For all these reasons, the effective management

8 See OECD (2015) *Pensions at a Glance 2015: OECD and G20 indicators* (OECD Publishing, Paris), http://dx.doi.org/10.1787/pension_glance-2015-en, 124, Architecture of National Pension Systems, for a detailed discussion of these various arrangements. In total, 18 OECD countries provide basic pensions, while 13 provide minimum pensions.

9 Larry Willmore, in an article written for the United Nations in 1998, makes the further distinction between forced and voluntary saving, noting that there is no consensus on whether the forced saving pillar should be administered by the public or the private sector, but noting that "public systems can . . . achieve a[n] equitable treatment of contributors while retaining low administrative costs and providing social insurance that is either expensive or unavailable in private markets". Willmore, Larry (1999) 'Public versus Private Provision of Pensions' (Discussion Paper of the United Nations Department of Economic and Social Affairs, revised June 1999), available at www.un.org/esa/esa98dp1.pdf.

10 For a full discussion of pension management and its implications, see Ambachtsheer, Keith P. (2016) *The Future of Pension Management: Integrating Design, Governance, and Investing* (Wiley).

11 See Kotlikoff, L.J. (1989) 'On the Contribution of Economics to the Evaluation and Formation of Social Insurance Policy' *American Economic Review*, Papers and Proceedings, 77, 184–190.

12 Social security has been shown to have a significant impact on labour supply decisions, particularly for women (who typically are more price-elastic). See Michael J. Boskin (1998) 'Sooner is Better in Social Security Reform' (National Academy of Social Science, Social Security Brief 2, September 1998) for a general discussion of the impact on the retirement decision. However, Kotlikoff has shown that, under assumptions of perfect capital markets, actuarial fairness and known lifespan, the provision of social security will not affect the retirement decision, because pensions simply substitute for private savings. Kotlikoff, L.J. (1979) 'Social Security and Equilibrium Capital Intensity' 93 *Quarterly Journal of Economics*, 233–253.

and regulation of pension schemes is of crucial importance for the efficient functioning of the economy, as well as for the welfare of retired people.[13] In order to explore what might, in principle, be the best way of organising a pension system, three different choices are discussed below: funding vs pay-as-you-go; defined benefit vs defined contribution; and privately vs publicly managed.[14]

Increasingly, pension providers around the world are using private institutions to manage the retirement savings of their account holders and members. This, plus switching from defined benefit to defined contribution schemes (which transfers risk to fund members), creates responsibility for regulatory agencies to ensure that members' interests are properly reflected in institutional behaviour. This point has recently been emphasised by Jeremy Cooper, chair of a recent review of the Australian superannuation system, who has argued that pushing responsibility for risk down to the individual creates a "high degree of cognitive and other inefficiencies" which need correcting.[15]

2.1.1 Funding vs pay-as-you-go

In a *fully funded* system each person makes contributions while working, which are used to purchase capital. Total available capital is then the sum of private capital and the publicly owned capital of the pension system. In a very simple pension system that pays benefits based on contributions, the following identity holds:

Pensions = Social Security Contributions plus interest = Capital plus return

Consumers are free to save in addition to the contributions they make to a pension scheme.[16] If they all do so, then any public saving simply replaces private saving and has no effect on the equilibrium outcome for the economy. However, if the system increases the savings rate (because some consumers are induced to save more), or if the rate of return on private savings differs from that on public

13 Of course, it is also important that other aspects of lifetime income support, for example the aged pension. These need to interact effectively with the superannuation system in order to facilitate effective whole-of-life income management. See Asher, Anthony (2010), 'Innovation and Imperatives in Financial Security Systems' (paper presented at the International Congress of Actuaries, 7–12 March 2010, Cape Town, South Africa), available at www.actuaries.org/EVENTS/Congresses/Cape_Town/Papers/Pensions,%20Benefits%20and%20Social%20Security%20%28PBSS%29/152_final%20paper_Asher.pdf for a discussion of how pension schemes fit into wider whole-of-life financial decisions.

14 The first two of these choices are discussed by Feldstein and Leibman in their seminal contribution, written in 2001. Feldstein, Martin and Jeffrey B. Liebman (2001) 'Social Security' in Alan J. Auerbach and Martin Feldstein (eds), *Handbook of Public Economics* (National Bureau of Economic Research, Elsevier).

15 Cooper, Jeremy R. (2014) 'Are Defined Contribution Pension Plans Fit for Purpose in Retirement?' 37 *Seattle University Law Review*, 511–532.

16 This third tier, consisting of voluntary savings, is also sometimes described as part of a pension system.

savings (for example, because of the development of an excessively costly private system), then a fully funded system may affect the equilibrium outcome.[17]

In contrast, a *pay-as-you-go* system does not own any capital. Instead, the pensions of the old are paid by the contributions of the next generation. Such a system leads to an intergenerational reallocation of resources, but can be welfare-improving for the current retired generation.[18] Systems that fall between the two extremes are termed *non-fully-funded.*

The public finance literature provides some helpful guidance as to whether funded or pay-as-you-go systems are preferable, in principle. It shows that there is potentially an efficiency-improving role for transfers from the younger generation to the older (i.e. for a pay-as-you-go system). Samuelson showed in 1958 that a pay-as-you-go financing system can

> provide every generation of workers with a better internal rate of return on their contributions than a capital funded system if the sum of the growth rates of the population (Samuelson's "biological rate of interest") and of the income per worker exceeds the rate of interest on productive investment.[19]

Aaron has further shown that such transfers raise the welfare of the older generation and leave that of all future generations unchanged, providing they persist in the future.[20] With technical progress and a growing population, incremental gains of this kind can be achieved on a continuing basis.

The problem facing most countries, including Australia, is that the currently retiring generation has not previously saved enough to pay for its own retirement, as a consequence of increased longevity, and publicly funded and corporate systems are proving increasingly unable to fill the gap. Introducing individually funded pensions now, however, will take many decades to come to maturity, during which time the retired population will be insufficiently supported.[21] Provided that future

17 For further development of the implications of pension schemes in such a system, see Myles, Gareth D. (2001) *Public Economics* (Cambridge University Press), 14.3 An Optimal Program, 432.

18 For discussion of the conditions under which a PAYG system is welfare-improving, see Sanchez-Marcos, Virginia and Alfonso R. Sanchez-Martın (2005) 'Can Social Security be Welfare Improving When There is Demographic Uncertainty?' (Departamento de Economıa, Universidad de Cantabria, Spain, revised version September 2005), available at http://personales.unican.es/sanchezv/ss.pdf.

19 Breyer, Friedrich (1989) 'On the Intergenerational Pareto Efficiency of Pay-as-you-go Financed Pension Systems', 145 *Journal of Institutional and Theoretical Economics*, 643.

20 Aaron, H. (1966) 'The Social Insurance Paradox', *Canadian Journal of Economics and Political Science*, 32, 371–374. In developing the so-called "Aaron condition", Aaron drew on previous work by Samuelson: Samuelson, Paul (1958) 'An Exact Consumption-Loan Model of Interest With or Without the Social Contrivance of Money' 66 *Journal of Political Economy*, 467–482.

21 And there is some recent evidence that this lack of sufficient savings may persist in future generations. A recently published UK report, International Longevity Centre (2017) *The Global Savings Gap*, compares the UK pension systems with that of 30 high income regions. It finds that young people in the UK need to save 18–20% of their incomes while working to achieve an "adequate retirement income", defined as two-thirds of an average pre-retirement salary. Despite recent *National Employment Savings Trust* (NEST) auto-enrolment into savings schemes, many people are still failing to save adequately, the report argues.

generations can be trusted to honour the promises made for previous generations, the problem of increasing poverty and lower living standards among the old can solved by requiring the currently working population to contribute to their pensions.[22] But this solution was not implemented in Australia, for reasons discussed in Chapter 3.

Samuelson set out in 1975 the basis for determining what might be an optimal social security programme, in a stylised economy (often termed a *Diamond Economy*[23]), under strong assumptions such as inelastic labour supply and no variation in the date of retirement.[24] Based on this, Myles provides a good explanation about how a pay-as-you-go social security programme can be developed that is feasible for the programme in all time periods,[25] and which leads the economy to the *Golden Rule*, in which a capital–labour ratio is achieved that maximises per capita consumption in the steady state.[26] He notes that a fully funded scheme does not have the same properties, and cannot restore efficiency to a system in the way that a pay-as-you-go system potentially can.

Myles also notes that the optimality result can be extended to show that "a social security program can be designed such that the implied steady state maximises the discounted sum of future utilities and achieves the *Modified Golden Rule*, providing that it is not fully funded".[27] Relaxing the Samuelsonian assumptions does not invalidate the basic conclusion that publicly administered pay-as-you-go systems are preferable to fully funded systems, even if the latter are operated efficiently.[28]

22 The impact of mistrust in the (power of) government, and its role in distorting public policy choices, is highlighted in Rein, Martin and John Turner (2001) 'Public–Private Interactions: Mandatory Pensions in Australia, the Netherlands and Switzerland' 10 *Review of Population and Social Policy*, 107–153.

23 This is named after Nobel Laureate Peter Diamond, who in 1965 wrote: Diamond, Peter (1965) 'National Debt in a Neoclassical Growth Model' 55 *American Economic Review* 5, 1126–1150. Diamond's work was a development of the original ideas put forward by Irving Fisher in his *Theory of Interest* (Fisher, Irving (1930) *The Theory of Interest, as determined by Impatience to Spend Income and Opportunity to Invest it* (Macmillan)). In the *Diamond Economy* each (identical) consumer works during the first period of their life and supplies one unit of labour inelastically. In the second period of life they are retired and do not work. Consumption in the second period is financed by savings plus accumulated interest. The population grows at a constant rate.

24 Samuelson, Paul (1975) 'Optimum Social Security in a Life-cycle Growth Model' 16 *International Economic Review*, 539–544. Other key assumptions are that capital does not depreciate, that the production function exhibits constant returns to scale and that production is chosen, in competitive markets, so as to maximise profits.

25 A *feasible pension system* must satisfy the identity that pension payments are equal to tax revenue plus return on capital holdings less investment in capital.

26 Myles, Gareth D. (2001) *Public Economics*, 434–436. Myles notes that "The system presently in operation in the US is of this form since the capital it owns would only fund approximately two months of benefit payments", citing Thompson, L.H. (1983) 'The Social Security Reform Debate' *Journal of Economic Literature*, 21, 1425–1467.

27 Gigliotti, G.A. (1984) 'Total Utility, Overlapping Generations and Social Security' *Economics Letters*, 15, 169–173. The *Modified Golden Rule* chooses the growth path of the economy to maximise the discounted sum of future utilities.

28 Breyer, Friedrich (1989) 'On the Intergenerational Pareto Efficiency of Pay-as-you-go Financed Pension Systems' 145 *Journal of Institutional and Theoretical Economics*, 643–658.

Hu has also explored a simple extension of the Samuelson analysis which shows that the decentralisation of the *Golden Rule* will not be desirable when the retirement decision is endogenous.[29] This is because the tax used to pay for pensions introduces a distortion into the choices made by each consumer.

The three main limitations of the analysis presented above relate to assumptions of exogenous wages and interest rates, so that the analysis strictly only applies to a small open economy; comparing a 'pure' funded system with a 'pure' pay-as-you go system, thus excluding the possibility that mixed systems may perform better than either; and consideration only of mature systems, so that windfall benefits to the generation founding a pay-as-you-go system are not considered. Samuelson explored the first issue, and showed that even for a closed economy, a pay-as-you-go system can lead to higher per-capita consumption provided the economy is "over-capitalised".[30] On the second limitation, Spremann has shown that a pay-as-you-go plan will always Pareto-dominate a funded plan unless the sum of population and wage growth is permanently smaller than the interest rate.[31]

The third limitation has led to extensive literature on the question of how to compensate future generations for the windfall benefits enjoyed by the founder generation, if the Aaron conditions (such as trust that the same privileges will be granted to themselves in retirement) fail to hold.[32] An interesting development of this question was provided by Townley, who suggested that the current retiree generation should be provided with pensions equivalent to those they would have enjoyed under a pay-as-you go system, but that this should be funded by a combination of government debt and employee contributions.[33] All generations are as well off as in a pay-as-you-go system until the government debt is paid off, after which subsequent generations can earn the full interest rate on their contributions.

Breyer summarised the literature discussed above, in 1989, as follows:

> When a pay-as-you-go financed public pension system is replaced by a funded system or by private savings, it is generally impossible to compensate the pensioners in the transition generation for the loss incurred without making at least one later generation worse off.[34]

29 Hu, S.C. (1979) 'Social Security, the Supply of Labor, and Capital Accumulation' *American Economic Review*, 69, 274–283.

30 Samuelson, P.A. (1975) 'Optimum Social Security in a Life-cycle Growth Model' 16 *International Economic Review*, 543.

31 Spremann, K. (1984) 'Intergenerational Contracts and Their Decomposition', 44 *Zeitschrift for Nationalokonomie*, 237–253. *Pareto-domination* means that this outcome can make one generation better off without hurting any other generation.

32 See, for example, Greene, K.V. (1974) 'Toward a Positive Theory of Intergenerational Income Transfers' 29 *Public Finance*, 306–324; and Browning, E.K. (1975) 'Why the Social Insurance Budget is too Large in a Democracy', 13 *Economic Inquiry*, 373–388.

33 Townley, P.G.C. (1981) 'Public Choice and the Social Insurance Paradox: A Note' 14 *Canadian Journal of Economics*, 712–717.

34 Breyer, Friedrich (1989) 'On the Intergenerational Pareto Efficiency of Pay-as-you-go Financed Pension Systems' 145 *Journal of Institutional and Theoretical Economics*, 655.

This replacement of a previous, albeit inadequate, pay-as-you-go system by a funded system is, however, what Australia's policymakers chose to do. Moreover, the funded system that has emerged is in many ways inferior to the idealised one discussed in the literature, because of the principal-agent problems, conflicts of interest and rent-seeking behaviour discussed in this book, which have led to lower investment returns than might otherwise have been achieved.

2.1.2 Defined benefit vs defined contributions

Members of pension funds face numerous risks, which include unexpected longevity and underperformance of invested assets (either because of unjustified costs or other mismanagement, or because of market fluctuations). Defined benefit schemes involve the pooling of these risks across all the members of the scheme, while defined contribution schemes mean that each individual bears his/her own risk.[35]

As Peter Orszag and Joseph Stiglitz pointed out, policymakers in many countries, including Australia, have too often interpreted the second pillar of a superannuation system as requiring personal saving which is translated into defined contributions.[36] They also argue that DB plans can reduce risks for members and that this can be achieved at lower cost than with DC schemes. Providing they are adequately funded, DB schemes ensure that retirees have sufficient income throughout their remaining lives, a certainty that can only be achieved with DC schemes through the subsequent purchase of annuities.[37]

However, others have argued that DB systems are susceptible to political interference, that relevant policy decisions can be captured by vested interests, and that the implicit subsidies that form part of such systems can be manipulated by those in privileged positions.[38] Corporate defined benefit funds place market and investment risk on the plan sponsor, which can lead to bankruptcy and hence

35 The implications of using predominately defined contribution schemes, especially failure to provide a predictable and adequate income stream in retirement, are discussed in Cooper, Jeremy R. (2014) 'Are Defined Contribution Pension Plans Fit for Purpose in Retirement?' 37 *Seattle University Law Review*, 511–532.

36 The first pillar is state provision through age pension and other welfare benefits. Orszag, Peter R. and Joseph E. Stiglitz (2001) 'Rethinking Pension Reform: Ten Myths about Social Security Systems' in Robert Holzman and Joseph E. Stiglitz (eds), *New Ideas about Old Age Security* (World Bank), 17. Orszag and Stiglitz argued that the second pillar should be based upon public management and DB schemes, both of which are mostly lacking in the current Australian system.

37 This, of course, requires that the DB scheme is itself properly funded, an issue that has come to the fore in many countries that rely on these schemes, such as the UK. For a discussion of DB deficits see Asher, Anthony (2014) 'Book Review: "Pension Finance: Putting the Risks and Costs of Defined Benefit Plans Back Under Your Control, M. Barton Waring, Wiley Finance"' 13 *Journal of Pension Economics and Finance* 1, 113–116.

38 For example, Asher, Anthony (2014), 'Redistribution and Capital Market Impacts of Social Security Retirement Systems: Principles and Scope for Actuarial Involvement' 2 *Australian Journal of Actuarial Practice*, 13–20.

unfunded pension liabilities.[39] Notional defined contribution (NDC) systems have been put forward as a method of overcoming some of these difficulties, although these “can also be mimicked by a set of rules in a conventional defined benefits PAYG system”.[40]

The choices to be made by those responsible for investing pension funds are sometimes difficult. For example, there is a trade-off between potential retirement income and protection from bad outcomes. Reducing the downside risk for an individual (as in a DC plan) requires holding more bonds, for example, and fewer equities or other higher-performing assets. But this may reduce the probability of higher returns, which could be achieved at a lower cost if there were more scope for pooling of the downside risk (as in a DB plan).[41]

While very rich individuals may be able to bear their own risks, and to afford the necessary advice and products to protect themselves from risk on an individual basis,[42] the majority have neither the resources nor the knowledge/expertise to do so. As a result of all these influences, defined benefit schemes, where the risks are managed on behalf of a substantial group of members, are in principle a more optimal policy choice than defined contribution.

2.1.3 *Privately vs publicly managed*

The encouragement of private sector management of contributed funds in Australia, rather than developing a state-controlled and managed system, resulted from both historical and ideological pressures. Historically, much superannuation provision in Australia had been run by the insurance companies and banks, and these institutions were seen to possess the necessary systems and technical skills. But perhaps more important was world-wide acceptance of the idea that the private sector was more efficient (and accountable to its customers through the operation of competitive markets, in which consumers can choose the best provider) than the public sector.[43]

39 See Stewart, F. (2007), ‘Benefit Security Pension Fund Guarantee Schemes’ (OECD Working Papers on Insurance and Private Pensions, No. 5, OECD Publishing) for a discussion of these issues and the policy responses of various countries.

40 Borsch-Supan, Axel (2004), ‘What are NDC Pension Systems? What Do They Bring to Reform Strategies?’ (Paper presented to the World Bank–RFV Conference on NDC Pensions, Sandhamn, Sweden, 29–30 September 2004), available at www.mea.mpisoc.mpg.de/uploads/user_mea_discussionpapers/fu66wudcl4okogdk_dp42.pdf.

41 Antolín, P., Sandra Blome, David Karim, Stéphanie Payet, Gerhard Scheuenstuhl, Juan Yermo (2009) ‘Investment Regulations and Defined Contribution Pensions’ (OECD Working Papers on Insurance and Private Pensions, No. 37, OECD Publishing), available at http://dx.doi.org/10.1787/222771401034.

42 For example, hedging instruments or a heavily diversified portfolio.

43 Perhaps the best-known exponent of these ideas is Milton Friedman. See Friedman, Milton (1977) *From Galbraith to Economic Freedom* (Institute of Economic Affairs, London, January 1977), available at https://iea.org.uk/wp-content/uploads/2016/07/From%20Galbraith%20to%20Economic%20Freedom.pdf.

Post-war enthusiasm for state-organised welfare provision in the UK and US waned during the 1970s, and by the early 1980s both countries had elected right-wing governments with a mandate to reduce the role of the public sector and to develop competitive markets. The apparent success of the 'Thatcher revolution' in the UK and 'Reaganomics' in the US led Australian policymakers to believe that handing over control of superannuation funds to lightly regulated private sector operators was beneficial for Australian's retirees. This belief matched the underlying philosophy of the Liberal governments that took power in Australia from the mid 1990s onwards, seeking to develop market-oriented policies and to reduce the size of government.[44]

A major difficulty with seeking to rely on competition and consumer choice to control the rent-seeking behaviour of the private sector is that consumers are not well informed about pensions. For most people, many financial matters are difficult to understand. In addition, the long-term nature of pension decisions means that they are often subordinate to more immediate concerns, particularly among younger people.

So, even if financial markets are competitive, members still need to rely on the trustees of the fund(s) in which their assets are invested to exercise choice on their behalf. A major problem, highlighted in a substantial literature on the subject, is that pension fund governance systems are not sufficiently robust to ensure that trustees have sufficient motivation and expertise to perform this function effectively.[45] Some commentators have also argued that the introduction of choice itself has been one of the reasons the Australian system has such high costs, because it requires funds to spend large amounts marketing their products, reduces the commitment of fund members to their funds (hence making them more disengaged from governance) and has allowed the most informed participants to escape to the SMSF sector.[46]

A further issue, which we discuss in more detail in Chapter 5, is that the greater the degree of separation between members and the agents who act on their behalf, the more diffused is the responsibility the agents feel for the welfare of the members they represent. In a multi-layered system with extensive outsourcing, such as that Australia has developed, key decisions are taken by those who have little or no contact with members, and whose own situation is barely affected by whether the decisions they make turn out to be in the long-term interest of fund members. This is a further reason why defined benefit plans are to be preferred, at least from the perspective of members. The focus of DB plan

44 On 2 March 1996, the incumbent Australian Labor Party, which had been in government for 13 years, led by Bob Hawke (1983–1991) and Paul Keating (1991–1996) was defeated in a landslide by a coalition of the Liberal Party and the National Party led by John Howard.

45 Stewart, F. and J. Yermo (2008) 'Pension Fund Governance: Challenges and Potential Solutions' (OECD Working Papers on Insurance and Private Pensions, No. 18, OECD publishing).

46 For a general discussion of these issues, see Asher, above n 20, Section 5.6, 16.

sponsors is more intense – because they in the end suffer more directly from the failure of their fund – than is the focus of those who simply have an advisory/management capacity for someone else's funds.

2.2 The cost of complexity

Economic exchange, locally or internationally, provides many opportunities for those who act purely in their own self-interest to extract 'unfair' rents. Sometimes the behaviour that facilitates this rent extraction is clearly disapproved of by the political system, for example the use of murder and extortion by the Italian Mafia, or the exploitation of market power by a recognised monopoly or cartel. However, in many more cases over-charging and misrepresentation goes unnoticed or takes a form that existing control systems are unable to prevent.

The Australian superannuation system that has resulted from the policy choices discussed above is complex, with over half a million funds of many different types, over 300 platform products, and with extensive outsourcing of key functions to numerous intermediaries.[47] This complexity is a major reason why many of the problems highlighted in this book go unchecked.

2.2.1 Manipulation by agents

Complexity leads to great opportunity for agents to manipulate their system for their own, rather than the principals', benefit. This manipulation can take a variety of forms including charging of excessive fees; misrepresentation of performance and risk; diversion of funds to activities that benefit the agent, or his associates, rather than the member; regulatory capture; and acquiescence by regulators and politicians in pro-industry policy changes. The ability of the members, or of trustees acting on their behalf, to completely check on an agent's performance or rent extraction is limited, and the legal and regulatory system only provides limited protection. Complexity also permits agents to play one principal off against another, relying on vague contracts or on imprecise legislation. Adverse outcomes (including higher than expected charges, unexpected losses, or low returns) can erode the basis of trust that is needed to develop effective co-ordination. Together, these prevent competitive response from disciplining agents, and permit conflicts of interest, rent-seeking and negligent behaviour to thrive without effective constraint.

2.2.2 Barriers to effective reform

Complexity also works against policy reform. The ability of those in positions of authority – which may be politicians, regulators, the courts or trustee boards – to implement and enforce appropriate controls and suitable disclosure is weakened,

47 See Section 2.5.3 for a more detailed description of the industry and its governance arrangements.

sometimes substantially, by lack of understanding of products, processes or industry structures. Even if politicians and officials are competent, well resourced, completely trustworthy, well-meaning and responsive to the requirements of the political system, complexity in product design and in industrial structure can still prevent the implementation of effective controls over rent-seeking behaviour. Allowing rent-seekers a role in the design of the system further enhances their ability to extract rents. Australian politicians, arguably, have wanted to believe that competitive pressures will produce an equitable and efficient outcome, without putting the necessary effort and political capital into ensuring that industry structure and governance mechanisms, in fact, deliver an appropriately competitive outcome.

2.2.3 Negotiation processes

These issues are at the heart of matters debated between George Akerlof, Robert Shiller and Joseph Stiglitz, which led to the awarding of the 2001 Nobel Prize.[48] The design and implementation of laws and regulations emerges through a negotiation process between a rent-seeking industry and those who seek to control it: the less the latter understand the system and its products, because of complexity, the stronger is the negotiating position of the former. The greater the number of decision points, the less likely is a beneficial change to be implemented, as multiple goals and multiple stakeholders can distort the original intention.

The same observation applies to the relationship between financial services boards and their managers, and between managers and their employees. The more knowledge (or ability to influence outcomes) rests in the hands of one participant in a negotiating situation, the stronger their bargaining position. It is no accident that remuneration issues have come to the fore following the GFC, or that major failures of governance have emerged within previously well-respected firms (for example, Société Générale and J.P. Morgan).[49]

The modern financial services industry is unusual among industrial sectors in the size of the rents that are available, and in the complexity of the value chain.[50] Governments continue to provide huge subsidies to the sector, and the expectation of bailouts creates severe moral hazard.[51] Political objectives (such as

48 See www.nobelprize.org/nobel_prizes/economic-sciences/laureates/2001/popular.html.

49 In the case of J.P. Morgan, the relevant trading took place in London rather than New York, although in principle the unit was run by the Chief Investment Officer.

50 Stout, Lynn (2010) *Cultivating Conscience: How Good Laws Make Good People* (Princeton University Press). Stout makes the observation that "Conscience needs breathing room to work" (p. 117) and that if the pay-off for self-interested behaviour is sufficiently great, it will crowd out any other-regarding instincts.

51 Boone, Peter and Simon Johnson (2010) 'Will the Politics of Global Moral Hazard Sink Us Again?' in Adair Turner, Andrew Haldane, Paul Woolley, Sushil Wadhwani, Charles Goodhart, Andrew Smithers, Andrew Large, John Kay, Martin Wolf, Peter Boone, Simon Johnson and Richard Layard (2010) *The Future of Finance and the Theory Which Underpins It* (London School of Economics), ch. 10, estimate that US and European taxpayers had by 2010 (the figure will be higher now) some 250% of their GDP in implicit obligations, which they observe contributes to moral hazard.

greater home ownership or attempts to hide lack of real earnings growth) may be fulfilled, again in the short term, through imperfectly understood financial instruments (such as derivatives, low-start/sub-prime mortgages, or complex products with substantial tail-risk), without politicians understanding, or caring about, the longer-term consequences of the risks that are being taken. As superannuation becomes dominant amongst financial assets, these realities create a need for innovative policy responses.

2.3 The need for regulation

The first welfare theorem of economics[52] argues that optimising consumers will buy a product up to the point where the marginal utility from a purchase is just equal to price, while optimising producers will produce the product up to the point where the marginal cost of production is also just equal to price.[53] In a competitive market both consumers and producers then face the same price. The competitive outcome is one in which marginal utility is exactly equal to marginal cost, which is the requirement for *Pareto optimality*.[54] In principle, therefore, regulatory intervention may not be necessary where there is effective competition and all participants are fully informed, as competition between providers should ensure the efficient provision of the desired services.

However, in real and complex markets such as financial services, market failures can prevent this from happening. The most important failures usually cited are (i) the existence of monopoly power, (ii) externalities, and (iii) information failure, including difficulties over assessing product quality.[55] Regulation has traditionally attempted to address these perceived market failures. The presence of systemic risk, the risk of contagion and the presence of moral hazard also create the need for prudential regulation, in order to maintain the stability of the financial system.

52 This theorem can be traced back to Adam Smith, *The Wealth of Nations* (Prometheus Books, first published 1776, 1991 ed.). Smith wrote: "Every individual necessarily labours to render the annual revenue of the society as great as he can. He generally indeed neither intends to promote the public interest, nor knows how much he is promoting it . . . He intends only his own gain, and he is in this, as in many other cases, led by an invisible hand to promote an end which was no part of his intention" at 364.

53 Formal proof of this theorem can be found in Lerner, A.P. (1934) 'The Concept of Monopoly and the Measurement of Monopoly Power' 1 *Review of Economic Studies* 157; and elaborated on in Arrow, Kenneth J. (1950), 'An Extension of the Basic Theorems of Classical Welfare Economics' (Paper presented at the Second Berkeley Symposium on Mathematical Statistics and Probability, University of California, 31 July – 12 August 1950) in Jerzy Neyman (ed.), *Proceedings of the Second Berkeley Symposium on Mathematical Statistics and Probability* (University of California Press, 1951), 507.

54 For a discussion of Pareto optimality and the application of such ideas, traced back to Pigou and Samuelson, see Brownstein, Barry P. (1980) 'Pareto Optimality, External Benefits and Public Goods: A Subjectivist Approach' IV *Journal of Libertarian Studies* 93. A policy change is said to be Pareto optimal if there is no reallocation that allows greater production of one utility or output without less of another.

55 For a discussion of how public policy needs to respond to market failures see Tirole, Jean (2014) *Market Failures and Public Policy* (Nobel Prize Lecture, December 8 2014), available at www.nobelprize.org/nobel_prizes/economic-sciences/laureates/2014/tirole-lecture.pdf.

Asymmetric information, conflicts of interest, principal agent problems and oligopolistic industry structures create the need for regulation aimed at customer protection.

Regulation in other industries, for example for utilities, is often focused on ensuring that services are provided at the desired quality,[56] with risks being suitably constrained, at a price no more than necessary. In the financial services industry, these services include providing financial intermediation to retail customers and providing capital allocation and risk insurance services to wholesale customers. In a wider social sense, regulation is also needed to ensure that households are appropriately protected from risk, especially for *key family assets* such as savings, pensions, homes, and children's education. Vulnerable/uninformed households need particular care.

The international literature contains considerable discussion of regulatory enforcement, and seeks to find ways in which regulators, politicians and the law can influence behaviour in the financial services sector in order to create better outcomes for clients and investors by mitigating market failures. International experience also contains numerous examples of practical attempts to solve principal-agent and conflict of interest problems.[57] This section, drawing both on literature and on international experience, is focused on the implications for the regulation of pension systems, in Australia and worldwide.[58]

2.3.1 Principal-agent issues

From the seminal work of Kenneth Arrow onwards, the description of financial activities as being guided by the interaction of principals and agents has been widely used in the economic, financial and organisational literature.[59] Arrow is,

56 In the case of financial services this includes the appropriate trade-off between risk and return for investment products.

57 For example, the original goal of the US Securities and Exchange Commission (SEC) was to regulate financial exchanges in order to reduce these problems. The original remit was to enforce the *Securities Act of 1933*, which is also known as the 'Truth in Securities Act' and highlights the need for uniform disclosure to increase public trust. SEC has subsequently developed a substantial apparatus requiring companies involved in securities trading to make appropriate disclosure, and facilitated a variety of self-regulatory arrangements. The history of financial regulation in the US is documented by the Securities and Exchange Commission Historical Society, available at www.sechistorical.com.

58 The need for such an approach has been highlighted by ASIC, see Medcraft, Greg (2013) 'Opening Address' (Speech delivered at the ASIC Annual Forum, Sydney, 25 March 2013), 5 (in which the ASIC chairman noted: "My position on this is clear – those selling complex products to unsuspecting investors need to wise up and do the right thing. They might get away with it for a while, but government and courts will inevitably rule in favour of investors.").

59 Arrow, Kenneth (1963) 'Research in Management Controls: A Critical Synthesis' (Paper presented at the Seminar on Basic Research in Management Controls, Stanford University, 1963) in Charles P. Bonini (1964) *Management Controls: New Directions in Basic Research: Papers* (McGraw-Hill). In this article, Arrow introduces the idea of moral hazard, using examples from the insurance industry; those ideas are further developed in Arrow, Kenneth (1971) *Essays in the Theory of Risk Bearing* (Markham); for a detailed survey of how agency theory was developed and its uses, see Eisenhardt, Kathleen M. (1989) 'Agency Theory: an Assessment and Review' 14 *Academy of Management Review* 57.

however, pessimistic about the ability of principals to monitor fully the actions of agents:

> [B]y definition the agent has been selected for his specialized knowledge and the principal can never hope to completely check the agent's performance.[60]

Laffont and Martimont have developed Arrow's concepts, providing a survey of the ways in which incentives affect the behaviour of agents, and in particular what they call the *Rent Extraction–Efficiency Trade-off*.[61] Almost inevitably, agents have different objectives from the principals they serve, a problem that can only be overcome through contract if the agents have no relevant private information. Once asymmetric information (which includes differential ability to understand and process available information) is introduced, it becomes possible for the agent to use this information to extract rent, either through 'hidden action' or through 'hidden knowledge'.[62] Laffont and Martimont also raise the issue of non-verifiability, where no third party (and in particular no court of law) can observe the information, even if it is available ex post to both principal and agent, which is also problematic for contract design.[63]

Susan Schapiro asks the question "How do agents understand and reconcile the duties delegated to them when they are receiving mixed messages and conflicting instructions—and incentives—from multiple principals?" (p. 267) noting that vague contracts and controversial or imprecise legislation give agents many opportunities to "play one principal off against another".[64] Schapiro also notes that agency relationships, and the conflicts inherent in them, are important in determining the actions of legislative or administrative agencies.

60 Arrow subsequently described the agency relationship as a 'pervasive fact of economic life', and distinguishes between two types of failure in the relationship – *Hidden Action* and *Hidden Information*. Arrow, Kenneth J. (1984) *The Economics of Agency* (Technical Report, Stanford University, October 1984).

61 Laffont, Jean-Jacques and David Martimort (2002) *The Theory of Incentives: the Principal-Agent Model* (Princeton University Press). Laffont and Martimort intended to develop the work to explore the situation with one principal and several agents (Volume II) and imperfections in contract design (Volume III), but this endeavour was prevented by Laffont's untimely death in May 2004.

62 See Nobel Media (2001) 'The Prize in Economic Sciences 2001' (Press Release, 10 October 2001), www.nobelprize.org/nobel_prizes/economic-sciences/laureates/2001/press.html, for an explanation of the contributions made by Akerlof and Stiglitz on asymmetric information, cited as the reason they were both awarded the Nobel Prize.

63 Laffont and Martimort draw heavily on the work of Williamson both in exploring the transactions costs created by informational asymmetry and non-verifiability through allocative inefficiency. Williamson, Oliver E. (1975) *Markets and Hierarchies, Analysis and Antitrust Implications* (Free Press); Williamson develops these ideas further in Williamson, Oliver E. (1985) *The Economic Institutions of Capitalism* (Free Press) where he explores the extent to which institutional design can be used to reduce the costs.

64 Schapiro, Susan P. (2005) 'Agency Theory' 31 *Annual Review of Sociology* 263; Stephen Ross further explores the issue of how principals can distinguish between the characteristics of multiple agents: Ross, Stephen (1973) 'The Economic Theory of Agency: The Principal's Problem' 63 *American Economic Review* 134.

Taken together, the international literature (of which the above is only a very small sample) on principal-agent problems highlights numerous issues that have potential to reduce the efficiency and probity of pension systems. It is hard for principals to fully monitor the actions of agents, asymmetric information makes creation and enforcement of suitable contracts difficult, while complexity makes the problems worse and makes the actions of opportunistic agents harder to control. In markets dominated by concern over short-term returns, agents are under considerable pressure to deliver what the market wants, even if this is to the long-term detriment of their clients.

2.3.2 Conflicts of interest

Conflicts of interest are a source of concern not only for individual principals but also for society and the State. Reflecting this, the European Union, for example, has introduced a variety of rules that provide for an administrative duty of loyalty, which is supplementary to the requirements of private law.[65] Investor protection legislation and arrangements, including rules of conduct for analysts and advisers, have been introduced in numerous countries. However, fiduciary duties have been eroded by the increasing ability of agents to 'contract around' such duties, as well as the development of corporate law to include, for example, the business judgement rule.[66]

In the last decade, conflicts of interest among financial agents have been the subject of considerable study. Recently, for example, the UK Financial Services Authority (FSA) published a report reviewing the arrangements for managing conflicts of interest in asset management firms.[67] The FSA emphasised the importance

65 These include the *UCITS Directive and the Directive on Markets in Financial Instruments*, *Council Directive of 20 December 1985* on the coordination of laws, regulations and administrative provisions relating to undertakings for collective investment in transferable securities (UCITS) (85/611/EEC) OJ L375/3, 1985 (hereafter 'UCITS Directive') and *Directive 2004/39/EC* of the European Parliament and of the Council of 21 April 2004 on markets in financial instruments, amending *Council Directives 85/611/EEC* and *93/6/EEC* and *Directive 2000/12/EC* of the European Parliament and of the Council and repealing *Council Directive 93/22/EEC*, OJ L 145/1, 2004 (MiFID).

66 Getzler, Joshua (2014) 'Ascribing and Limiting Fiduciary Obligations' in Nicholas Morris and David Vines (eds), *Capital Failure: Rebuilding Trust in Financial Services* (Oxford University Press, 2014), ch. 9; However, as described in O'Brien, Justin, 'Professional Obligation, Ethical Awareness and Capital Market Regulation', in Morris and Vines (eds), ibid., ch 10, the question of whether principals have the necessary knowledge and information to provide such consent has been tested in recent court cases, including *Wingecarribee Shire Council v Lehman Brothers Australia Ltd (in liq)* [2012] FCA 1028. The business judgment rule, which has been part of the Common Law for two centuries, recognises, at its simplest, that Directors should not be held liable for honest mistakes or unpopular business decisions. The difficulties with interpretation and implementation of this rule are covered in depth in Samuel, Arsht, S. (1979) 'The Business Judgment Rule Revisited' 8 *Hofstra Law Review* 1, 93–134.

67 Financial Services Authority (2012) 'Conflicts of Interest between Asset Managers and their Customers: Identifying and Mitigating the Risks' (Report, November 2012). The reviews were carried out between June 2011 and February 2012.

of the “relationship of trust between the industry and its customers. This means that when making investment decisions, or buying products and services for customers, asset managers must always act in customers’ best interests and put customers’ interests ahead of their own”. However, the FSA found that “in most cases senior management failed to show us they understood and communicated this sense of duty to customers or even that they had reviewed or updated their arrangements for conflicts management since 2007. In these firms, employees too often lacked awareness of situations where short-term business goals conflicted with the long-term interests of customers”.[68]

Bahar and Thevenoz have set out the various forms that conflicts of interest take in financial services, exploring the problem in selected specific situations including asset management and the distribution of financial products.[69] In particular, they note difficulties with the definition of conflicts of interest and of the types of relationships that trigger a duty of loyalty, from both a legal and an economic perspective. The duty of loyalty embodied in agency law clearly requires that agents protect and promote the interests of the other party.[70] Conflicts of interest are not limited to individual relationships, and if they are widespread the “effects can plague entire markets”.[71] If investors regard the agency costs of equity as too high, or if they cease to trust their agents, they will either reduce their investment, or avoid the use of asset managers or collective investment schemes.[72]

Freeman and Brown have reviewed conflicts of interest in the funds management industry in the US.[73] They concluded that

> unfortunately . . . decades of SEC-commissioned studies, rule-making, and jawboning have led to a system that, for the most part, works beautifully for those who sell funds to the public, or sell services to funds, but much less admirably for the industry’s investors.

They explore, and reject, the industry’s claim that competition means that fees are kept at reasonable levels, and cite cases where high fees are charged even for passive investment management.[74] They blame the high fees and charges on

68 Ibid. 4.

69 Bahar, Rashid and Luc Thévenoz (2007) ‘Conflicts of Interest: Disclosure, Incentives, and the Market’ in Luc Thévenoz and Rashid Bahar (eds), *Conflicts of Interest: Corporate Governance and Financial Markets* (Kluwer Law International) 1.

70 Simonart, V. (1997) ‘Conclusions générales’ in *Les Conflits d’intérêts* (Bruylant) 303. This is true in both common law and civil law jurisdictions, and Bahar and Thévenoz, ibid. 2, regard it as “indisputable that directors and officers everywhere owe a duty of loyalty to their companies, and that asset managers owe a similar debt to their clients”; for an overview of this issue in corporate governance, see Roe, Mark J. and Jeffrey N. Gordon (eds), *Convergence and Persistence in Corporate Governance* (Cambridge University Press, 2004).

71 Bahar and Thévenoz, above n 69, 4.

72 Arguably the rapid growth of SMSFs in Australia may reflect, in part, concerns of this kind.

73 Freeman, John P. and Stewart L. Brown (2001) ‘Mutual Fund Advisory Fees: the Cost of Conflicts of Interest’ 26 *Journal of Corporation Law* 609.

74 Ibid. 639.

"watered-down fiduciary standards, weak, misguided regulation, Congressional indifference, and either poor advocacy on the part of investors' lawyers or excessive judicial deference to fund managers' contentions".[75] Further, they argue that

> the gap between prices charged [to] funds for advisory services versus prices fetched elsewhere in the economy for those same services represents the bill paid by fund shareholders for the advisory conflict of interest that is both the fund industry's hallmark and its stigma.[76]

The UK's Financial Conduct Authority (FCA) has recently published a final report on an asset management market study carried out in 2015.[77] The UK industry manages over £1 trillion for individual investors, £3 trillion for UK pension funds and other institutional investors and £2.7 trillion for overseas clients, making it the second largest such market in the world. Important findings were weak price competition, evidence of a negative relationship between net returns and charges, poor investor awareness, and lack of investor benefits from economies of scale. These echo many of the concerns reported in this book about conflicts in the Australian market. The FCA suggested a strengthening of duties (to act in the best interests of clients), consistent and standardised disclosure, a single all-in fee, and regulation of investment consultants.

Compensation arrangements can create conflicts of interest if they include misguided incentives, even if they have in principle been agreed between the fiduciary and the principal. This is because the perverse incentives contained in, for example, equity-based plans, management shareholdings, and bonus plans, can encourage the fiduciary to take action that contravenes his (direct or delegated) duty of loyalty.[78]

Investment management brings another set of, largely institutionalised, conflicts. Soft commissions are often paid by stockbrokers to investment managers and advisers, perhaps in the form of research services or terminals/software that are provided free of charge. Such commissions are rarely disclosed in superannuation fund accounts. Investment managers may be required to pay 'shelf fees' to be listed on a master trust, and such payments may bias the decisions of the fund administrator. If investment managers also manage particular investment opportunities – for example, in property or in 'small cap' companies – conflicts will arise between their desire to raise capital and their (delegated) duty towards the fund member. Investment managers may also have an incentive to generate excessive trading in order to maximise commissions for related parties or to increase revenue. Financial

75 Ibid. 671.

76 Ibid. 672.

77 Financial Conduct Authority (2017) *Asset Management Market Study: Final Report* (FCA Market Study MS15/2.3, June 2017), available at www.fca.org.uk/publication/market-studies/ms15-2-3.pdf.

78 See Bolliger, Guido and Manuel Kast (2007) 'Executive Compensation and Analyst Guidance: The Link Between CEO Pay and Expectations Management' in Bahar and Thévenoz, above n 69, 137.

advisers may also have an incentive to recommend investments in which they have a personal interest, although this clearly creates a conflict.

In the case of investment analysts, whether there is a conflict depends partly on whether they are buy-side or sell-side analysts. If they are advising the investor, then they have a contractual relationship that creates a duty of loyalty, and any advice that favours their employers or maximises their own remuneration to the detriment of the investor is a clear conflict. In contrast, if they are a sell-side analyst, hired and paid by analysts or M&A advisers, their duty is clearly to those who hired them and there is no conflict with investors' interests provided they do not represent themselves as providing impartial advice.[79] Sell-side analysts who also act as underwriters have implicit incentives to issue favourable reports, which can create conflicts if not fully disclosed.

In the particular case of conflicts of interest relating to investment research, Abegglen suggests that, in contrast, rules developed in Switzerland could be applied more generally.[80] Swiss Rules only permit an agent to act if there is no risk that a principal will be put at a disadvantage. Thevenoz calls for prohibition of conflicts of interest to be the default, but suggests allowing contracting out by mutual consent based on appropriate disclosure.[81]

Although there have been attempts to improve the professional skills of trustees, to permit them to carry out the arduous and difficult task of representing members in such a complex environment, in practice most trustees can best be described as 'lay' (non-expert).[82] Because of lack of knowledge, time or expertise, trustees face enormous pressure to delegate decisions to professionals. These professionals, however, do not have the same primary duty to members and are usually motivated by their duty to their employers (which usually means maximisation of profit for the employer). This motivation is often accentuated by remuneration systems.

Nevertheless, although the practical ability of trustees to fulfil their duties may be limited, they would generally recognise that they owe a duty to the members they represent and that they must themselves avoid any hint of conflict. However, once they delegate functions to service providers, this duty gets severely diluted, partly because the service providers themselves have other duties, and partly because the business judgement rule has often been allowed by the courts to override any delegated duty to investors.[83]

79 For further discussion of conflict resolution in investment research, see Abegglen, Sandro (2007) 'Investment Research: How to Solve Conflicts of Interest More Efficiently', in Bahar and Thévenoz, above n 69.

80 Abegglen, ibid. 171.

81 Thévenoz, Luc (2007) 'Conflicts of Interest in the Distribution of Investment Funds' in Bahar and Thévenoz, above n 69, 337.

82 Despite calls, for example from Myners, for the introduction of paid professional trustees, there has only been limited progress in this direction. HM Treasury (2001)*Institutional Investment in the UK: A Review* (*The Myners Report*, March 2001).

83 See, e.g., §4.01(c) American Law Institute Principles of Corporate Governance; Aronson v Lewis, 473 A 2d 805, 812 (Del, 1984); Smith v Van Gorkom, 488 A 2d 858 (Del, 1985).

2.3.3 Rent-seeking behaviour

There is considerable evidence worldwide that the management of funds attracts rent-seeking behaviour by the financial services industry which erodes much of the potential return.[84] In the words of John Bogle "fundamental changes in the mutual fund industry during the past 60 years have benefited mutual fund managers, not mutual fund investors",[85] and of Michael Johnson "intermediaries have . . . put upward pressure on distribution costs, ultimately reducing investor returns".[86] Numerous studies have highlighted the problems for pension schemes with substantial contributory components.[87] Experience in several Latin American countries, and elsewhere, has shown the dangers of introducing inadequately regulated market-oriented pension systems with compulsory contributions.[88]

Emphasis on competition and choice to control this rent-seeking behaviour has, however, failed in many countries and in numerous different contexts. Noel Whiteside reviews the UK experience, where the view that competition and choice provide foundations for better public services has dominated policymaking. She notes that

> Far from allowing the state to withdraw . . . the resort to markets has enmeshed it in a quagmire of new duties and obligations, creating expensive administrative complexities that destroy the very market signals that were the supposed advantage of new systems.[89]

84 For a summary of past research on this issue, see Congleton, Roger D., Arye L. Hillman, and Kai A. Konrad 'Forty Years of Research on Rent Seeking: An Overview', available at www.tax.mpg.de/fileadmin/TAX/pdf1/2008-introduction_rent_seeking_june_16_2008.pdf. Academic work on these issues dates mostly from the 1960s and 1970s, and especially the work of Gordon Tullock, see Tullock, Gordon (1967) 'Welfare Costs of Tariffs, Monopolies, and Theft' *Western Economic Journal* 5, 224–32 and Tullock, Gordon (1980) 'Efficient rent seeking', in James M. Buchanan, Robert D. Tollison, and Gordon Tullock (eds), *Towards a Theory of the Rent-Seeking Society* (Texas A&M University Press, College Station), 97–112.

85 Bogle, John C. (2005) 'The Mutual Fund Industry 60 Years Later: For Better or Worse?' 61 *Financial Analysts Journal* 1, 30. John Bogle was CEO and founder of the Vanguard Group, and a pioneer in the development of passively managed, low cost, funds.

86 Johnson, Michael (2012) *Put the Saver First: Catalysing a Savings Culture* (Centre for Policy Studies, London).

87 For example, the studies carried out by the American Association of Retired Persons (AARP) Public Policy Institute highlight unsatisfactory experience with voluntary carve-outs in the UK, and how mandatory contributions in Australia have created huge complexities and 'perverse labour force and financial behaviour patterns'.

88 The Latin American changes, which also started in the 1990s, largely followed the recommendations of *Averting the Old Age Crisis*, a study published by the World Bank in 1994, and also relied on privately-managed defined contribution funds. The new systems were criticised over fund performance, governance, and fiscal costs: for a discussion see David de Ferranti, Danny Leipziger, and P.S. Srinivas (2002) 'The Future of Pension Reform in Latin America' 39 *IMF Finance & Development* 3.

89 Whiteside, Noel (2011) 'Creating Public Value: the Theory of the Convention' in John Benington and Mark H. Moore (eds), *Public Value: Theory and Practice* (Palgrave Macmillan), 74. Whiteside makes the point that "[e]fficiency depends not just on 'topdown' regulation by government, but also on careful negotiation with key participants, allowing deliberations that both explain mechanisms and identify possible future problems", implying that these processes failed in the UK: ibid. 75.

Australia has followed the UK in developing many aspects of its regulatory system and hence has also sought to rely heavily on competition and choice to curtail rent-seeking.

There is a large US literature on the development and performance of managed funds, which has resonance for the present situation facing Australian superannuation. Many of the problems identified in that literature – extra costs caused by delegation of management, poor value-for-money from active trading, increasing speculation, hidden costs, large advertising expenses, multiple layers – also occur in Australia. A seminal *Wall Street Journal* article by John Bogle provided estimates that in the period 1984 to 2002 when the S&P 500 rose by 791%, the average equity fund in the US rose by 442%, and the return to the average investor was only 66%. Of the remaining 725% of return that might have been obtained by investing in the S&P 500, Bogle estimated that 349% went in "bad trades and unacknowledged costs".[90]

In later published work Bogle reviewed major changes in the mutual fund industry during the past 60 years, and evaluated the impact of those changes on the returns earned by mutual funds and on the returns earned by their investors.[91] He attributes many of the industry's problems to inadequate governance and to the "industry's peculiar operating structure, in which fund directors delegate all of a fund's operations to an external management company".[92]

Bogle's findings are supported by more recent literature, for example Cuthbertson, Nitzsche and O'Sullivan, who find that economic gains to investors even from 'winner' funds may be quite marginal, after load fees, expenses and turnover are taken into account.[93] They observe that sensible advice for most investors would be to hold low cost index funds.[94]

2.3.4 Inadequately managed risk

A further market failure that requires regulatory intervention is the difficulty that members have in acquiring suitable products to help them manage risk. Their need to do this on an individual basis has been created by the policy choices described above. In the DC environment of Australian superannuation, individuals face both longevity and market risks (including the risk of needing to pay excessive fees because of principal-agent, conflict of interest and rent-seeking problems).

As they do not know how long they are going to live they need to pool longevity risk with others, something that would have happened automatically if they had a

90 Paul Samuelson is a Nobel Laureate and noted economist, inter alia author of a key textbook on economics, quoted in Slater, Robert (1997) *John Bogle and the Vanguard Experiment: One Man's Quest to Transform the Mutual Fund Industry* (McGraw-Hill).

91 Bogle, above n 85.

92 Ibid. xxiii.

93 Cuthbertson, Keith, Dirk Nitzsche and Niall O'Sullivan (2010) 'Mutual Fund Performance: Measurement and Evidence' (Working Paper, New York University).

94 Ibid. 171.

DB pension.[95] The generally accepted method of doing this is to purchase an annuity on retirement.[96] However, annuity markets around the world have not succeeded in providing a product that has become recognised as 'fair' enough to command widespread adoption. Actuarial unfairness has been identified in many studies as a key reason for this failure.[97] An "annuity is said to be actuarially fair . . . if the benefit stream discounted by an interest rate and annual survival probabilities equals the premium paid", but even this calculation understates the problem, because annuities also involve a loss of liquidity.[98] This loss of liquidity is important because most households also face uncertainty about their possible long-term care costs.

In a recent paper, Boon et al. compare the collective arrangement of DB schemes, which distributes longevity risk among members, with market-provided annuity contracts. They show that, even if the latter is priced at its best estimate, it still yields lower individual welfare than the collective arrangement, and that the "annuity provider is incapable of adequately compensating its equity-holders for bearing longevity risk".[99] They therefore observe that market-provided annuity contracts are unlikely to co-exist with collective schemes.

Households also face difficulties in acquiring suitable hedges for other aspects of the risks they face, including price indexation, a problem highlighted by Bodie et al. as far back as 1988:

> DB plans create implicit securities that can be welfare improving and that are neither currently available in capital markets, nor likely to be created in capital markets in the future. Some examples of these "securities" are factor-share claims, price-indexed claims, and perhaps deferred life annuities at fair interest rates.[100]

95 The current advice from *Industry Super* in Australia is that "These days, if you're looking for a defined benefit product they are few and far between. If you do find one that's still open, it's likely that the income guaranteed will be much less than with the old ones." See www.industrysuper.com/retirement-info/income-streams/defined-benefit-pension/.

96 An annuity provides a guaranteed income stream for life (or for a specified period) in return for an up-front payment. Fair pricing of such a product requires that appropriate life expectancy tables are used, and that the overall return to the provider is not excessive. Mitchell, Olivia S., James Poterba, Mark J. Warshawsky, and Jeffrey R. Brown (1999) 'New Evidence on the Money's Worth of Individual Annuities' 89 *American Economic Review* 5, 1299–1318. See also Abraham, Katherine and Benjamin H. Harris (2015) *Better Financial Security in Retirement? Realizing the Promise of Longevity Annuities* (Brookings Institutions Economic Studies, February 2015).

97 Webb et al. have observed that "for the average household, the expected value of the income, discounted by a rate of interest and annual survival probabilities, is considerably less than the premium paid". Webb, Anthony, Guan Gong and Wei Sun (2007) 'An Annuity That People Might Actually Buy' Issue in Brief 7–10 (Center for Retirement Research, Boston College, July 2007). They explore the idea of an Advanced Life Deferred Annuity (ALDA) which would take effect from, say, age 75.

98 See, for example, Webb, Anthony (2010) 'The United States Longevity Insurance Market' (Pension Research Council Working Paper PRC WP 2010–17, September 2010).

99 Boon, Ling-Ni, Marie Brière and Bas J.M. Werker (2017) 'Longevity Risk: To Bear or to Insure?' (paper presented at the 25th CEPAR Superannuation Colloquium, UNSW, Sydney, 6 July 2017).

100 Bodie, Zvi, Alan J. Marcus, and Robert C. Merton (1988) 'Defined Benefit versus Defined Contribution Pension Plans: What Are the Real Trade-offs?', Chapter 5 in Zvi Bodie, John B. Shoven, and David A. Wise (eds) *Pensions in the U.S. Economy* (University of Chicago Press), 139–162.

The retrenchment of DB schemes in Britain, for example, has been rapid since the mid 1990s, a trend some commentators put down to 'herd behaviour' by private sector management.[101] Defined benefit schemes are increasingly unavailable to individuals, and, following recent problems (for example, at British Home Stores (BHS) and Tata Steel) the sustainability even of existing DB schemes is under intense scrutiny.[102] The capital requirements to underpin such products are large, and the willingness of financial institutions to tie up capital in this way is limited.

Regulation is clearly needed to assist individuals in the management of these risks, with reduction of asymmetric information problems being a key requirement. Regulators need to ensure adequate disclosure of all pertinent information, and its presentation in a way that is accessible to ordinary members.[103] Ensuring that products, such as annuities, are priced fairly – i.e. that appropriate life expectancy tables are used for each member, and that interest rate assumptions are reasonable – is an essential part of the regulatory task.

2.4 Pension systems around the world

Many countries, for example most of Western Europe, the USA and Japan, use what is often called a 'social insurance' approach, in which the working generation is required to contribute to a fund that is then used to pay the pensions of those currently retired. Such systems are mostly pay-as-you-go, but some choose to set rates that permit accumulation of funds and thus are partially funded. Faced with the steep rises in required payments caused by longevity, and the consequent increase in funding requirements, a number of countries have instituted reforms that seek to contain costs, including changing the period of earnings required, making benefits subject to an income test, changing indexation rules and raising the statutory age of retirement.[104]

There is growing international pressure for the use of compulsory, self-funded, schemes, including in the UK. Net replacement rates – the share of

101 Bridgen, Paul and Traute Meyer (2005) 'When Do Benevolent Capitalists Change Their Mind? Explaining the Retrenchment of Defined-benefit Pensions in Britain' 39 *Social Policy and Administration* 7, 764–785.

102 Franklin, Ben and Dean Hochlaf (2017) 'The End of the Beginning? Private Defined Benefit Pensions and the New Normal' (Ince and Co, January 2017), available at www.ilcuk.org.uk/images/uploads/.../ILC-UK_-_The_End_of_the_Beginning.pdf.

103 Anthony Asher has considered these issues in the particular context of linking home finance to salaries. He notes, however, that "Moral hazard and anti-selection risks are likely to restrict the market to employees of large institutions". Asher, Anthony (2011) 'Salary Linked Home Finance: Reducing Interest Rate, Inflation and Idiosyncratic Salary Risks' 17 *Australian Actuarial Journal* 1, 117–148, available at www.actuaries.asn.au/Library/AAJ/2012/AAJ_Vol17_iss1_web.pdf.

104 Hinrichs, Karl and Julia F. Lynch (2010) 'Old-Age Pensions' in Francis G. Castles, Stephan Leibfried, Jane Lewis, Herbert Obinger, and Christopher Pierson (eds) *The Oxford Handbook of the Welfare State* (Oxford University Press).

net pre-retirement earnings, net of income taxes and social security contributions paid by workers and pensioners – from public pensions vary widely between countries from lows, at average earnings, of 39% (UK) to highs of 97% (Netherlands) and the rates also vary between earnings levels.[105]

With the notable exceptions of the UK, Denmark and some South American countries, most have chosen to retain a pay-as-you-go basis, and continue to rely primarily on defined benefit schemes. Many countries that have in the past opted for funded schemes have been reversing these decisions as financial realities, especially following financial crises, have become apparent, and some have diverted previously accumulated funds to pay-as-you-go pensions. Countries that have opted for defined contribution schemes are now finding they need to introduce new policies (such as compulsory annuitisation) to assist scheme members with risk management. Where private sector management has been encouraged, competition, facilitated by providing members with choice of provider, does not seem to work well enough to constrain costs (and indeed, as discussed above, providing choice seems to escalate costs by more than the benefits it provides).

Chile preceded Australia in the introduction of compulsory contributions, but recent reviews have highlighted the many problems it now faces, including high costs and member disenchantment, and it is now considering a full or partial move back to PAYG. New Zealand's Kiwisaver provides an example of a simple system which is voluntary but has automatic enrolment should members make no alternative choice. European countries, following Bismarck's 1889 legislation in Germany, mostly rely on publicly administered, pay-as-you-go, defined benefit systems. The Netherlands has introduced risk sharing for occupational schemes between employers, employees and pensioners. Denmark is unusual in having introduced a compulsory, fully funded DC scheme, publicly administered, in addition to a tax-financed general basic pension. Switzerland has obligatory occupational schemes, and tax incentives for voluntary saving, with pensions paid mostly on a DB basis.

The United Kingdom, after the Second World War, developed a pension system based on compulsory *National Insurance Contributions,* which pays a non-means-tested pension to all who satisfy contribution and age conditions. Its second tier consists mostly of occupational pension schemes, with benefits mostly paid on a DB basis. However, recent changes in policy have caused a move away from defined benefit towards defined contribution schemes, have permitted (through Pension Freedoms) the early withdrawal of pension assets, and have introduced an auto-enrolment workplace pension. The United Kingdom pension industry today shares many of the principal-agent, conflict of interest and rent-seeking problems faced by Australia.

105 For example, UK replacement rates are around 66% at half average earnings and only 24% at twice average earnings. See OECD (2015) *Pensions at a Glance: OECD and G20 Indicators*, Figure 1.7, 28, available at www.oecd.org/publications/oecd-pensions-at-a-glance-19991363.htm, for detailed data on replacement rates across OECD countries. The lowest replacement rate in the OECD analysis for average income earnings was Mexico at 28% and the highest was Turkey at 105%.

Although the primary United States pension scheme is funded on a pay-as-you-go basis, funded schemes in the US have around US$15 trillion in funds under management, 60% of the OECD total. DB plans predominate, but DC plans have grown in importance in recent years. Canada provides a universal, flat-rate benefit for all seniors and an earnings-related scheme financed by compulsory contributions, both on a pay-as-you-go basis. In addition, tax incentives encourage additional savings. Japan has a universal flat rate basic pension that is mostly financed on a pay-as-you-go basis, while 90% of private enterprises provide some form of occupational benefits at retirement, mostly on a DB basis. The Japanese Government Pension Investment Fund is the largest single pool of retirement savings in the world (US$1.28 trillion).

In what follows, we set out these features of the different countries' pension systems, and their evolution, in a little more detail, and relate what has happened there to the problems faced by Australia.

2.4.1 Chile

Chile's pension system until 1980 was based on pay-as-you go contributions, but this was replaced in 1980/81 by a fully funded system based on individual capital accounts, managed by entities known as *Administradoras de Fondos de Pensiones* (AFPs). To reduce political opposition at the time of the reforms, workers that opted for the new regime were given an 11% effective increase in net wages as well as *recognition bonds* which were deposited in the transferring workers individual capital accounts. AFPs are allowed to charge fees and commissions for managing individual capital accounts, but must charge the same percentage fee to all contributing members irrespective of the investment option they choose.[106] However, there are strict regulations as to which assets the AFPs can invest in, in order to encourage safety and profitability, with risk categories defined by a *Risk Classification Commission*.[107] Where members do not make a choice of funds they are allocated to a default fund. These features are somewhat more prescriptive than in the Australian case, with the AFPs more tightly regulated than Australian funds.

The Chilean government provided several guarantees that underpinned the system. Where contributions had been made for at least 20 years, a minimum pension was guaranteed. Second, the government also expected a minimum return from each AFP, and would liquidate any AFP that was unable to deliver this. Third, the government guaranteed pension payments to pensioners of any insurance company that became bankrupt.[108] Guarantees of this kind do not exist in Australia.

106 Chant West (2016) 'Chilean Pension System: Updated Comparison with Australia' (Research Paper, Sydney). There are restrictions on the investment fees payable to external fund managers: these are disclosed to regulators on a monthly basis and published on the Superintendence of Pensions' website.

107 Superintendence of Pensions (2010) *The Chilean Pension System* (Government of Chile, Santiago).

108 Barr, Nicholas and Peter Diamond (2016) 'Reforming Pensions in Chile' 1 *Polityka Społeczna* 4–9, available at www.ipiss.com.pl/?lang=en.

Chile's initiative, which was praised by the World Bank,[109] led to similar reforms being started in many other Latin American countries,[110] and later several Eastern European countries introduced funded individual accounts.[111] However, moving worker's contributions into funds meant that they were not available to finance current pensions, so that past promises then needed to be financed from elsewhere.[112] Following the Global Financial Crisis many countries have reversed the process. In some cases, this has led to the retention of individual accounts but diversion of some of the funds to pay-as-you-go benefits.[113] In others, individual accounts have been abandoned altogether and the stock of assets and contributions have been transferred back to the PAYG system.[114] This reversal of the initial funding decision and the trend back to a PAYG basis, which as we describe below is continuing, provides a useful comparator for Australia, which is at an earlier stage in the development of its funded system.

In Chile, the *Marcel Commission* of 2006 led to the introduction of a non-contributory *solidarity pension* for the bottom 60% by income and of an auction mechanism for AFP rights in both the accumulation and draw-down phases. In 2008 a tender system was introduced under which AFPs bid for new entrants to the workforce. This was an attempt to increase competition between AFPs and also to reduce marketing fees associated with encouraging workers to choose a particular AFP.[115] This attempt to increase competition between providers, and put downward pressure on costs, is also something that, as argued below, is needed in Australia.

In 2015, the *Bravo Commission* identified numerous continuing problems, including inadequate pensions, low coverage, continued high charges, hostility towards the AFP system and low financial literacy. It recommended 58 actions

109 World Bank (1994) *Averting the Old Age Crisis* (Oxford University Press).

110 These reforms all sought to ensure the funding of pension systems in the medium-to-long term. They began in Peru (1993), followed by Argentina (1994), Colombia (1994), Uruguay (1996), Bolivia (1997), Mexico (1997), El Salvador (1998), Ecuador (2001), Costa Rica (2001), the Dominican Republic (2003–2005), and Panama (2005–2007). Rofman, R., I. Apella, and E. Vezza (eds) (2015) *Beyond Contributory Pensions: Fourteen Experiences with Coverage Expansion in Latin America* (The World Bank, Washington DC).

111 Hungary (1998), Poland (1999), Latvia (2001), Bulgaria (2002), Estonia (2002), Lithuania (2004), Slovakia (2005) and Romania (2008). Funded individual accounts were also introduced in China (1998) and Hong Kong (2000).

112 The problems faced by Argentina's pension system following the 2001 economic collapse are discussed in Bertranou, Fabio M., Rafael Rofman and Carlos O. Grushka (2003) 'From Reform to Crisis: Argentina's Pension System' 56 *International Social Security Review* 2, 103–114.

113 Examples include Estonia, Latvia, Lithuania, Poland and Romania.

114 Notably Hungary and Argentina. See Bielawska, K., Chłoń-Domińczak, A., Stańko, D. (2016) *Retreat from Mandatory Pension Funds in Countries of the Eastern and Central Europe in Result of Financial and Fiscal Crisis: Causes, Effects and Recommendations for Riscal Rules* (Warsaw School of Economics, Warsaw); and Simonovits, A. (2011) 'The Mandatory Private Pension Pillar in Hungary: An obituary' 64 *International Social Security Review* 3, 81–98.

115 Shelton, A. (2012) 'Chile's Pension System: Background in Brief' (Congressional Research Service, Washington DC).

to improve the system and recommended a partial or full move back to PAYG.[116] Its proposals included the introduction of compulsory annuitisation (to deal with the risks faced by members in the decumulation phase), including a person's education or average income in the pricing of annuities (to reflect the fact that poorer people have lower life expectancies) and the encouragement of a group bidding process for annuities.[117] Chile's introduction of risk management mechanisms such as annuitisation is something that is needed in Australia in the near future: early attempts to do this are described in Section 2.5.4 below.

Chile's experience has demonstrated that, in that country at least, private supply plus competition are not enough to keep costs down; that the idea of the fully informed consumer doesn't hold; and that providing choice is costly and often welfare-reducing. The model of a fully funded, defined contribution system, for which Chile has been a world pioneer, has been shown to be problematic both because of the persistent high costs of administering the funds and of continuing problems with the management of risks. The result is that a move back to PAYG is under way, and seems likely to accelerate if the Bravo Commission recommendations are implemented. Active government input has been needed to improve competition, including the auctioning of rights to be a provider; and risk management mechanisms such as compulsory annuitisation have been found to be needed in a predominately DC environment.

2.4.2 New Zealand

New Zealand's public pension system, which was initially set up in 1898, provides flat rate benefits of between 60% and 72.5% of average earnings to all residents over 65, paid from general tax revenues on a pay-as-you-go basis. Occupational schemes covered around 22% of the population (4% government, 18% private) until the mid 1990s, but this coverage fell to around 15% after tax concessions were removed.[118] In July 2007, following concern over savings rates and potentially large falls in post-retirement living standards for middle-class New Zealanders, an automatic-enrolment but voluntary savings scheme called *Kiwisaver* was introduced.[119] The idea of auto-enrolment seems to be an effective way of dealing with consumers who do not, in fact, exercise the choices available to them, a lesson from which Australia can learn.

116 Under 'Global Proposals', the second of which would add a tax-financed match to the social security accounts of poorer people and the third which would involve a flow of existing contributions into a new PAYG, defined benefit system.

117 Barr and Diamond, above n 108.

118 Rashbrooke, Geoff (2014) 'New Zealand's Experience with the KiwiSaver Scheme', Chapter 5 in Richard Hinz, Robert Holzmann, David Tuesta and Noriyuki Takayama (eds), *Matching Contributions for Pensions: A Review of International Experience* (World Bank), Figure 5.1, 104.

119 New employees were given eight weeks to opt out, after which they were required to stay in the scheme for at least 12 months.

Kiwisaver has an estimated 2.6 million members and around NZ$35 billion in funds under management.[120] Incentives to invest in Kiwisaver include a tax-free government 'kick-start' of NZ$1,000; member tax credits; and compulsory employer contributions (of 2% of earnings). After three years of contributing to Kiwisaver, a first home deposit subsidy of up to NZ$10,000 may be available.[121] Inland Revenue assigns those who do not choose a scheme to one of six government-appointed providers.[122] These various incentives to join a government-run scheme, and the fact that the New Zealand government has been willing to evaluate providers before entrusting them with citizen's savings, both provide useful lessons for Australia.

New Zealand's pension system is generally recognised to be the simplest in the OECD, with no means testing and only a basic residential test. Kiwisaver involves voluntary contributions of 3%, 4% or 8% of salary, deducted from employee earnings through the tax collection system, which are then sent directly to providers in addition to a 2% contribution from employers.[123]

There is some agreement in the policy literature that the New Zealand system has merit.[124] New Zealand has the lowest relative poverty rate among the over 65s in OECD countries, with only 1.5% having incomes less than half median income.[125] Although the accumulated funds are privately managed it avoids some of the principal-agent, conflict of interest and rent-seeking problems highlighted in this book through close supervision of the government-appointed providers.[126]

2.4.3 Europe

Germany was the first country that compulsorily insured almost all employees, under Bismarckian legislation of 1889.[127] Means-tested benefits are payable from

120 Financial Markets Authority (2016) *Kiwisaver Annual Report* (New Zealand Government). For a summary, see 'Kiwisaver in a nutshell' at www.kiwisaver.govt.nz/new/about/summary/.

121 Rashbroke, above n 118, 109.

122 The default providers are required to meet additional reporting requirements, and face limits on the fees they can charge.

123 There are now over 30 providers in the New Zealand system. Rashbrooke, Geoff (2009) 'Simple, Effective and (Relatively) Inexpensive: New Zealand Retirement Provision in the International Context' 36 *Social Policy Journal of New Zealand*, 97–110.

124 See, for example, Rashbrooke, above n 123; and www.forbes.com/sites/nextavenue/2014/07/17/why-new-zealands-retirement-system-works-so-well/#3df144716312.

125 Rashbrooke, above n 118, 106.

126 For a recent review of the effectiveness of Kiwisaver funds management, see Heuser, Andreas, Jack Kwok, Daniel Snethlage and Dillon Watts (2015) 'Review of the KiwiSaver Fund Manager Market Dynamics and Allocation of Assets' (New Zealand Treasury, September 2015), available at www.treasury.govt.nz/publications/research-policy/tp/kiwisaver/tp-kiwisaver.pdf. However, the authors observe that "returns to members have not outperformed benchmarks chosen by us and are mixed compared to the investment performance of the Crown financial institutions".

127 *Old Age and Disability Insurance Law, 1889.*

a fixed retirement age,[128] and are intended to supplement earnings from continued employment, savings, family support or private pensions from former employers. This public system[129] continues to provide the vast majority of pensions, while voluntary occupational schemes – which cover some 50% of employees – provide only around 5% of pensions.[130] The system is funded on a pay-as-you-go basis. A particular recent initiative is the introduction of voluntary, but heavily subsidised, private *Riester* pensions.[131] Germany thus provides a good example of a stable, well-run, pension system that follows the principles of relying on pay-as-you-go funding.

France has a large number of pay-as-you-go schemes (about 120 basic and 400 supplementary), for both public and private sector employees. Retirement age, contribution rates, and benefit rules vary considerably between different schemes. The ordinary retirement age of 60 was introduced in 1982. Funded pension schemes play only a very minor role.[132] France is, however, a rather special case, where long-established societal controls provide confidence that funds will, in the main, not be misappropriated despite the complexity of the system. Lessons for Australia include that, in this well-functioning democracy, the choice has been to use PAYG and DB systems with significant public control.

Italy introduced in 1919 a compulsory scheme for all employees whose earnings were under a certain threshold, following the Bismarckian model. Despite recent reforms, the Italian pension system is still the most expensive among OECD countries, partly because early retirement is encouraged (particularly in the public sector), partly because pensions also play an income support role, and partly because of adverse demographics.[133] The system is very fragmented, with many funds for different professional groups, and is particularly generous to public employees and to the self-employed.[134]

128 This was initially 70, then reduced to 65, currently 67. Earlier retirement is permitted for women, those with long contribution records, and for the unemployed and handicapped.

129 *Gesetzliche Rentenversicherung* (GRV).

130 Gern, K.-J. (1998) 'Recent developments in old-age pension systems: An international overview' (Working Paper no. 863, Kiel Institute of World Economics).

131 On average, the government provides one euro for every two euros of household savings into these schemes. Börsch-Supan, Axel H., Michela Coppola and Anette Reil-Held (2012) 'Riester Pensions in Germany: Design, Dynamics, Targeting Success and Crowding-in' (NBER Working Paper 18014), available at www.nber.org/papers/w18014.

132 Börsch-Supan, Axel (2006) 'European Welfare State Regimes and their Generosity toward the Elderly' (Working paper 279, The Levy Economics Institute).

133 For a fairly recent summary, see Aben, Maurits (2011) 'Overview of the Italian Pension System' (APG World of Pensions Scholarship, Working Paper, March 2011), available at https://core.ac.uk/download/pdf/11830242.pdf.

134 For discussion of the recent development of Italian pensions, see Natali, David (2016) 'Two Decades of Pension Reforms in Italy: Shedding Light on a Series of Mirror Images', Chapter 2 in Ascoli, Ugo and Emmanuele Pavolini (eds), *The Italian Welfare State in a European Perspective: A Comparative Analysis* (Policy Press), 49–70.

The Netherlands provides a universal basic pension financed on a pay-as-you-go basis,[135] which is part of a broader social security scheme that also covers nursing care and disability. The benefits are generous, providing 70% (100% for married couples) of the statutory minimum wage after 40 years of contributions. The second tier consists of well-established occupational pensions that cover most of the workforce, on a DB basis. In recent decades there has been a migration from a final-salary to an average-salary basis for determining pension rates. Should a plan become insufficiently funded, employers, employees and pensioners all contribute to its recovery.[136] The Netherlands also implemented 'Defined Ambition' pension plans from 2015 onwards, where the guarantee inherent in DB schemes is replaced by 'soft real rights', which are adjusted annually to reflect achieved investment returns and longevity.[137] These innovative approaches to risk management, involving all relevant stakeholders, provide models that could be useful in the Australian case as it seeks to 'retrofit' suitable risk controls on its DC system.

Denmark has a tax-financed general basic pension, which is partly means-tested. The second tier consists of a compulsory, fully funded, public DC scheme,[138] and funded DC pension plans established through the collective bargaining system and supported by tax incentives. The Swedish public pension system includes a flat rate basic pension and an income-related supplementary pension (ATP), both financed on a pay-as-you go basis.[139] Sweden has also introduced competitive tendering to be permitted to be a provider in its second tier. Finland has a basic pension, which is nationally administered and financed by contributions on a pay-as-you go basis, supplemented by a compulsory employment scheme that is partly funded. The Scandinavian experience shows how these democracies have, with the exception of Denmark, chosen to use a PAYG basis and how societal controls can be useful in reducing the impact of rent-seeking behaviour.

Switzerland has a three-pillar system consisting of a government-run old age insurance program,[140] which is financed on a pay-as-you-go basis, obligatory occupational pension schemes financed on a funded basis,[141] and voluntary saving promoted by preferential tax treatment. Swiss occupational pensions are mostly paid on a DB basis, dependent on individual earnings and number of years of

135 *Algemeene Onderdomswet* (AOW).

136 OECD (2016) *Pensions Outlook 2016*, 30.

137 Goudswaard, Kees Pieter, Roel Maria Wilhelmus Jozef Beetsma, Theo E. Nijman and Paul Schnabel (2010) *Report of the Committee on Sustainability of Supplementary Pension Contracts (Toekomstbestendigheid Aanvullende Pensioenregelingen)*, (Lieden University, January 2010), available at http://media.leidenuniv.nl/legacy/kpg-2010-02.pdf.

138 *Arbejdsmarkedets Tillaegspension* (ATP).

139 Although this system can be regarded as partially funded, as surpluses have been built up over time.

140 *Alters und Hinterlassen Enversicherung* (AHV).

141 These were established after a referendum in 1985.

contributions. Switzerland's choice of PAYG and DB as the basis for their system reinforces the arguments presented above that these provide a superior basis for a sustainable pension system. The Swiss government currently provides a system-wide guarantee of a minimum investment return.[142]

Taken as a whole, European practice has been to retain pay-as-you-go funding, pay benefits on a DB basis, and rely mostly on public administration and provision. Denmark is an outlier, having chosen to introduce a compulsory, fully funded DC scheme, albeit publicly administered and tightly regulated. Risk sharing between employers, employees and the government is an innovative, and helpful, aspect of the Netherlands system.

2.4.4 United Kingdom

Following the Second World War and the *Beveridge Report*, the UK introduced *National Insurance Contributions* that fund flat-rate payments for unemployment, sickness, disability and old age.[143] A State Earnings-Related Pension Scheme (SERPS) was introduced in 1978, with arrangements for opting-out, but this was downgraded in 1986 and has been gradually phased out since.[144] Exchequer costs of pensions have been further reduced by increasing the statutory pension age and by technical changes to indexation and other rules.[145] The UK's state pensions today are among the lowest in Europe.

Occupational pensions are an important, and well established, part of the UK pension system,[146] but recent governments have developed these in different ways. The Thatcher–Major governments of 1979 to 1997 made private supplementary pension provision voluntary, but used tax incentives to encourage such saving, relying on competition to keep charges under control.[147]

142 This guarantee was set at 1% for 2017, but it has been proposed that this rate be replaced by the average market yield on seven-year Swiss government debt, but this has yet to be implemented. See Cooper (2014), above n 15, 528.

143 Beveridge, William H.B. (1942) *Social Insurance and Allied Services: Report by Sir William Beveridge*. (London: H.M. Stationery Office).

144 Dilnot, Andrew, Richard Disney, Paul Johnson and Edward Whitehouse (1994) *Pensions Policy in the UK: An Economic Analysis* (London: Institute for Fiscal Studies).

145 For a detailed summary of the regulatory arrangements for UK pensions prior to the mid 1980s, see Morris, Nicholas (1988) 'Competition, Regulation and Deregulation in Pension Fund Portfolio Management: The Case of the United Kingdom', in Leslie Hannah (ed.) *Pension Asset Management: An International Perspective* (Pension Research Council, Wharton School, University of Pennsylvania).

146 For recent statistics on occupational schemes in the UK, see Office for National Statistics (2016) 'Occupational Pension Schemes Survey, UK: 2015', available at www.ons.gov.uk/peoplepopulationandcommunity/personalandhouseholdfinances/pensionssavingsandinvestments/bulletins/occupationalpensionschemessurvey/2015/pdf.

147 However, it was left to the market to determine the structure and efficiency of pension schemes. The result was schemes that exhibited very high front-loaded charges, because retail customers tend not to be skilled at assessing the cost-effectiveness of retail financial products (Office of Fair Trading 1997, 1999).

In contrast, the Blair–Brown governments of 1997–2010 imposed restrictions on pension schemes, which were intended to reduce charges.[148] Despite these various initiatives, as noted above, there is still concern about the extent to which pension assets are managed wisely, about the multi-layered structure of the pensions industry, and about the rent extraction which occurs there. These concerns mirror many of those set out in this book as problems with the Australian system.

The UK pension industry shares many of Australia's principal-agent, conflict of interest and rent-seeking problems, which have led to continued concern over the structure of the pension system.[149] The UK Centre for Policy Studies published a report in 2012 containing 104 detailed proposals for reform of the UK pension industry, which it regarded as deeply flawed.[150] In this report Michael Johnson described how the UK industry has severe principal-agent problems, exacerbated by excessive delegation of responsibility for the management of pension funds. He attributed these problems to a lack of effective competition in the industry; information asymmetry; asset mispricing; and rent capture. Moral hazard is a widespread problem, including stock lending (which exposes investors to additional but undisclosed risk). Product innovation is rarely in the customer's interest. Johnson notes how there can be up to seven intermediary layers between the market and a potential customer in the UK. Johnson identified the main sources of charges as transaction costs, fiduciary costs, fund management charges, life company product wraps, platforms that provide a distribution capability, platform consolidators and advisers. He also cited excessive trading as a significant source of undisclosed costs and performance drag.[151] Johnson argued that trustees in the UK were falling well short of performing what ought to be a pivotal role within the industry and that they should demand more transparency, the unbundling of charges, and the disclosure of hidden counterparty risks.[152]

Recent governments have introduced numerous reforms, mainly to reduce the burden on the exchequer but also to provide more flexibility for retirees by permitting easier access to pension assets on retirement. *Pension freedoms* introduced in April 2015 have led to early withdrawal of pension assets, with the majority opting

148 The evolution of UK pension policy during the Thatcher, Major and Blair governments is described in detail in Blake, David (2002) 'The United Kingdom: Examining the Switch from Low Public Pensions to High-Cost Private Pensions' (National Bureau of Economic Research: Social Security Pension Reform in Europe, Conference Report edited by Martin Feldstein and Horst Siebert, The University of Chicago Press, Chicago), 317.

149 Johnson, above n 86.

150 Ibid.

151 SCM Private (2011) *Research into Dealing Activity and Costs of UK Individual Pension Funds* (Report, November 2011). SCM Private analysed 1,287 individual pension funds comprising £392.5 billion of assets.

152 Johnson also estimated additional implicit charges (principally bid-offer spreads) at £7.3 billion per annum.

for drawdown rather than the purchase of a subsequent annuity.[153] The general trend of policy change is to move away from defined benefit towards defined contribution schemes, and to place further responsibility on individuals for the management of their retirement incomes.[154] By 2030 the Department of Work and Pensions estimates that workplace DC schemes will hold £1.7trn, five times the £340bn held in 2015.[155] A Green Paper on the future of DB schemes in the UK was published in February 2017,[156] and a White Paper is expected later this year.[157] Perhaps surprisingly, given the evidence presented in a now well-developed international literature on the subject, and the emerging problems in both Chile and Australia, the UK seems well established in its move down the DC path.

A particular innovation introduced under the UK Pensions Act 2008[158] is the *National Employment Savings Trust* (NEST), a government-initiated auto-enrolment workplace pension. This is provided free for employers to use, and, following New Zealand Kiwisaver's example, has a single charging structure whatever fund is chosen.[159] There are currently some 370,000 employers using the system. The success of this initiative also provides helpful guidance for Australia as it seeks to fix some of the the problems highlighted in this book.

2.4.5 USA

The United States relies on the Old Age, Survivors, and Disability Insurance (OASDI) system, a DB pension scheme financed by payroll tax.[160] Benefits are

153 Financial Conduct Authority (2017) *Retirement Outcomes Review: Interim Report* (FCA MS16/1.2, July 2017). The FCA is concerned that many are opting for the first drawdown option offered to them and few are taking advice on the choice.

154 This has led to concern by regulators over the state of the decumulation market and that distrust of pension providers is causing members to withdraw all their funds. See www.professionalpensions.com/professional-pensions/analysis/3013725/fca-we-must-get-decumulation-market-into-better-shape-as-dc-grows.

155 Financial Conduct Authority (2017) *Retirement Outcomes Review: Interim Report* (FCA MS16/1.2, July 2017), 3.

156 Department for Work and Pensions (2017) *Security and Sustainability in Defined Benefit Pension Schemes* (Cm 9412, February 2017). This green paper emphasised the deficits estimated to be faced by existing defined benefit schemes, with estimates ranging from £459 billion (August 2016) to £197 billion (January 2017). There are currently an estimated 11 million members of DB schemes in the UK, with £1.5 trillion in funds-under-management. The green paper was published as a response to "some commentators [declaring] that there is a fundamental problem with the funding and regulation of these schemes", a claim the department refutes.

157 Among other things, the White Paper is expected to give the pensions regulator "more proactive powers" to deal with the problems created by the switch from DB to DC. See www.professionalpensions.com/professional-pensions/news/3013752/dwp-to-launch-db-white-paper-this-winter-to-give-tpr-more-proactive-powers.

158 UK Government (2008) *Pensions Act 2008* (Chapter 30).

159 For details of NEST, see www.nestpensions.org.uk/schemeweb/NestWeb/public/whatisnest/contents/whatisnest.html. The charges are 1.8% on new contributions and 0.3% of funds under management as an *annual management charge* (AMC). There are no other charges, for example for switching funds or changing retirement date.

160 Currently 12.4% subject to an upper limit.

based on earnings during the best 35 years of an individual's career and are indexed to the consumer price index. The OASDI is required to be financially balanced over a period of 75 years. There are many company and (state, federal and local) government employee retirement funds, mostly operated on a DB basis.[161] In recent years, DC plans have grown in importance, including 401(k) plans[162], employee stock ownership plans (ESOPs) and individual retirement arrangements (IRAs).[163] Funded schemes in the US have a total of $15 trillion of funds under management, some 60% of the total in all OECD countries.[164] Some DC schemes manage their funds efficiently, for example the US Thrift Savings Plan, which has around $300 billion in net assets and approximately 4.5 million members. This scheme (which is available to civilians who are, or were, employed by the government or were members of the armed services) uses a passive management strategy and charges fees to its members of only 2.5 basis points (0.025%) per year.

However, a recent study by Joshua Rauh for the Hoover Institution has found that unfunded pension liabilities in the US may exceed $3.8 trillion, and may lead to further civic bankruptcies in the next five to ten years.[165] Several commentators believe that this problem has potential to create another major financial crisis in the US.[166] The US does not now have enough workers to support what is actuarially necessary as a payroll tax or pension contribution, hence the move towards DC plans.[167] This expansion of the DC component

161 Examples are the National Railroad Retirement Investment Trust, the civil service retirement and disability fund, Railroad Retirement Board, judicial retirement fund, military retirement fund, and the foreign service retirement and disability fund.

162 These take advantage of Section 401(k) of the Internal Revenue Code, under which employees are allowed to make before-tax contributions from their salaries.

163 See Antolin, P., S. Payet and J. Yermo (2012) 'Coverage of Private Pension Systems: Evidence and Policy Options', OECD Working Papers on Finance, Insurance and Private Pensions, No. 20, OECD Publishing, Paris, available at http://dx.doi.org/10.1787/5k94d6gh2w6c-en.

164 OECD (2017) *Pension Funds in Figures* (May 2017), available at www.oecd.org/daf/fin/private-pensions/Pension-Funds-in-Figures-2017.pdf.

165 Rauh, Joshua D. (2017) 'Hidden Debt, Hidden Deficits: 2017 Edition – How Pension Promises are Consuming State and Local Budgets' (Hoover Institution Essay, May 2017), available at www.hoover.org/sites/default/files/research/docs/rauh_hiddendebt2017_final_webreadypdf1.pdf. Rauh's research follows similar analysis of 56 US public pension schemes by Moody's, the ratings agency that put the total deficit at around US$7 trillion. Mooney, Attracta (2016) 'Problems Pile up for US Public Pensions' (Financial Times, 17 March 2016). See also http://uk.businessinsider.com/us-government-7-trillion-pension-shortfall-2016-4?r=US&IR=T.

166 See, for example, www.marketwatch.com/story/collapsing-pensions-will-fuel-americas-next-financial-crisis-2017-03-14; www.forbes.com/sites/oliviergarret/2017/06/09/the-disturbing-trend-that-will-end-in-a-full-fledged-pension-crisis/#645984db6620. For more detail on the issue of unfunded pension liabilities see Wachter, Susan M. (ed.) (2016) *Public Pensions and City Solvency* (University of Pennsylvania Press, Philadelphia).

167 For detailed discussion of this issue, see Hsiao, William C.L. (2008) 'Demographic Changes and Funding for Pension Plans', available at www.bostonfed.org/-/media/Documents/conference/16/conf16b.pdf?la=en.

of pension provision has recently been criticised as causing "a massive retirement crisis in the United States by leaving most workers unprepared for retirement".[168]

2.4.6 Canada

The Canadian public pension system consists of a universal flat benefit for all seniors, supplemented by a means-tested *Guaranteed Income Supplement* (both financed from tax revenues)[169] and an earnings-related scheme financed on a pay-as-you go basis by compulsory contributions.[170] In addition, there are tax incentives to encourage participation in *Registered Pension Plans* (RPPs) and *Registered Retirement Savings Plans* (RRSPs), with the latter targeted on the self-employed.[171] All of these elements date from the 1960s.[172] In the mid 1990s, contribution rates were increased to create funds to finance future benefits, following concern about the long-term sustainability of the *Canada Pension Plan*.[173] Canada's pension system is usually regarded as well-run, and active government intervention has ensured that it remains sustainable.

Canada's largest pension funds are recognised as being well run and operated in the interests of members. The top ten have invested more than $400 billion in Canada, and also participated in major infrastructure deals worldwide.[174] They manage about 80% of funds internally, with an average cost of around 0.3% of FUM.

168 Secunda, Paul M. (2016) 'The Behavioural Economic Case for Paternalistic Workplace Retirement Plans' 91 *Indiana Law Journal*, 505–547. Secunda goes on to say "The voluntary, inaccessible, employer-centered, expensive, and consumer-driven natures of these plans have combined to make retirement a type of corporate-inspired elder abuse in America" (p. 505) and highlights how employees making improper choices with regards to their 401(k) plans have "helped to fuel the current retirement crisis".

169 This includes Old Age Security [OAS] and income tested supplements (the Guaranteed Income Supplement [GIS] and Spouse's Allowance [SPA]).

170 Currently 6.1% of covered earnings.

171 Upon maturity the assets can be used to purchase a life annuity, or placed in a Registered Retirement Income Fund (RRIF) which provides more flexible timing of the withdrawals.

172 Beland, Daniel and John Myles (2006) 'Stasis Amidst Change: Canadian Pension Reform in an Age of Retrenchment', Chapter 12, 252–273, in Giuliano Bonoli and Toshimitsu Shinkawa (eds) *Ageing and Pension Reform around the World; Evidence from Eleven Countries* (Edward Elgar, 1 Jan 2006).

173 Contributions were increased from 5.6% to 9.9% by 2003, with the intention of creating funds capable of paying five years of benefits. The surplus was to be invested in a diversified portfolio of securities. Martin, Paul (1998) 'Finance Minister's Statement on the Seniors Benefit' (Ottawa, Government of Canada, 28 July), www.fin.gc.ca/news98/98-071e.html.

174 See Lakoff, David (2013) 'The Top Ten: Investing for Canada on the World Stage', available at https://hoopp.com/docs/default-source/newsroom-library/research/top-10-pension-funds-in-canada.pdf?sfvrsn=6. Investments include "one of the largest electricity transmission and distribution companies in the US, seven UK airports including Heathrow, three Chilean water utilities and one of the largest and most profitable insurance providers in South Korea".

2.4.7 Japan

Japan has a universal flat rate basic pension that is mostly financed on a pay-as-you-go basis. Benefits are proportional to the number of years of contributions, with a statutory retirement age of 60. A second tier, known as the *Employees Pension*, provides earnings-related benefits and is funded by a government-run fund. The public pension system is funded by a national government subsidy (of around 2% of GDP) and by contributions. In total, 90% of private enterprises provide some form of occupational benefits at retirement, and it is possible to contract out of the *Employees Pension* into selected occupational schemes.

The Japanese Government Pension Investment Fund (Nenkin Tsumitatekin Kanri Un'yō Dokuritsu-gyōsei-Hōjin or GPIF) holds the largest single pool of retirement savings in the world, with assets under management of 145 trillion yen (US$1.28 trillion). Japan also has average life expectancy of 83 years and a corresponding dependency ratio (the ratio of those aged over 65 years to the working age population), which is expected to rise from 38% in 2010 to 57% by 2030, the highest in the world.[175] The fiscal challenges this presents are intense. Various reforms have been suggested to reduce the annual government subsidy, including increasing the age for eligibility, clawing back benefits from wealthy retirees, and collecting contributions from dependent spouses.

2.5 Australia's challenges

The introduction of compulsory superannuation contributions[176] was intended to provide a well-financed retirement for Australia's people.[177] The creation of the Australian superannuation system is regarded by some as one of Australia's great achievements.[178] However, there is today a growing sense of unease about

175 Kashiwase, Kenichiro, Masahiro Nozaki, and Kiichi Tokuoka (2012) 'Pension Reforms in Japan' (IMF Working Paper WP/12/285, December 2012). Pension benefit spending in FY2010 was around 10.6% of GDP.

176 The Superannuation Guarantee Charge concept was introduced by Paul Keating, shortly after becoming Prime Minister in 1991. Australia is unique among developed countries in requiring all employees to make such contributions.

177 A statement of the political intent behind this decision is to be found in John Dawkins, Security in Retirement: Planning for Tomorrow Today (Australian Government Publication Service, 1992).

178 See, e.g., Bill Shorten's claim that "[s]uperannuation has proved to be a terrific idea; blessing Australia with a national institution that almost every developed economy in the rest of the world would give their eye teeth for". Shorten, Bill (2011) '20 Years of Superannuation' (Speech delivered at the ASFA Superannuation Guarantee Dinner, Parliament House, Canberra, 16 August 2011). Shorten was Minister for Financial Services and Superannuation at the time. The system has also been described recently as being of "high quality", see KPMG (2017) *Super Insights Report 2017*, 4.

the level of retirement income that the system will provide,[179] a lack of trust in the industry and its advisers,[180] and a steep rise in the numbers of those who are choosing self-management of their superannuation fund.[181] The recent *Financial System Inquiry*[182] has led to both the Reserve Bank of Australia and the Australian Treasury, questioning whether the transfer of risk to members and the large costs of the system are appropriate.[183]

Chapter 3 focuses on the policy choices made by Australia that led to this situation, and in particular on three major influences. First, it examines the role of the unions and how and why compulsory superannuation contributions emerged as a by-product of the wage bargaining process. Second, it reviews the decision to hand over strategy and management of superannuation assets to the private sector. Third, it notes the complex institutional and governance structures that have emerged, the division of responsibility between multiple regulatory agencies, and the weakening of protections provided by the legal system.

179 See, e.g., Hewett, Jennifer (2010) 'The Great Superannuation Delusion', *The Australian* (Sydney, 13 March 2010). She quotes John Brogden of the Investment and Financial Services Association as saying "The fact of the matter is that the vast majority of Australians are going to retire on less money than they can live on. They are going to get a rude shock when they realise that in their early 50s."

180 See Brandweiner, Richard (2012) 'Trust is a Central Issue for Super Fund Managers', *The Australian* (Sydney, 6 March 2012). Brandweiner, President of the Chartered Financial Analysts' Society of Sydney, also notes that "[t]he average return on default superannuation schemes over the past 10 years has underperformed the returns on cash and has barely beaten inflation". A 2013 survey of the views of members carried out by the Financial Services Council and ING (Financial Services Council and ING (2013) Superannuation – Australia's View, 9) reveals that only 50% of those surveyed had trust in superannuation funds and providers, and only 49% had confidence in the superannuation system. 66% stated that superannuation funds, their fees and the way they work were not transparent enough. Concern about lack of trust is sometimes also expressed by advisers, see, e.g., Brown, Robert M.C. (2012) 'The Public's Lack of Trust Is No Conspiracy Theory – It's Real' 45 *Professional Planner* 22.

181 Through self-managed superannuation funds ('SMSFs'). Slattery, Andrea (2011) 'The Rise and Rise of SMSFs' (Speech delivered at the Self-managed Superannuation Funds Professionals' Association of Australia National Conference, 13 July 2011) estimated the size of SMSF funds at 31 March 2011 as $432 billion. Concern is sometimes expressed about the dangers of unregulated SMSFs being responsible for such large sums, see, e.g., Gettler, Leon (2013) 'The Rise and Rise of SMSFs' 127 *InFinance: The Magazine for Finsia Members* 2, 9.

182 The *Financial System Inquiry*, chaired by David Murray AO, was announced by the Prime Minister, Tony Abbott, on 20 November 2013; see Prime Minister of Australia, *Financial System Inquiry* (20 November 2013), available at www.pm.gov.au/media/2013-11-20/financial-system-inquiry.

183 Reserve Bank of Australia (2014) 'Submission to the Financial System Inquiry' (RBA, March 2014); Department of Treasury (2014) 'The Department of the Treasury's Submission to the Financial System Inquiry' (Cth, 3 April 2014). Peter Costello, Australian Treasurer from 1996 to 2007, highlighted in a speech in October 2017 the high costs of the current system, and proposed that funds over which members make no active choice should be managed by a publicly run body. Costello, Peter (2017) 'The Uncertain Path of Superannuation Reform' (speech to the SuperRatings & Lonsec 'Day of Confrontation 2017', Melbourne, 12 October 2017), available at www.petercostello.com.au/media/LonsecSpeech-12Oct2017-Uncertain-Path-of-Super-Reform.pdf.

The introduction of compulsory contributions was in part necessary because Australia had been slow to introduce effective state provision for those not in the public sector or in the larger companies that ran their own schemes. As discussed below, the result is that Australia has a worse problem of poverty among the old than most other OECD countries, and a particularly poor income replacement rate for retirees.

Faced with the challenge of demographic change and an inadequate publicly funded pension system, Australia's politicians and union leaders of the early 1990s chose to create a predominately funded system.[184] This is the opposite of what the economic theory set out above would suggest was optimal, which would have been to require current workers to make contributions that then paid for improved pensions for the currently retired generation.[185] The major losers from this choice are mostly those who are retired now, and those who retire before the new system reaches full maturity. However, as also discussed in Chapter 3, it may, nevertheless, have been the best that could be achieved given Australian political realities. For the current working generation to provide the necessary contributions to fund their parents' pensions requires a degree of trust that the political system will, in fact, extend the same privilege to themselves in future.

The role of the unions was particularly important during the 1960s and 1970s, when a number of sector-specific schemes were established, and in the run-up to the introduction of compulsory superannuation contributions. Initially, there were various discussions about establishing a national scheme, and then about making superannuation an integral part of the wage bargaining process, but eventually the government decided that legislating for compulsory contributions was the way forward. A crucial factor was the inability of unions to achieve desired wage rises through the wage bargaining process (partly because of concerns over inflationary pressures), with employer superannuation contributions seen as more easily achievable.

The second choice that was made was to encourage defined contribution pensions. As noted above, this transfers longevity and market risks, as well as the risks associated with principal-agent, rent-seeking and conflicts of interest problems, to the individual. This denied Australian retirees the benefits of risk sharing, yet little attention was given at the time to how to protect individuals from the various risks. As discussed below, attempts are now being made to retrofit systems such as Comprehensive Income Products for Retirement (CIPRs).

The third choice was to hand over responsibility for management of the accumulated funds largely to private sector providers. This has led to many of the problems identified in this book. In particular, the creation of a complex and multi-layered industry in which many responsibilities are delegated to third parties has created a degree of separation between the members and those who

184 Although the scheme was announced in the 1991 budget, it was introduced in July 1992.

185 Several commentators have suggested that the primary reason for the policy choice was that government wished to use pensions legislation to establish a pool of funds in order to alleviate balance of payments problems. See, for example, Scheiwe, Dan (1999) 'Why Australia's Pension System Is Not a Good International Model' (Queensland University of Technology).

make decisions on their behalf. This has led to a less efficient system and worse outcomes for members.

2.5.1 Pension adequacy[186]

In the late 2000s, Australia's income replacement rate for the over 65s was the lowest among 34 OECD countries (69% of national mean income compared with the OECD average of 86.2%).[187] Poverty in Australia among those aged over 65 is worse than in most other OECD countries, estimated at over 33%.[188] This is despite the fact that Australia provides a basic pension to those who do not have enough personal assets, which in 2014 provided income of about 27% of the average wage.[189] Challenger has attempted an evaluation of pension system adequacy based on poverty rates, poverty gaps and the relative incomes of the over 65s: on this basis, Australia ranks a lowly 25 out of 34 OECD countries.[190]

Analysis by Burnett, Davis et al. suggests that compulsory contributions to a retirement savings account at current levels during an entire working life would generate a median consumption level during retirement of less than half the median equalised income of the whole population.[191] So even if the accumulated funds were administered and invested efficiently, there is still a problem of pension adequacy in the future. Further, Bateman has highlighted the accumulated amounts affected by taxes and by administrative charges.[192] She calculated that 2% administrative costs per annum, and taxes, can reduce an effective 9% superannuation guarantee to 3.4–3.8%, a level that she also estimates will not be sufficient to provide adequate incomes in retirement.

186 For a recent discussion of the overall situation in Australia, see O'Loughlin, Kate, Colette Browning and Hal Kendig (eds) (2017) *Ageing in Australia: Challenges and Opportunities* (International Perspectives on Aging, Volume 16, Springer), in particular Chapter 9: Bateman, Hazel, Rafal Chomik and John Piggott (2017) 'Retirement Incomes'.

187 Challenger (2014) *An International Comparison of Pension System Performance in Delivering Adequate Retirement Incomes*, 3. This analysis is based on OECD estimates taken from OECD (2013) *Pensions at a Glance 2013: Retirement-Income Systems in OECD and G20 Countries*, www.oecd.org/pensions/pensionsataglance.htm

188 Latest available year. OECD (2015) *In it Together: Why Less Inequality Benefits All* (OECD Publishing, Paris), available at http://dx.doi.org/10.1787/9789264235120-en, 56, Table 1.A1.1. The OECD defines the poverty threshold as 50% of median disposable income in each country (slightly above the level of the basic Australia Age Pension – so many Australians are only marginally 'in poverty'). Most OECD countries had a poverty rate among over-65s of less than 15%, for example the UK (13.4%), Germany (9.4%), Sweden (9.4%), Spain (6.8%), Norway (4.1%), France (3.8%). Even the United States has a lower poverty rate among over-65s, of 21.5%.

189 This basic provision is often described as a 'first tier' pension. New Zealand provides a first tier pension of 40% of average earnings, and has a poverty rate among over-65s of around 8%.

190 Challenger (2014) above n 187, 13, Figure 2.8. This poor performance on pension adequacy is, however, reflected in a high score on fiscal sustainability, in which Australia ranks second.

191 Burnett, J., K.T. Davis, C. Murawski, R. Wilkins and N. Wilkinson (2014) 'Measuring Adequacy of Retirement Savings' (Melbourne Institute Working Paper, Vol. 2014, No. 5).

192 Bateman, Hazel (2002) 'Retirement Income Strategy in Australia' 32 *Economic Analysis and Policy* 49; see especially Table 1, 50.

These high costs may have an impact on retirement behaviour.[193] Bateman has also observed that there seems likely to be a principal-agent issue with employer choice of fund, in that employers may not seek the most cost-effective fund for their employees, but instead focus on funds which meet other corporate objectives.

2.5.2 Legal and regulatory constraints

The commercial law framework for superannuation funds in Australia is based on the law of trusts. Superannuation funds are usually 'express trusts' and the trustees of superannuation funds are in principle 'status-based' fiduciaries.[194] Prime responsibility for the viability and prudent operation of the superannuation fund thus rests with trustees. Trustees may be either a company with a Board of Directors or a group of people (who may also be the members). Trustees, in their role as fiduciaries, are in principle subject to an 'inflexible rule' that prevents them putting themselves in a position where their interest and duty conflict.[195]

Australian legislation defines many responsibilities of trustees. For example, s 56(2) of the *Superannuation Industry (Supervision) Act* 1993 (SIS Act) prevents the use of a trust instrument to exempt a trustee from liability for dishonest or intentionally or recklessly careless breaches of trust., and s 52(2) of the SIS Act requires that trustees covenant to act honestly, with due care and diligence, and in the best interests of members. In practice, however, trustees often do not have the expertise, knowledge or motivation to intervene effectively on behalf of their members.[196]

Fiduciary duty is frequently set aside in financial services, where apparently well-informed consent is given, and the courts have usually regarded contracts as taking precedence over fiduciary duties. In addition, trust law has limited effectiveness in a world of member choice and flexibility of trust deed.[197] Trustees' fiduciary responsibilities therefore need to be strengthened. This may require the adjustment of some aspects both of legislation and of policy, including ensuring

193 Bateman, Hazel, Geoffrey Kingston and John Piggott (2001) *Forced Saving: Mandating Private Retirement Incomes* (Cambridge University Press).

194 But see Edeleman, James (2013) 'The Role of Status in the Law Of Obligations: Common Callings, Implied Terms and Lessons For Fiduciary Duties' (Paper presented at the DePaul University Conference, Chicago, 19–20 July 2013). Edelman notes that the courts usually regard status as simply informing about what the fiduciary has undertaken to do, see *Beach Petroleum v Kennedy* (1999) 48 NSWLR 1, 188.

195 See *Bray v Ford* [1896] AC 44, 51;*Phipps v Boardman* [1967] 2 AC 46, 123; Glover, John (2002) 'Conflicts of Interest in a Corporate Context' in Gerald Anselm Acquaah-Gaisie and Julia Snip (eds), *Corporate Crime Workshop 2002, 13 February 2002: Papers* (Monash University Department of Law and Taxation, 2002).

196 Only trustees of public offer funds were licensed by APRA pre-2004, and it was not until after 2004 that changes made to the SIS Act required all trustees of APRA-regulated funds to be licensed.

197 Donald, M. Scott (2007) 'The Prudent Eunuch: Superannuation Trusteeship in an Environment of Member Investment Choice' (University of New South Wales Australian School of Business).

that design of the trust deed does not reduce trustees' fiduciary responsibilities and preventing member choice from diluting the trustee's ability to take a holistic view of members' needs. We explore how trust law might be further enhanced in Section 6.4.

A variety of inquiries into the Australian system, reported in Annex C, have highlighted inadequate governance and disclosure arrangements. The complexity of the industry, and of the contractual structures it relies on, make the identification and prevention of de facto collusive behaviour and anti-competitive use of cross-subsidies very difficult for regulators (such as the Australian Competition and Consumer Commmssion (ACCC), the Australian Securities and Investments Commission (ASIC), and the prudential regulators), or the courts to identify and combat.

There are too many regulatory agencies, with inadequate focus on investment management costs. Various legislative changes have weakened the force of trust law and fiduciary duties. The legal and governance framework has failed to prevent principal-agent and conflict of interest problems, including inadequate enforcement and recognition of fiduciary duties and duties of care.

2.5.3 Organisation and governance

The Australian superannuation industry comprises three distinct types of superannuation funds – retail (run by the major banks, insurance companies and other financial institutions), not-for-profit and self-managed superannuation funds.[198] Retail funds are all 'public offer funds', which means that they are open to the general public. The not-for-profit funds comprise single employer corporate funds, public sector funds and multi-employer industry funds (initially created to provide superannuation for particular occupational groups but now extended to a wider clientele). These were traditionally 'closed' to all except employees of the constituent firms or industries, but increasingly also operate as public offer funds.

Governance differs by fund type, with some not-for-profit funds governed by trustee boards with equal representation of employee and employer directors, and retail funds governed by 'corporate trustees', where the board comprises mostly employees of the associated financial services provider. The trustee boards in Australia generally delegate a large proportion of asset management to external managers and rely on external third parties for a range of other services, including member account administration, custodial services, insurance, actuarial services and auditing. This creates many 'degrees of separation' between the beneficiaries and those who manage their pension assets.

The superannuation funds interact extensively, with the retail funds subcontracting aspects of various tasks to each other, and the industry funds outsourcing

198 While self-managed superannuation funds comprise one third of superannuation assets, they account for less than 5% of members. Self-managed funds comprise four or fewer member-directors. They are not included in the analysis presented in this paper.

many activities to investment managers and consultants who may in turn be employed by banks or insurance companies. Specialist 'funds of funds' and 'fund platforms' are commonplace, and delegation of custody, strategy, portfolio selection, investment management and administration to third parties is widespread. There is strong interplay between life assurance and pension provision, and as a result the life insurance companies have also become major players in the funds management industry.

A 2011 survey of funds management in Australia summarised the wider investment management industry thus:

> Australia's wealth management market is comprised of 300 investment managers in Australia and about 450 investment managers which source Funds under Management (FUM) from offshore, 440,000 superannuation funds, 320 platform products, several thousand managed funds and 18,000 financial advisers. These market participants are supported by a range of service providers that include investment consultants as well as custodians, fund administrators, accountants and legal advisers.[199]

Although the Australian superannuation industry on the surface looks diverse, in practice those involved in the system are grouped into a small number of entities, through operational, financial, collaborative and social links, which has implications for system stability and for the emergence of effective competition.[200]

The Australian superannuation system places heavy reliance on the accumulation of funds in the name of each individual. Most individuals will end up participating in several funds as they change jobs or make additional contributions. In total, there are over 579,500 funds with a total of over 29 million members.[201] The costs of administering such a system are inevitably high.

In practice, trustees in Australia face numerous pressures to act against the interest of their members in permitting payments to intermediaries.[202] In employer

199 Dunnin, Alex (2011) *Fund Management in Australia: Market Entry Report* (Rainmaker Information), 4.

200 Donald, Scott, Hazel Bateman, Ross Buckley, Kevin Liu and Rob Nicholls (2016) 'Too Connected to Fail: The Regulation of Systemic Risk within Australia's Superannuation System', 2 *Journal of Financial Regulation* 1, 56–78; Donald, Scott, Bruce Arnold, Hazel Bateman, Ross Buckley and Kevin Liu (2013) 'The Implications of Complexity for Systemic Risk in the Superannuation System' (Working Paper No. 13-3, Centre for Law, Markets and Regulation, UNSW, August 2013), 11.

201 APRA (2017) *Annual Superannuation Bulletin* (June 2016, updated February 2017), Table 3. Figures as at 30 June 2016. The large number of members, greater than the total population of Australia, reflects the fact that many people are members of several funds.

202 These issues are discussed in detail in Taylor, Sue, Anthony Asher and Julie Anne Tarr (2017) 'Accountability in Regulatory Reform: Australia's Superannuation Industry Paradox' 45 *Federal Law Review* 257, 290; Campbell, Joe (2017) 'Some Aspects of the Civil Liability Arising from Breach of Duty by a Superannuation Trustee' (Sydney Law School Legal Studies Research Paper No. 17/31, April 2017).

sponsored, non-public-offer funds, the trustees are often also directors or managers of the employer, thus facing conflict between their Corporations Act duties and their duties as trustee. This conflict is particularly acute when reductions in employer contributions to the fund are being discussed. Trustees of industry funds may have direct links to employer sponsors, and rely on these or unions to attract union members and this may lead to arrangements which are not in the interest of members.

Trustees of retail funds in Australia are judged on the growth and profits of their funds, and in turn are dependent on active marketing through life companies, bank branches or advisers. Where outsourcing is done to a related party, trustees face a conflict between their duty to the wider employer and their duty to members. Trustees also face a conflict in determining their own fees and expenses. Their remuneration may be, and often is, linked to the profitability of the trustee firm or of the wider group within which the firm is nested.

2.5.4 Work in progress

Perhaps the best that can be said about the Australian superannuation system is that it is still a work in progress. Pension adequacy is poor by OECD standards, and poverty among the old remains a serious concern. The current generation of retirees face retirement on incomes that are low by international standards. The development of pension policy as a by-product of the wage bargaining process has meant that the system lacks systematic design, and as a result a complex and expensive industry has been allowed to emerge. Longevity and market risks have been imposed on individuals who are ill-equipped to manage them. Although there is clearly scope for the legal and regulatory system to control more effectively the principal-agent, conflict of interest, rent-seeking problems highlighted in this book, to date the political system has not chosen to bring these under effective control.

As noted above, many of these problems are the result of making three particular choices: to fund the system, rather than operating it on a pay-as-you-go basis; using defined contribution rather than defined benefit schemes; and delegating much of the administration and fund management to a rent-seeking private sector. These policy failures are considered further in Chapter 5, which also summarises recent attempts at reform. Some solutions are suggested in Chapter 6, while Chapter 7 provides brief conclusions. Chapter 3 provides detail on how and why the system evolved as it did, while Chapter 4 provides some empirical evidence on the outcomes of the last 25 years.

3 The evolution of the Australian pension system

3.1 Origins

The origins of the modern superannuation system go back to the management of wealth created by the Gold Rush of the nineteenth century. Federation gave the Commonwealth Government taxation powers, and tax concessions were used to encourage pension provision. However, apart from public sector pensions and some concessions to corporate schemes, occupational pensions for the majority remained limited until the 1980s. The means-tested Age Pension has never been intended to provide adequate income protection in retirement for anyone other than the poorest, and attempts to introduce state-run earnings-related schemes (three times between 1913 and 1938, in the 1970s, and in the 1980s) all failed to be implemented. Instead, demands by the unions for better treatment for their members led eventually to agreed contributions by employers in lieu of wage rises, and also led to the decision in 1991 to introduce the *Superannuation Guarantee Charge*.

Prior to Federation, provision for the non-wealthy aged was limited to that provided by voluntary charitable organisations, and normally took the form of institutionalised care focused on alleviation of only the worst poverty.[1] Occupational pension schemes commenced in the 1840s, the first being for employees of the Bank of New South Wales (now Westpac). The depression of the 1890s placed the voluntary system of aged care under strain and led to general recognition that support for the aged was a collective responsibility.[2] This followed the introduction of insurance or pension schemes in Germany (1882), Denmark (1891), Belgium (1894) and New Zealand (1898).[3] In 1900, New

1 See Herscovitch, Andrew and David Stanton (2008) 'History of Social Security in Australia' 80 *Family Matters* 51 for a detailed history of the evolution of Australian social security. See also Kewley, Thomas Henry (1973) *Social Security in Australia, 1900–72* (Sydney University Press), 15.

2 Dixon, John (1977) *Australia's Policy towards the Aged: 1890–1972* (Canberra College of Advanced Education).

3 Department of the Treasury (2001) *Towards Higher Retirement Incomes for Australians: a History of the Australian Retirement Income System since Federation* (Department of the Treasury, Economic Round Up Centenary Edition, 14 May 2001), 65–92.

South Wales, Victoria and Queensland introduced a means tested old age pension funded from general revenue.[4]

Life insurance companies in Australia first emerged in the 1830s through branches of British companies, while the Australian life insurance industry mostly has its origins in mutual associations formed during the mid-nineteenth century.[5] Organisations such as Australian Mutual Provident (AMP), founded in 1849, dominated sales of life insurance products for over a century, and enjoyed strong consumer support.[6] These associations accumulated a large capital base, originally from Gold Rush earnings, and were relatively lightly regulated, partly reflecting their original status as philanthropic organisations.[7] Although the mutual associations faced some competition from the British life insurance companies, this was limited by the preference of Australians to deal with local providers, and from 1884 by the introduction of a requirement that probate duty be paid on the policies of British companies.

The rapid growth of Australian cities between 1870 and 1890 and rising real incomes led to substantial increases in life industry earnings and in the number of life insurance companies.[8] The mutual form of association was popular, with the directors seen as "men of probity and honesty".[9] Partly because Australian death rates were lower than British, the profitability of the early industry was impressive.[10] The dominance of a few firms, and aggressive protection of their market share, led to a very concentrated industry.[11] The fact that the Australian associations, led by AMP and Mutual Life Association, provided life cover that had fewer conditions than that normally required by British firms, reinforced their competitive position.[12] Non-price competition, a large network of offices

4 New South Wales did consider the introduction of a compulsory contributory insurance scheme of the type introduced by Bismarck in Germany, but rejected this on the grounds that it was not suited to NSW's small and underdeveloped society. Kewley, above n 1, 33.

5 In 1890, mutual firms accounted for 90% of all new policies sold. Keneley, Monica (2006) 'Mortgages and Bonds: The Asset Management Practices of Australian Life Insurers to 1960' 16 *Accounting, Business and Financial History* 99, 103.

6 AMP was originally established as a Friendly Society to create a 'modest life office' for the benefit of clergymen and other professionals. Richmond, George William and Francis Henry Sheriff (1930) *Pitman's Dictionary of Life Assurance* (Pitman) 130.

7 Keneley, Monica (2001) 'The Evolution of the Australian Life Insurance Industry' 11 *Accounting, Business and Financial History* 145. The Friendly Societies Acts, which protected the personal liability of members, also included regulation of policy cover and the investment of premium income. However, these restrictions were subsequently relaxed by a special act of Parliament in New South Wales.

8 Real GDP in Australia grew at an average of 4.8% in the period 1861 to 1889, while per capita real GDP expanded at a rate of 1.3%. Maddock, Rodney and Ian W. McLean (1987) *The Australian Economy in the Long Run* (Cambridge University Press) 14.

9 Keneley, above n 7, 149.

10 Yet the industry initially used British life tables.

11 The top five firms accounted for 74% of new policies in 1880, rising to 77.5% in 1890. *Australasian Insurance and Banking Record* (AIBR, 1870–1930, 1881: 98; 1891: 52), quoted in Keneley, above n 7, 152.

12 Spratt, Walter (1968) 'Lessons Learned: British, American and Colonial Life Insurance in Australia, 19th Century' 92 *Australasian Insurance and Banking Record* 132.

and branches, and agencies in country towns further reinforced the dominance of the larger firms. The life associations were also able to generate non-premium income through investment in property and mortgages.

However, speculative investment in land and housing, financed by borrowing overseas, led to a land price bubble that burst in 1889, revealing massive frauds by some of Victoria's leading financiers.[13] Although the life associations emerged from the depression of the 1890s stronger than many other parts of the finance industry, decline of new business and losses on mortgages reduced assets and earning capacity, and in turn affected their ability to pay bonuses.[14] Many companies amalgamated as an alternative to liquidation, and investment portfolios were restructured to reduce dependence on mortgages and include more government securities.[15] By the end of the nineteenth century, a smaller number of life insurance offices were established as a major element in the Australian financial system, with substantial and growing assets.[16]

The origins of legal and regulatory control of financial services in Australia lay in the fiduciary obligations placed on trustees by company law. Investment companies from the eighteenth and nineteenth centuries onwards were typically controlled by trustees who had obligations to act in good faith, in the interests of investors, and for a proper purpose.[17] However, alternative investment arrangements avoided the restrictions of company law, and so were not subject to government oversight and control.

3.2 Age pensions and tax incentives after Federation

The *Constitution* gave the Commonwealth Government power from 1901 to legislate for provision of old age and invalid pensions, in addition to those provided by the states.[18] This power was formalised in a national act in 1908, which introduced a national means-tested pension for those over 65.[19] In 1910 the

13 Cannon, Michael (1986) *The Land Boomers* (Melbourne University Press).

14 Building societies declined and the number of trading banks was reduced by half. Thomson, Dianne and Malcolm Abbott (1998) 'The Life and Death of Australian Permanent Building Societies' 8 *Accounting, Business and Financial History* 73; Schedvin, Carl Boris (1970) *Australia and the Great Depression: a Study of Economic Development and Policy in the 1920s and 1930s* (Sydney University Press).

15 Keneley, above n 7, 155.

16 The value of life association assets doubled from £11.5 million in 1890 to £23 million in 1900. Conversely, those of trading banks fell from £151.5 million in 1890 to £116.5 million in 1900, whilst those of building societies fell from £22.5 million to £4.5 million. Keneley, above n 7, 156.

17 For a discussion of the evolution of the unit trust as a vehicle for investment, see Hughes, Robert Allan (1991) *The Law of Public Unit Trusts* (Longman Professional), 26–35; Sin, Kam Fan (1997) *The Legal Nature of the Unit Trust* (Oxford University Press), 7–32.

18 *Australian Constitution* s 51(xxiii).

19 *Invalid and Old-age Pensions Act 1908* (Cth). The 1908 Act required claimants to have been continuously resident in Australia for 25 years, subsequently reduced this to 20 years to match the residency requirement of the superseded Victorian and Queensland schemes. The residency requirement was reduced to 10 years in 1962, and from 1973 Australians became entitled to draw the pension regardless of where they lived.

pension age for women was reduced to 60 and in 1912 the Act was amended to exclude the family home from the means test.[20] The *Income Tax Assessment Act* of 1915 allowed tax deductibility of employer contributions and the exemption of superannuation fund earnings from taxation.[21]

These initiatives started the 'three pillar' system of old age support. Australia's pension system until the 1980s thus relied on the means-tested Age Pension and on charitable support for the poorest, on occupational schemes, and on voluntary savings for retirement encouraged by tax concessions.[22] At the beginning of the First World War some major companies provided corporate pensions, and there were a variety of public sector schemes, but their initial coverage only extended to a minority of the population. The state pension did not attempt to provide income replacement for those not covered by public sector or corporate schemes.

Development of the modern superannuation system is best considered in a series of epochs, punctuated by the two world wars and culminating in the 1991 decision to introduce compulsory superannuation contributions, which in turn led to the development of the modern industry.

Epoch 1 (1918–1945) covers the inter-war period, during which pressure grew for the introduction of better pension provision, and attempts were made to introduce a national earnings-related scheme. However, a combination of political change, the economic crisis of the 1930s, and the outbreak of war prevented these being implemented. The period also saw rapid growth of the life insurance industry and the emergence of the managed funds industry.

Epoch 2 (1945–1970) covers the post-war development of the welfare state, the use of the tax system to provide incentives for superannuation, and the continued tightening of bank regulation. This encouraged the entry of foreign insurance companies and the emergence of investment banking.

Epoch 3 (1970–1991) started with a further call for the introduction of an earnings-related scheme, which again failed to be implemented because of a change of government. This in turn created industrial relations pressure for the introduction of wider superannuation, which in due course led to the introduction of compulsory contributions. The epoch also saw major changes to the structure of the financial services industry, partly in response to tax changes, privatisation and deregulation, and further involvement of foreign players.

20 The 1908 Act replaced similar provisions in three States. The Australian Act was introduced in the same year Lloyd George introduced the Old Age Pensions Act in the UK. At the time, life expectancy for men was such that individuals were not expected to survive in retirement for many years. The pension introduced on 15 April 1909 was ten shillings a week, or £26 per year, with eligibility based on means, race, age, character and residency. The British pound was used in Australia until 1910, when Australia introduced its own currency, the Australian pound (A£), which in turn was replaced by the Australian dollar in 1966.

21 Nielson, Leslie (2010) 'Chronology of Superannuation and Retirement Income in Australia' (Background Note, Parliamentary Library, Parliament of Australia).

22 The Age Pension has always been paid out of general revenue, and is generally recognised not to provide sufficient income in retirement for the citizens of a rich country such as Australia. Tax concessions were formalised under the *Income Tax Assessment Act 1936* (Cth), and extended in the *Income Tax and Social Services Contribution Assessment Act 1961* (Cth).

Epoch 4 (1991 to the present) began with the introduction of the *Superannuation Guarantee Charge*, and has seen the rapid growth of the superannuation industry, as well as Asian and global financial crises. The modern, multi-agency, system of regulation emerged mostly during this period, as did the extensive delegation of management to intermediaries. The institutional structure which has emerged resulted from complex interplay between the regulatory and taxation regimes, the wider evolution of the financial services system (in particular the insurance industry and the major banks), demutualisation, and increasing participation by overseas firms.

In what follows, the major events of each of the epochs are discussed, and then the relevant development of the legal and regulatory system and the wider evolution of the financial services industry during the period are analysed. In the light of these developments, the emergence of the modern superannuation arrangements is considered.

3.3 Epoch 1: early inter-war attempts to introduce a unified system

State social security and pension provision developed during the 1920s, with Queensland introducing unemployment insurance in 1923, and New South Wales introducing a widow's pension in 1926, family allowances in 1927, and employment injury benefits in 1928. The first unified superannuation scheme for government employees was established by the Superannuation Board in 1922 and this scheme gradually absorbed other public-sector schemes.[23] Most schemes were operated on a defined benefit basis, and provided generous retirement benefits, with assets invested mostly in government bonds.

Despite two detailed attempts to introduce a national earnings-related scheme in 1923 and 1938, and several subsequent attempts to introduce a comprehensive superannuation scheme run by the government, Australia did not introduce one.[24] The Bruce Government established a Royal Commission in 1923 which explored options for a comprehensive national insurance scheme for retirement, sickness and disability.[25] This led to the introduction of a *National Insurance Bill* in 1928, but this lapsed in 1929 when the government was defeated.[26]

Following the Wall Street crash of 1929, the incoming Labor government led by James Scullin introduced the 'Premier's Plan', which included a reduction of 20%

23 For example, the Defence Force Retirement Fund, set up in 1948, was transferred to the Superannuation Board in 1959. The *Commonwealth Superannuation Scheme* was established in 1976. Barbetti, Annette and Stephen Kendal (2008) 'Australian Government Civil and Military Service Pensions' 14(1) *Commonwealth Innovations* 21.

24 Bateman, Hazel, Geoffrey Kingston and John Piggott (2001) *Forced Saving: Mandating Private Retirement Incomes* (Cambridge University Press). See especially Appendix 1, 'Mandatory Retirement Saving in Australia', 190.

25 *Royal Commission on National Insurance* (7 Sept 1923 – 5 Oct 1927).

26 The introduction of national insurance also faced opposition from employers and a 'lukewarm response from unions,' Herscovitch and Stanton, above n 1, 54.

in government spending, reductions in interest rates and increases in taxation.[27] Orthodox fiscal policy, including downward pressure on wages, was also pursued by the subsequent Lyons government.[28] Fiscal pressure led to some tightening of pension provision and reductions in other benefits, including the introduction of a means test for the maternity allowance.[29] The *Financial Relief Act* of 1932 reduced the aged pension rate, but also introduced indexation based on the retail price index for food and groceries.[30] Unemployment in Australia peaked at 29% in 1932, followed by a slow recovery until the outbreak of the Second World War in 1939.[31]

Against this background, calls for improved health and pension provision emerged, but there was considerable disagreement over whether this should be funded through national insurance contributions (preferred by the medical profession) or from taxation revenue (preferred by the Labor Party). A capitation fee of 11 shillings per patient per year was proposed, a voluntary scheme for the self-employed was developed, and medical benefits for dependants of members of the compulsory scheme were also introduced.[32] This led to the passing of the *National Health and Pensions Bill* in 1938.[33] However, implementation was delayed, partly because of pressure from interest groups, and then abandoned after the outbreak of war.[34]

The growth of superannuation provided further business for the dominant and well-resourced insurance firms. In part this growth was encouraged by tax concessions, including for contributions from 1914 and for lump sum payments from 1936.[35] In the inter-war period the life insurance industry grew and diversified, moving into industrial insurance and widening the customer base to include lower income groups. The value of assets held by life companies grew rapidly, and increasingly the industry assisted the government to finance the rapid development of Australian infrastructure.[36] Because the industry was

27 This plan was heavily influenced by the British banks, represented by Sir Otto Niemeyer, who were concerned about the possibility of debt defaults. See Bassett, Jan (1996) *The Oxford Illustrated Dictionary of Australian History* (Oxford University Press, paperback ed.), 228–9; Macintyre, Stuart (1999) *A Concise History of Australia* (Cambridge University Press).

28 Jack Lyons led the newly formed United Australia Party, which was elected in December 1931.

29 Herscovitch and Stanton, above n 1, 53.

30 An amending act to the *Financial Relief Act* restored the rate to pre-1932 levels in 1937.

31 Although there are claims that the total was somewhat higher, see Lowenstein, Wendy (1998) *Weevils in the Flour: an Oral Record of the 1930s Depression in Australia* (Scribe Publications, first published 1978, 1998 ed.), 14; and lower, see Potts, David (1990) 'A Reassessment of the Extent of Unemployment in Australia during the Great Depression' 24 *Australian Historical Studies* 378.

32 After rank-and-file concern that this level was too low an inquiry was announced, but this was subsequently dropped as preparations for war took precedence for government attention.

33 Robert Menzies resignation as Attorney General in 1938 was attributed to the repeal of some of the pensions' provisions in this bill. He later became Prime Minister after Lyons died.

34 Herscovitch and Stanton, above n 1, 54; enabling legislation was passed in 1938, but implementation was deferred indefinitely on account of the Second World War: *Superannuation and Family Benefits Act 1938* (Cth).

35 Smith, Julie P. (2004) 'Taxing Popularity: The Story of Taxation in Australia' (Research Study No. 43, Australian Tax Research Foundation).

36 Keneley, above n 7, 155.

stable relative to other parts of the financial industry, and was perceived as having effective self-regulation, government intervention was limited, a situation that persisted into the post-war period. At the end of the war, in contrast, the regulation of banks became intrusive, wartime controls having been formalised into the *Commonwealth Bank Act* and the *Banking Acts* of 1945.[37] This gave the life industry a competitive advantage, as banks and other financial intermediaries were limited in the deposits they could accept and the loans they could make. Life companies became active in mortgage lending, for example, satisfying demands the banks were not permitted to meet.[38]

The origins of the Australian managed funds industry can be traced back to the formation by Hugh Walton of Australian Fixed Trusts (AFT) and the First Australian Unit Trust (FAUT) in 1936,[39] and of Unit Trusts Ltd in 1938. The new unit trusts, which mostly followed a conservative fixed investment strategy and were closed-ended, competed with recently established investment companies, for example JB Were and Son.[40] When FAUT was wound up in 1951, it had out-performed both broker-based and fixed interest investments. In response to poor cash inflow in the early 1950s, AFT introduced direct marketing, sending circulars to names selected from the telephone directory. By 1961, AFT had established its own direct-mailing company, Australian Mailing Service (AMS) and also ran a sizeable network of sales agents.

3.4 Epoch 2: post-war development of the welfare state and tightening of regulation

A cross-party Commonwealth Parliamentary Joint Committee on Social Security was formed in 1941 and during the next four years developed a blueprint for an Australian welfare state.[41] State schemes for child endowment and widows' pensions were adapted and expanded nationwide, and a new Department of Social Services was established.[42] Fixed rate unemployment and sickness benefits, means-tested and funded from general revenue, were established in 1945. A referendum in 1946 confirmed the Commonwealth's power to legislate in respect

37 Banks were licensed in 1941 and regulated by the Commonwealth Bank (acting in the capacity of central bank). Profits were restricted to pre-war levels: Commonwealth, Ken Wallis (Chair), *Financial System Inquiry: Final Report* (1997), ch. 14; The *Life Insurance Act 1945* (Cth) defined supervision of life companies.

38 Commonwealth, *Financial System Inquiry*, ibid. 579.

39 'First Australian Unit Trust, A Fixed Trust Type of Investment' *Australian Financial Times* (Sydney, 1936). Walton had been encouraged by the successful development of unit trusts in Britain from 1931 and a favourable English Board of Trade review in 1936.

40 Founded in 1928.

41 Shaver, Sheila (1987) 'Design for a Welfare State: The Joint Parliamentary Committee on Social Security' 22 *Australian Historical Studies* 411.

42 The states 'temporarily' ceded their income tax powers to the Commonwealth as a wartime measure, never to regain them. Herscovitch and Stanton, above n 1, 55.

of social security. The various items of legislation developed during the war were brought together into a single *Social Services Act* in 1947.[43]

In 1945, the Chifley Government set up a 'National Welfare Fund', to be funded by a levy on personal income tax and a payroll tax on employers. The intention was to provide a basis for the establishment of a national superannuation fund. However, the government failed to establish a formal link between contributions and benefits, so that the fund was largely an accounting device until its abolition in 1985 and the 'Social Security Contribution' simply became an extra tax on income. However, the generosity of the basic pension was improved, income and assets limits for the means test were increased in 1946 and 1954, free medical and hospital treatment for pensioners was introduced in 1951, additional support was provided in 1958 for pensioners paying rent, and a higher rate of pension for those living alone was introduced in 1963.

In 1953 the Waterside Workers Federation (WWF) began a campaign, which continued for ten years and included industrial action, to establish superannuation for stevedores with more than 20 years' service.[44] The Stevedoring Employees Retirement Fund (SERF) was finally established in 1967 and involved employers paying 60% of contributions, compulsory retirement at 65 and early retirement at 60, redundancy provisions and better long-service leave. The Seaman's Union of Australia established a similar fund, the Seafarers Retirement Fund (SRF) in 1973.[45]

In 1954, the *Victorian Statute Law Revision Committee* heard "considerable evidence, with regard to unit and option certificates, lots, concessions, and other forms of interests in the undertaking of business", which led it to conclude that "this field provides opportunity for fraudulent practice".[46] So emerged the 1955 Victorian regulation of managed funds. Unit issuers were required to provide a prospectus, adopt an approved deed and appoint a trustee. Other Australian jurisdictions followed the Victorian model from the 1960s onwards.

Federal government focus, now under a Liberal–Country Party coalition government,[47] was then turned to the use of the taxation system to provide incentives for the private development of superannuation funds (and the provision of funds for other government purposes), and in 1961 superannuation funds were granted

43 *Social Services Consolidation Act 1947* (No. 26 of 1947).

44 Twenty-four hour strikes were held every two weeks during 1965 in all the major ports in Australia. Government response was to fine the union, changes were made to the *Stevedoring Industry Act 1949* (Cth) to deregister WWF, and ASIO investigated criminal activities on the wharfs. St Anne, Christine (2012) *A Super History: How Australia's $1 Trillion+ Superannuation Industry Was Made* (Major Street), 7.

45 See Maritime Super, *Our Story* www.maritimesuper.com.au/WebPage/AboutUs/frmAboutMaritimeSuper.aspx. SRF and SERF merged to create Maritime Super in 2009.

46 Statute Law Revision Committee, Parliament of Victoria, *Amendments of the Statute Law to Deal with Fraudulent Practices by Persons Interested in the Promotion and/or Direction of Companies and by Firms* (1954).

47 Elected in 1954. The Labor party had campaigned on the basis of abolition of the means test. Herscovitch and Stanton, above n 1, 59, note 10.

tax exemption by the *Income Tax and Social Services Contribution Assessment Act* if they held required amounts of Commonwealth Bonds.[48] This use of taxation power to control superannuation was challenged in the courts, but in 1965 the High Court upheld the Commonwealth's right to do so.[49] The exemption from tax of superannuation funds that held Commonwealth bonds triggered a steep rise in the number of superannuation businesses.

Means-testing of the pension developed so that by the late 1960s means were assessed on the basis of income plus a proportion of assets (excluding the family home). A major liberalisation of the means test occurred in 1969, including abolition of means tests for the blind, and replacement of one-for-one reductions under the means test with a more tapered system. By then, about 70% of people qualifying on the basis of age received some pension, a proportion that has persisted since.[50]

Regulation of banks was tightened considerably during the war and in the following two decades, leading to a further decline in their market share and a shift of investment management activities to finance companies and to separate superannuation funds.[51] The life insurance industry also grew rapidly in the 1950s and 1960s. In 1950 there were 22 life insurance offices in Australia, rising to 37 in 1960 and 48 in 1970. Although only three were foreign-owned in 1950, by 1970 this had risen to 35.[52]

Unit trusts rapidly became popular in the 1950s as their good performance was publicised, with assets under management growing from A£500,000 at the end of World War II to A£18 million by 1955.[53] Universal Flexible Trusts (UFT) was founded in Melbourne in 1955 and also grew rapidly. The Bank of New South Wales bought Unit Trusts Ltd in 1958 and was the largest bank involved in unit trusts until the early 1980s. A new industry group, the Unit Trust Association of Australia was founded in the late 1950s.

48 *Income Tax and Social Services Contribution Assessment Act 1961* (Cth). The right of the Commonwealth Government to control superannuation through tax concessions was upheld in the High Court in 1965, *Fairfax v Commissioner of Taxation* (1965) 114 CLR 1. In total, 30% of assets were required to be in government securities, 20% of which had to be Commonwealth. The '30/20' rule remained until 1984 when it was abolished on the recommendation of the *Campbell Committee*. For more discussion see Keneley, above n 7, 163.

49 *Fairfax v Federal Commissioner of Taxation* (1965) 114 CLR 1.

50 Whiteford, Peter and Gregory Angenent (2002) 'The Australian System of Social Protection—an Overview' (Department of Family and Community Services Occasional Paper No. 6, Second Edition, June 2002), available at www.dss.gov.au/sites/default/files/documents/05_2012/no.6.pdf.

51 Section 2.3 explains how wartime controls were consolidated into the *Commonwealth Bank Act 1945* and the Banking Acts of 1945.

52 Commonwealth (1985) *Annual Report of the Life Insurance Commissioner*. Nevertheless, the majority of business was still carried on by locally owned firms: only one third of business written between 1950 and 1970 was by foreign-owned firms.

53 Mees, Bernard T., Monica S. Wehner and Pamela F. Hanrahan (2006) 'Fifty Years of Managed Funds in Australia' (Research Report, Investment and Financial Services Association Limited), 72.

The main competitors to the unit trusts were the early investment bankers, both within the major banking groups and as independents. ANZ founded the 'Public Retirement Fund – Self Employed' in 1959, which is today the oldest managed fund in Australia.[54] Also in 1959 Ian Potter and Co. launched the Australian Capital Fund (ACF), the first Australian US-style mutual fund.[55] Perpetual Trustees emerged during the same period as the leading custodial organisation. Open-ended funds gradually became more common. Although the first local Merchant Banks (such as Ian Potter and Co.) appeared in Australia at the end of World War II, it was not until the 1960s that foreign merchant banks opened in Australia. These included Darling and Co, Hill Samuel, and Bankers Trust (BT).[56] Overall, funds under management in Australia grew from A£1.5 million in 1945, to A£50 million by 1960 and to A£125 million by 1965.[57]

The early Australian managed funds were largely what today would be called 'tracker funds', focused on passive management of member's assets. For example, AFT's 'Selected Securities Fund' invested in the shares of 200 companies from 1946 onwards, a pattern that was followed by many other equity funds at the time. Diversification was offered mostly by the holding of a variety of companies, rather than across types of asset. Steady income was emphasised more than growth.[58] However, by the late 1950s, funds targeted on growth began to emerge. Combined income and capital returns of 12% or more were projected, although these were rarely delivered subsequently. Mutual funds that had emphasised the benefits of investing in resources performed badly, while metal stocks soared in the nickel boom, accelerating the withdrawal of funds and creating liquidity problems for the mutual funds.

The development of the wider Australian financial services industry prior to 1970 occurred to some extent through trial and error, with changes to investment strategies and industry structure responding to the booms and busts of the business cycle. First equities, then property, then metals, then specialist and international funds, waxed and waned in popularity as bubbles inflated and burst. Increasing internationalisation, following trends in UK, US and Canada, encouraged local innovation and in due course the entry of foreign players to the Australian marketplace. The first Australian futures market, the Sydney Greasy Wool Futures Exchange, opened in 1960. In 1963, savings banks were allowed to offer personal loans and in 1965 the RBA relaxed guidelines on bank lending which had previously restricted lending to particular classes of customer.[59]

54 This fund is still active, though now closed to new members.

55 With the backing of the Commercial Banking Company (CBC) of Sydney.

56 BT was an early pioneer in the 1970s in the development of superannuation funds.

57 The Australian Pound, introduced in 1910, persisted until 1966 when it was replaced by the Australian Dollar as part of the decimalisation process.

58 Mees, Wehner and Hanrahan, above n 53, 45.

59 Commonwealth, *Financial System Inquiry*, above n 37, 570.

3.5 Epoch 3: pressures for wider superannuation coverage from 1970 onwards

By the 1970s, some unions had introduced superannuation schemes for their officials and members. The Victorian Federated Storemen and Packers Union (FSPU), for example, set up a fully vested fund in 1974, an early example of an accumulation scheme with portability.[60] However, occupational superannuation was mostly limited to those employed by major companies and in the public services, and only some 30% of the working population were covered by such schemes.[61]

Pressure continued for better pension provision, especially as economic conditions improved. A new wives' pension was introduced in 1972. The *Henderson Commission of Inquiry into Poverty* (1972–1976) identified significant problems with poverty in Australia, though mostly focused on families and aborigines.[62] Its findings, and the previous work of Henderson and colleagues, were influential in establishing poverty as a significant ongoing problem in Australia, including among the elderly.[63]

Successive governments fiddled with means-testing. The means test was abolished for those aged 75 and over in 1973, and for those aged 70–74 in 1975, changes that were reversed in 1978 and 1983. The assets component of the means test was removed in 1976, but reintroduced in 1985 in a different form. In 1977 automatic increases in the age pension to allow for inflation were introduced, and in 1984 a pension was introduced for carers of a spouse with disabilities.

In March 1973 the Whitlam Government established a *National Superannuation Committee of Inquiry (NCSI)*, under the chairmanship of Keith Hancock, with broad terms of reference including examination of overseas practice.[64] However, the Whitlam government had a reduced majority after the 1974 election, and the superannuation bill which resulted from the *Hancock*

60 The fund was an accumulation fund with a 10% contribution from employees. However, the rules for payout were complex and opaque. St Anne, above n 44, 4.

61 Kewley, Thomas Henry (1980) *Australian Social Security Today: Major Developments from 1900 to 1978* (Sydney University Press); Bateman, Hazel and John Piggott (2001) 'Australia's Mandatory Retirement Saving Policy: A View from the New Millennium' (Discussion Paper No. 23160, World Bank, March 2001).

62 The Henderson Commission was established by Liberal Prime Minister William McMahon in August 1972, and expanded by the Whitlam government that was elected later that year; Henderson Commission (1975) *Poverty in Australia* (Parliament of Australia). For discussion, see Senate Community Affairs Committee (2004) *Poverty and Inequality in Australia: A Hand Up Not a Hand Out: Renewing the Fight Against Poverty* (Parliament of Australia) 33–53.

63 Mendes, Philip (2008) *Australia's Welfare Wars Revisited: the Players, the Politics and the Ideologies* (University of New South Wales Press, revised ed.). Mendes is critical of the influence of neo-liberal and economic rationalist ideas, arguing that welfare-state ideals would have served the country better.

64 Swoboda, Kai (2014) 'Chronology of Major Superannuation and Retirement Income Changes in Australia' (Commonwealth Parliamentary Library, Parliament of Australia), 3.

Inquiry was one of 21 major bills defeated in the Senate.[65] Also in 1974, the Rae Committee proposed mandatory disclosure in response to criticism of the regulatory regime, leading to the creation, five years later, of the *National Companies and Securities Commission* (NCSC).[66]

The NCSI interim report set out the advantages of a national earnings-related scheme,[67] and its final report was delivered to the Fraser Government in 1976.[68] This recommended the introduction of a partially contributory, universal, pension system with an earnings-related supplement.[69] The Fraser government rejected these proposals in 1979,[70] and opted to continue to rely on voluntary contributions. This rejection led to union leaders, notably Simon Crean and Bill Kelty, seeking to pursue superannuation as an industrial relations issue rather than through political channels. The Fraser government then established a task force to consider the role of occupational superannuation in providing for retirement. This reported in 1983, a few months before Fraser was replaced by Bob Hawke as Prime Minister.[71]

In 1978 the FSPU entered into talks with employers in the skin and hide industry, which led to the formation of the Labour Union Co-operative Retirement Fund (LUCRF).[72] LUCRF was invested entirely in equities, and achieved much higher returns for its members than the other funds of the time.[73] FSPU then sought in 1979 to extend superannuation to the Victorian wholesale grocery sector, a

65 St Anne, above n 44, 23.

66 The NCSC was renamed the *Australian Securities Commission* (ASC), which in turn became the *Australian Securities and Investment Commission* (ASIC) in 1991. ASIC is an independent Commonwealth body operating under the direction of three full-time Commissioners appointed by the Governor General, but nominated by the Federal Treasurer.

67 National Superannuation Committee of Inquiry (1974) *National Superannuation in Australia: Interim Report, June 1974* (Parliament of Australia).

68 National Superannuation Committee of Inquiry (1976, 1977) *A National Superannuation Scheme for Australia: Final Report, Part 1* (1976); *Part 2* (1977) (The *Hancock Inquiry*: Parliament of Australia).

69 The timing of this recommendation coincided with similar debates in the UK, which led to the introduction of the State Earnings Related Pension Scheme (SERPS) in 1978. The *Hancock Inquiry* recommended a partially contributory, universal pension system with an earnings-related supplement. A minority report to the *Hancock Inquiry* suggested a flat rate universal pension, a means-tested supplement and expansion of occupational superannuation.

70 Cabinet Decision 3435, 20 July 1977 in response to Cabinet Submission No. 1394, 1977. The NCSI report identified numerous shortcomings with company superannuation schemes, including the use of funds for takeovers and in-house investment schemes. St Anne, above n 44, 24. The rejection occurred partly because of concerns over the burden that contributions would place on low to middle-income earners. Social Welfare Policy Secretariat (1983) *Approaches to National Superannuation.*

71 Commonwealth Task Force on Occupational Superannuation (1983) *Final Report of the Task Force on Occupational Superannuation* (Parliamentary Paper No. 27/1983, Parliamentary Library, Parliament of Australia).

72 LUCRF introduced the representative trustee model, which included at least 50% employer representation on the Board. St Anne, above n 44, 74. Votes required a two-thirds majority.

73 St Anne, above n 44, 14.

move that was resisted by employers.[74] After six weeks of strike action, Woolworths offered a generous wage increase instead of superannuation, which FSPU accepted.

By 1980 superannuation business, which had started through endowment policies but evolved into specific savings schemes, had become a major area of insurance company activity.[75] In 1982 the five largest local firms were AMP, National Mutual Life, Mutual Life and Citizens, Colonial Mutual Life and T&G Mutual Life.[76]

In 1981 the *Campbell Inquiry* suggested separate legislation for collective investment schemes,[77] in 1985 Federal Treasurer Paul Keating recommended increased taxation of unit trusts,[78] and in 1987 the *Insurance and Superannuation Commission* (ISC) was established.[79] In 1988 the *Companies and Securities Law Review Committee* recommended extensive reform to the regulation of prescribed interests, and in 1990 the *NCSC Unit Trusts Task Force* recommended a full-scale review.

The life offices had not launched unit trust products in the 1950s and 1960s, merely adding complexity (e.g. in the form of bonus provisions) to their life assurance and endowment policies. However, as the size of the superannuation market grew in the 1970s, and competition from specialist superannuation funds emerged, the life offices accelerated product development.[80] National Mutual and Capita moved aggressively into retail managed funds.[81] National Mutual, AMP, Legal and General and Prudential utilised financial planners and public accountants as sales channels, with the older funds managers increasingly unable to compete with

74 The Chairman of Woolworths at the time was also a director at AMP, and Woolworths already had an 'invitation only' superannuation scheme for long-serving employees. The employers were opposed to the introduction of superannuation for the majority of workers. St Anne, above n 44, 14–7.

75 Keneley, above n 7, 162.

76 Lewis, Mervyn Keith and Robert Henry Wallace (1997) *The Australian Financial System: Evolution, Policy and Practice* (Longman).

77 The *Campbell Inquiry* made wide-ranging recommendations including abolition of limits on offshore investment, the formal introduction of foreign banks, the floating of the dollar, and the merger of numerous life offices. Govt (1981) *Committee of Inquiry into the Australian Financial System, Australian Financial System: Final Report* (Keith Campbell, Chair).

78 IFSA (1985) 'Capital Gains – The Tax That Benefits No-One' 3 *Unit Trust News* 1; 'Taxation Reform' (IFSA Archive Box, 1985) 10.

79 The purpose of the ISC was mainly to administer guidelines by which superannuation schemes operated in order to be eligible for tax concessions. The guidelines were codified in the *Occupational Superannuation Standards Act 1987* (Cth) ('OSSA'), which represented the first formal regulation of the superannuation industry.

80 By the 1980s, the assets of the superannuation funds were similar to those of the life offices. Lewis, M.K. and R.H. Wallace (1993) *The Australian Financial System* (Melbourne: Longman Cheshire), 285.

81 National Mutual was previously City Mutual, which had bought the Royal Bank of Canada's CMT. Capita expanded into capital-guaranteed products after the 1987 stock market crash, which led to its being absorbed into Lend Lease MLC. This was the first of a series of demutualisations that occurred during the 1990s. See Reserve Bank of Australia (1999) 'Demutualisation in Australia' (Bulletin, January 1999). National Mutual Funds Management was formed in 1985. It also suffered from a move into capital guaranteed products.

the dominant firms or with the emergent managed funds. AMP, Colonial Mutual, Legal and General, Prudential, Mercantile Mutual and MLC all developed retail funds, although much of the management of the funds was outsourced.[82]

Government policy influenced the development of life offices, and in particular their investment strategies, through tax concessions.[83] The extensive deregulation of the banking industry that followed the *Campbell Inquiry* in the 1980s permitted banks to sell life products and also to take over life companies.[84] This combined with technological innovation and privatisation to generate a steep rise in the size of the financial services sector, from around 100% of GDP in the early 1980s to over 200% by 1992. New banks and other financial institutions, including foreign-owned, entered the market and life offices grew rapidly, with some demutualisation. This began a process through which the major banks re-established their dominance, both through organic growth and through acquisitions. Life companies, in response, diversified into other financial markets, and even entered the banking sector themselves. AMP, for example, attempted to negotiate a joint venture with the Chase Manhattan Bank,[85] while later Colonial Mutual acquired the State Bank of New South Wales to form Colonial Bank.[86]

Funds invested in equities were increasingly unable to offer sufficiently competitive rates of return from the mid-1960s onwards, and in an attempt to improve this situation managed funds invested heavily in property.[87] An Australian 'fund of funds' also emerged briefly as an unsuccessful attempt to improve returns. However, the investment management companies still provided better returns in this period, so the funds management industry declined.[88] In 1971 the Garretty Group and Mineral Securities Australia (MinSec) collapsed, which further reduced investor interest in Australian managed funds.[89] A survey carried out

82 For example, MLC outsourced the management of its equities fund to Rothschild and County Natwest.

83 As previously noted, the 30/20 rule gave tax concessions if life offices kept a minimum of 30% in public sector securities, with 20% of this in Commonwealth government securities. Keneley, above n 7, 163.

84 Govt (1981), above n 77.

85 Blainey, Geoffrey (1999) *A History of the AMP 1848–1998* (Allen and Unwin), 288–289.

86 This acquisition occurred in 1994, during the next epoch.

87 The ratio of investment in equities versus property changed from 78.5%: 9.4% in 1962 to 15.7%: 72% in 1978 – the remainder was invested in fixed interest, mortgages and debentures. Mees, Wehner and Hanrahan, above n 53.

88 Between 1965 and 75 investment companies average return was 15.6% per annum, compared with 5.4% for managed funds. Mees, Wehner and Hanrahan, above n 53, 18.

89 The Garretty Dividend Fund had invested heavily in speculative metals during the minerals boom of the late 1960s. Ibid. 19. "The collapse of a variety of Garretty funds and companies, with losses to shareholders exceeding $1 million, as well as the failure of several stockbrokers and other firms associated with the mining boom, led to widespread concern over the security of the financial system and the establishment of the Senate Select Committee on Securities and Exchange headed by Senator Rae in March 1970". MinSec sponsored and under-wrote the launch of two mutual funds, in order to raise funds for investment in industrial and mineral securities. See Senate Select Committee on Securities and Exchange (1974) *Australian Securities Markets and their Regulation* (Parliament of Australia), 14.58.

by the University of Melbourne in 1974 reported that "investors are becoming increasingly disillusioned with the investment alternatives so eagerly sought in the past", and hence preferred banks as repositories of their funds.[90]

Other forms of investment gradually emerged. In 1972 Trustees, Executor and Agency Co. (TEA) launched a money-market investment service.[91] 1974 saw the largest stock market crash since 1929, accompanied by falls in property prices. Property groups, financiers and the CBC all failed.[92] However, at the time most of the trusts and funds in Australia were quite small and many survived nevertheless.[93] Funds under management started to increase again in the mid-to-late 1970s, and a number of new funds were launched.[94] The growth of the funds management industry in the 1980s, and the growing dominance of the largest banking groups, was facilitated by a number of legislative changes including removal of restraints on investment in foreign equities and the de-regulation of the banking industry.[95] International fund managers expanded their activities in Australia from 1983 onwards, bringing with them sophisticated marketing focused on corporate image.[96] Funds held by public unit trusts increased by 300% between September 1985 and June 1989, to A$26 billion.

In 1980, Hill Samuel introduced a cash management trust (CMT), a move that was followed by AFT, Were Securities, AUC and foreign banks (Bank of America and Royal Bank of Canada).[97] On the formation of Macquarie Bank in 1985, the Hill Samuel CMT became Macquarie CMT.[98] Early success with CMTs was facilitated by marketing via brokers and other investment advisers.[99] Bankers Trust (BT)

90 Lampe, Anne (1974) *Financial Review* (20 August 1974), 3, cited in Mees, Wehner and Hanrahan, above n 53, 78.

91 TEA was founded in the late nineteenth century. However, it subsequently expanded its cash management accounts and started to speculate in property in the early 1980s, which led to its collapse.

92 CBC subsequently merged in 1978 with National Australasia Bank, creating the National Australia Bank (NAB).

93 Mees, Wehner and Hanrahan, above n 53, 21: "most. . .trusts and funds [had] market values of under $2 million and averaging only about 1000 investors each (the largest fund, the AFT Saving Trust, having 3692 different unit-holders at the end of 1978)".

94 By 1978, funds under management were $488.3 million. New funds included the Javelin Fund launched in 1974 by the Australian subsidiary of NM Rothschild and Sons (and subsequently renamed the Five Arrows trust in 1983). Oceanic launched its first property fund in 1978, and Westfield floated its first listed trust in 1979: Mees, Wehner and Hanrahan, above n 53, 21, 50.

95 The historical background to deregulation and the deregulatory measures which were implemented during the 1980s are described in House of Representatives Standing Committee on Finance and Public Administration (1991) *A Pocket Full of Change: Banking and Deregulation* (Parliament of Australia), ch. 2.

96 Gregg, B.M. (1988) *A Survey of the Australian Fund Management Industry* (MBA Thesis, University of Melbourne), 3.

97 The Equitable Group CMT faced a run in 1982 and had to be bailed out by its parent, QBE.

98 Macquarie CMT now has funds under management in excess of $10 billion.

99 Skully, Michael T. (1987) *Merchant Banking in Australia* (Oxford University Press), 18.

subsequently entered the retail market in 1982.[100] When the stock market crashed again in 1987, BT performed relatively well (as its managers had built up defensive positions) and this improved its reputation in the market. Balanced products began to decline in popularity and asset consultants advised clients to invest in an array of sector-specific wholesale funds.[101] Increasing consumer demands at the retail level led to the production of an array of investment handbooks, and adoption of master trust structures. Increasingly, savings began to be channelled once again into managed funds instead of traditional bank deposits.

Banks' market share fell to a low of 57% in 1982, eroded by less-heavily-regulated institutions such as life offices, unit trusts and investment managers.[102] Financial deregulation then reversed the relative decline of the banks, and their market share recovered to around 80% by 1994, similar to the dominance they had enjoyed in the 1960s.[103] International banks (such as Citibank and HSBC) entered the market, and established new non-bank financial institutions (NBFIs) both separately and in joint venture with local banks. Financial deregulation also triggered a credit boom, which contributed to the growth of the sector, and fuelled asset price rises which in turn enabled investment funds to achieve exceptional returns.

Specialist suppliers, such as mortgage managers and advisers, also emerged from the 1980s onwards. Technological changes made possible the introduction of a wide range of new products and delivery systems, which reinforced the trend towards diversity and the complexity of the industry. A variety of non-bank financial institutions (NBFIs), notably building societies, converted to banks in the late 1980s and early 1990s.[104] Foreign-owned fund managers (such as Hambros, Jardine Fleming, Bankers Trust (BT) and Fidelity) rose to prominence in the mid-1980s, while firms such as Potter Warburg Asset Management developed through a series of mergers.[105] New international entrants (such as Norwich Union and County NatWest) launched capital-guaranteed products and master trusts, and moved into the retail market.[106]

With the failure of Estate Mortgage[107], Tricontinental[108] and Aust-Wide in 1990, property portfolios once again went out of fashion. The unlisted property

100 Haigh, Gideon (1999) *One of a Kind: The Story of Bankers Trust Australia 1969–99* (Text Publishing), 124.

101 Such as Towers, Perrin, Foster and Crosby.

102 Edey, Malcolm and Brian Gray (1996) 'The Evolving Structure of the Australian Financial System' (Research Discussion Paper No. 9605, Reserve Bank of Australia, October 1996), 7.

103 Although the banks were now more diversified, and had reabsorbed many of the NBFIs they had set up to circumvent the previous regulatory regime.

104 Building Societies were permitted to apply for banking licences after 1984.

105 Of Potter Partners with SG Warburg in 1987, with the equities management division of Hambros, and with Elders in 1990.

106 In 1990, Norwich Union in Australia merged with ANEV Life, which had developed the Navigator master trust.

107 Sykes, Trevor (1996) *The Bold Riders: Behind Australia's Corporate Collapses* (Allen and Unwin, 2nd ed.) 33–55, 349–73. Investors were able to recover only about $150,000 from the insurers of Burns Philp Trustee.

108 Partly because of bad loans made to companies associated with the Bond Corporation. One of the consequences of the Tricontinental collapse was the partial floating of the Commonwealth Bank after the acquisition of Tricontinental's parent the State Bank of Victoria.

sector declined, a number of mergers and takeovers resulted and many assets were transferred to listed property trusts (LPTs). Property trusts had grown by 49% between June 1988 and 1990 (to a peak of $17.9bn), but declined by 30% to June 1992 ($12.6bn).[109] These collapses led to renewed focus on the role of trustees, and UTAA (which had been re-branded in 1991 as the Investment Funds Association, IFA) argued for the establishment of a single responsible entity (RE), a change that was subsequently implemented in 1998.[110] Australian LPTs were increasingly successful during the 1990s, and encouraged the growth of real estate investment trusts (REITs) in many Asian countries.[111] The recession also facilitated the arrival of new foreign players, most notably Citibank who launched the first locally offered hedge fund (in Japanese equities) in 1989.

The Australian financial system changed from a closed, oligopolistic structure focused mostly on traditional banking activities in the 1950s and 1960s,[112] albeit with a vibrant life insurance industry and a relatively small managed funds sector serving wealthier customers,[113] to a much larger multi-layered system with a wide array of providers and intermediaries. This change occurred in response to growth in demand for financial services from a wider range of customers, driven by increasing wealth among middle-class families, increased desire to save in anticipation of greater longevity, concern to avoid the effects of inflation, and to optimise taxation. However, the changes were also guided by numerous political and regulatory interventions, notably deregulation (in the 1980s), the introduction of award superannuation and industry funds (from 1986), compulsory superannuation contributions (from 1991 onwards), and the privatisation of state-owned financial institutions. Between 1970 and 1990, the size of the financial sector in Australia grew from around 100% of GDP to over 200%, with much of the growth occurring first in life offices and then in superannuation funds.[114]

3.6 Epoch 4: the introduction and development of compulsory superannuation contributions

There are many reasons why the decisions that were taken seemed, at the time of the introduction of compulsory superannuation contributions in 1991, to be good policy. Australia had a state pension system that would not provide adequately for the retirement of the majority of the population. The idea of introducing a national, publicly administered, scheme had been explored on several previous occasions and rejected. Developing and maintaining an adequate state

109 Mees, Wehner and Hanrahan, above n 53, 59.

110 Bowerman, R. (1991) *BT Calls for a Fresh Approach to Trusts* (14 February 1991) Money Management; *Managed Investments Act 1998* (Cth).

111 Keng, Tan Yen (2003) *Strategic Investment Issues for Listed Property Trusts* (PhD Thesis, University of Western Sydney), cited in Mees, Wehner and Hanrahan, above n 53, 39.

112 In 1953 banks accounted for 88% of the total assets managed by financial intermediaries. Edey and Gray, above n 102, 4.

113 Comprising insurance, superannuation funds and investment vehicles such as unit trusts.

114 Edey and Gray, above n 102, 6.

pension funded by taxation, even if means-tested, in the light of demographic changes was predicted to be prohibitively expensive.[115]

'Blue collar' workers were seen to be disadvantaged relative to their 'white collar' counterparts, and especially to those employed by the public sector.[116] Demographic changes and greater longevity were understood to result in substantially greater need for retirement income for much larger numbers of people.[117] So policies that encouraged greater private saving were seen as reducing the burden on the exchequer in future as well as safeguarding the living standards of workers in retirement.[118]

As discussed in more detail below, the development of the current Australian superannuation system was triggered by the unions, and facilitated by the accords between the Australian Labor Party (ALP) and the Australian Council of Trade Unions (ACTU). Employer superannuation contributions were agreed in lieu of wage rises, partly to reduce inflationary pressures and partly because the unions believed a more generous overall package for their members was possible by this means. In 1989, the government endorsed the 'twin pillars' of age pension and privately funded superannuation, explicitly rejecting a national pay-as-you-go superannuation scheme (and playing down the third pillar of occupational schemes).

The 1991 Budget announced the introduction of the *Superannuation Guarantee Charge* (SGC).[119] This required all employers to make contributions on behalf of their employees to a complying superannuation fund. This crucial decision was a reaction to the Australian Industrial Court's rejection of a further 3% increment to productivity award superannuation (PAS), despite the fact that this was supported by both the government and the unions.[120] The SGC was implemented in July 1992, and superannuation contributions were increased progressively from 3% to 9% over the period to 2002.[121] The governance and

115 Dawkins, John (1992) *Security in Retirement: Planning for Tomorrow Today* (Australia Treasury).

116 Less than 40% of full-time workers were covered by occupational superannuation by the 1980s. Bateman, Hazel (1997) *Three Essays on the Economics of Mandatory Private Retirement Saving* (Unpublished PhD Thesis, University of New South Wales), 195 Table 5.1.

117 Ibid., vol 2, 273–6.

118 See Keating, Paul (2007) 'The Story of Modern Superannuation' (Speech delivered at the Australian Pensions and Investment Summit, Sanctuary Cove, Queensland, 31 October 2007) www.keating.org.au/shop/item/the-story-of-modern-superannuation-31-october-2007.

119 Kerin, John (1991) 'Budget Speech 1991–2' (Speech delivered at the Second Reading of the Appropriation Bill (No. 1), Parliament House, 20 August 1991).

120 Bateman et al., above n 24, 191. The introduction of PAS had previously increased superannuation coverage to about 80% of the work force.

121 *Superannuation Guarantee Charge Act 1992* (Cth), supported by the *Superannuation Guarantee (Administration) Act 1992* (Cth) ('SGAA'). The Liberal Coalition, despite its original opposition to compulsory superannuation, agreed to continue with the previous government's policy of increasing the SGC to 9%. This was previously announced in a speech by Peter Costello, then Shadow Treasurer, in November 1995: Costello, Peter (1995) 'Address to Australian Superannuation Funds Association (ASFA)' (2 Nov 1995); St Anne, above n 44, 200.

regulation of the superannuation industry was formalised by the *Superannuation Industry (Supervision) Act 1993* (SIS Act).

By 1993, 80% of all employed persons had superannuation contributions made on their behalf.[122] These contributions have now generated funds in excess of $2.2 trillion, and spawned a large, complex and costly industry to manage the funds. One simple indicator of this complexity is the large number of member accounts: in 2016, there were some 29 million accounts for a working and retired population of around 15 million.[123]

The *National Corporations Law 1991* finally brought all managed funds under a direct supervisor, the *Australian Securities and Investment Commission* (ASIC). The previous approach of mandatory pre-sale disclosure following a 'checklist' was replaced by a more general requirement to disclose "all information that an investor and their professional advisers would require to make an informed investment decision".[124] Importantly, the new law required each scheme to be constituted under an approved deed, to be managed by a company that held a dealer's licence, and to have an approved trustee.[125] However, the problems of unlisted property trusts that also emerged in 1991 led to emergency action to freeze redemption rights, later encapsulated in the *Corporations (Unlisted Property Trusts) Act 1991.*

Under the new law, management companies became important both as promoters of trusts and as asset managers. Trustees monitored compliance with the Corporations Law and promoted the interests of members.[126] However, this division of responsibilities came under almost immediate criticism from the *Companies and Securities Advisory Committee* (CASAC) and the *Australian Law Reform Commission* (ALRC). Their concern, expressed in an influential joint report, was that neither trustees nor managers were effectively accountable to investors.[127] So they recommended that the requirement to appoint both a management company and an independent trustee be replaced by a requirement for a

122 Australian Bureau of Statistics, 'Superannuation Australia, November 1995' (Catalogue No. 6319.0, 1995).

123 Number of accounts from Australian Prudential Regulatory Authority (2017), 'Statistics: Annual Superannuation Bulletin June 2016' (revised ed., February 2017), 48; Working and retired population estimated from Australian Bureau of Statistics (2013) 'Retirement and Retirement Intentions, July 2012 to June 2013' (Catalogue No. 6238.0, 9 December 2013); and Australian Bureau of Statistics (2014) 'Labour Force' (Catalogue No. 6202.0, 13 March 2014).

124 Mees, Wehner and Hanrahan, above n 53, 104.

125 *Corporations Law 1991* (Cth) pt 7.12, div 5.

126 ASIC (1995) 'Policy Statement 89' (6 February 1995), 22–8; For a detailed discussion of the respective roles of the management company and the trustee under the prescribed interest laws, see *Australian Securities and Investments Commission (ASIC) v ABC Fund Managers Ltd (2001)* 39 ACSR 443, 125 (Warren J); See also Hanrahan, Pamela F. (1998)*Managed Investments Law and Practice* (CCH, 1998), 2–300; von Nessen, Paul (1998) *A Practical Guide to Managed Investments* (LBC Information Services) 9–20.

127 Law Reform Commission (1993)*Collective Investments: Other People's Money* (Report No. 65, joint with Companies and Securities Advisory Committee), especially 12.3.

single 'responsible entity', which was expected to act honestly and to "prefer the interests of the investors to its own interests".[128] Investors were to be given the right to replace the responsible entity, wind up the scheme, and amend its constitution. These ideas eventually led to the *Managed Investment Act 1998* (MIA).[129] In 1999, the *Corporate Law Economic Reform Program Act (CLERPA)* strengthened the regulation of acquisitions of managed investment companies.[130]

In 1993, the *Fitzgerald Report* advocated increasing household savings through superannuation, providing further support for the rising SGC.[131] The World Bank also endorsed the new Australian system in a 1994 report.[132] In 1995, Treasurer Ralph Willis outlined plans to pay tax cuts directly into an employee's superannuation funds and for the government to make matching contributions for the lower paid.[133]

The first budget of the Howard Government introduced a *Superannuation Surcharge* in 1996.[134] A wide variety of changes to the arrangements for superannuation were made during the next ten years, including a commitment to choice of fund legislation,[135] the introduction of retirement savings accounts (RSAs) in 1998,[136] an amendment in 1999 to the SIS Act to permit Self-Managed Superannuation Funds (SMSFs),[137] the introduction of revised licensing and disclosure rules,[138] allowing temporary residents to withdraw accumulated benefits before their preservation age,[139] rules about division of superannuation assets on

128 Ibid. 10.8.

129 The process that eventually led to this bill is covered in Law Reform Commission (1992) 'Collective Investment Schemes' (LRC Discussion Paper No. 53); The *Superannuation Industry (Supervision) Act 1993* (Cth) was an intermediate step.

130 *Corporate Law Economic Reform Program Act 1999* (Cth) ('*CLERPA*'). *CLERPA* applied similar principles on takeovers to those contained in Chapter 6 of the Corporations Law. See also Explanatory Memorandum, Corporate Law Economic Reform Program Bill 1998 (Cth).

131 FitzGerald, Vince W. (1993) 'National Savings: A Report to the Treasurer' (Report, June 1993).

132 World Bank (1994) *Averting the Old Age Crisis: Policies to Protect the Old and Promote Growth* (Oxford University Press).

133 Willis, Ralph (1995) 'Budget Speech 1995–96' (Speech delivered at the Second Reading of the Appropriation Bill (No. 1), Parliament House, 9 May 1995); Willis, Ralph (1995) *Saving For Our Future* (Australian Government Publication Service).

134 Costello, Peter (1996) 'Budget Speech 1996–97' (Speech delivered at the Second Reading of the Appropriation Bill, Parliament House, 20 August 1996).

135 This legislation took seven years to be accepted, due to resistance in the Senate, which gave the Industry Funds sufficient time to become established before it took effect; St Anne, above n 44, 211.

136 RSAs were bank deposits with the same tax benefits as superannuation funds. The Coalition idea was to give individuals freedom to save. However, RSAs failed to achieve the returns which were available through the main superannuation funds and so did not grow; St Anne, above n 44, 205–6.

137 *Superannuation Legislation Amendment Act (No. 3) 1999* (Cth) ('SLAA3'); SMSFs have been regulated by the Australian Taxation Office (ATO) since 8 October 1999.

138 Under the *Financial Services Reform Act 2001* (Cth); The arrangements commenced in March 2002.

139 *Superannuation Industry (Supervision) Regulations 1994* (Cth), ss 6.20A, 6.20B, 6.24A; These arrangements do not apply to New Zealand residents; later, in 2008, proposals for the ATO to confiscate unclaimed superannuation were introduced by the Minister for Superannuation and Corporate Law, Nick Sherry, in Sherry, Nick (2008) 'Payment of Temporary Residents' Superannuation to the Australian Government' (Media Release No. 016, 5 May 2008); These were enacted in the Temporary Residents' Superannuation Legislation Amendment Act 2008 (Cth); Tax rates on departing temporary residents were increased in April 2009.

divorce,[140] the reduction of the superannuation surcharge from 15% to 12.5% to 10% to zero, followed by its subsequent reintroduction in a different form,[141] the introduction of a government co-contribution for low income earners,[142] the requirement for all superannuation trustees of large eligible funds to be licensed,[143] portability of money between different superannuation accounts,[144] extension of tax free payments to same sex couples and where financial dependency exists,[145] the introduction of transition to retirement arrangements,[146] government co-contributions,[147] and contributions splitting with spouses.[148]

The *Financial Services Reform Act 2001* (FSRA) was designed to enhance standardisation within the financial services industry. It provided for licensing of dealers in financial products and services as well as for fund operators, and set out requirements for the provision of information to members, and defined conduct rules.[149] In June 2004, the *SIS Act* was amended to require all superannuation trustees to become a *Registrable Superannuation Entity* (RSE) licensee, and to demonstrate to APRA that they have adequate resources, appropriate skills and risk management systems.[150] These increased regulatory requirements led to the closure of some smaller superannuation funds and contributed to a steep decline in the number of corporate funds as superannuation for company employees was outsourced to the retail sector.

In 2006, Treasurer Costello announced plans to simplify superannuation, including the exemption from tax of benefits for those aged over 60, removal of tax on lump sums, the abolition of reasonable benefit limits (RBLs) and easier rules for transfer between funds, arrangements that took effect on 1 July 2007.[151] Further amendments permitted those with a terminal illness to receive tax free benefits,[152] made enhancements to employees' ability to recover superannuation amounts from employers that have ceased operating,[153] and made

140 *Family Law Act 1975* (Cth), pt VIIIB, as amended 28 December 2002.
141 In 2003, 2004 and 2005.
142 In 2003.
143 *Superannuation Safety Amendment Act 2004* (Cth).
144 *Superannuation Industry (Supervision) Regulations 1994* (Cth), ss 6.28, 6.29.
145 Ibid. ss 10(1), 10A
146 Ibid. s 6.01. Retirement pensions can be received without having to leave the workforce or retire.
147 St Anne, above n 44, 218.
148 *Superannuation Industry (Supervision) Regulations 1994* (Cth), ss 6.40–6.46, amended 2006.
149 The aim of the financial disclosure rules was to provide information to allow ordinary people to make decisions about choice of super fund and investment options.
150 From 2004, the *Superannuation Safety Amendment Act 2004 (Cth)* required all superannuation trustees to be licensed. There is no such requirement for SMSFs, which has been argued to give SMSFs a competitive advantage, and be partly responsible for their recent growth; St Anne, above n 44, 221.
151 Costello, Peter (2006) 'Budget Speech 2006–07' (Speech delivered at the Second Reading of the Appropriation Bill No. 1, Parliament House, 9 May 2006); *Tax Laws Amendment (Simplified Superannuation) Act 2007* (Cth).
152 *Tax Laws Amendment (2008 Measures No. 1) Bill 2008* (Cth) sch 2; *Income Tax Assessment Act 1997* (Cth) s 303–10, as amended in September 2007.
153 *Corporations Act 2001* (Cth) s 556(1)(e), as amended on 31 December 2007.

further adjustments to the treatment of same-sex couples.[154] The rate at which the government co-contribution was paid was reduced temporarily between 1 July 2009 and 30 June 2014 and limits on concessional contributions were also reduced from 2009.[155] The Superannuation Guarantee Charge was intended to be increased gradually from its current level of 9.5% to 12% by 2019–20.[156]

3.7 The union movement and the push for universal superannuation

For 'blue collar' union leaders, the fact that government officials and 'white collar' workers enjoyed retirement benefits while their members did not was a source of substantial concern. The early pioneers of wider superannuation also saw the benefits of unions providing a financial service to their members and of the voting power of major shareholding in the largest Australian companies.

The role of the unions during the 1960s and 1970s, when a number of sector-specific schemes were established, was important, as it was in the run-up to the introduction of compulsory superannuation contributions. Initially, there were various discussions about establishing a national scheme, and then about making superannuation an integral part of the wage bargaining process, but eventually the Labor government decided that legislating for compulsory contributions was the way forward. As noted above, a crucial factor was the inability of unions to achieve desired wage rises and hence arguing for employer superannuation contributions which were seen as more easily achievable. This combined with the desire of union leaders to develop their roles and influence in the face of declining union membership.

Following the 1979 ACTU Congress, a committee was set up to examine superannuation issues.[157] ACTU developed a blueprint for a national superannuation scheme that had full vesting and union members dominating the fund's board. Despite misgivings from left-wing union leaders (who believed that adequate retirement incomes were a responsibility of the government) over the next few years most accepted the advantages of including superannuation in wage

154 *Same-Sex Relationships (Equal Treatment in Commonwealth Laws — Superannuation) Act 2008* (Cth).

155 *Tax Laws Amendment (2009 Budget Measures No. 1) Act 2009* (Cth) sch 2–3.

156 Australian Taxation Office (2013) 'Changes to Employers Superannuation Obligations from 1 July 2013', 1. However, there have been calls for the implementation of the increases to be delayed and draft legislation has been prepared to delay the next increase by two years. In the budget speech of 2014, the Government announced changes that will hold the super guarantee rate at 9.5% until 30 June 2018 and then increase it by 0.5 percentage points each year until it reaches 12%. See www.ato.gov.au/rates/key-superannuation-rates-and-thresholds/?page=23.

157 The committee included Simon Crean, Bill Kelty and Gary Weaven. Weaven had previously been involved in the superannuation scheme for the Victorian Municipal Officers Association in the 1970s. St Anne, above n 44, 28.

negotiations.[158] The employer groups, such as the *Business Council of Australia* (BCA) and the *Confederation of Australian Industry* (CAI) were, however, opposed, regarding occupational superannuation as a threat to company schemes, and expressing concerns over unions managing workers' money.[159]

The evolution of the Australian wage bargaining system and the election of a labour government in 1983 led to a closer relationship between the unions and the government. However, achievable increases in wages were still constrained by concerns about inflation, and union leaders saw an opportunity to obtain a better deal for their members through compulsory superannuation contributions made by employers. They also perceived, correctly, that the development of industry funds would enhance their role and influence. The following decade thus led to the gradual acceptance of employer superannuation contributions as part of wage awards, and in due course to the introduction of the SGC.

The accord signed between the ACTU and the ALP in February 1983, shortly prior to the election of the Hawke government, promised that an immediate priority would be consideration of a national superannuation scheme. FSPU led strike action over rewards for productivity increases, again arguing for these to be channelled into superannuation, and also argued successfully that the *Conciliation and Arbitration Commission* should regard superannuation as an industrial issue. In the same year, the building unions agreed to the creation of *Building Unions Superannuation* (BUS) during industry negotiations. The *Allied Unions Superannuation Trust* (AUST) was established in 1984.[160] By late 1985 a number of other industry superannuation funds had been established, including two in the building industry and an FSPU-sponsored fund in the paint industry.[161] FSPU also engaged in further strike action over superannuation, this time in the oil industry, leading to petrol rationing in Victoria.

Paul Keating, the new Treasurer, was a supporter of the superannuation movement, but nonetheless raised taxes on superannuation payments in May 1983.[162] However, subsequent adjustments permitted retirees to roll over their lump sum payments at concessional rates. The 1984 ALP National Conference supported "a portable national superannuation scheme providing entitlements to cover all persons".[163] In December 1985 guidelines for occupational superannuation

158 This was originally the view of Norman Gallagher, the leader of the Building Labourers Federation. Perceived advantages of including superannuation included less inflationary pressure than an equivalent wage rise.

159 St Anne, above n 44, 43.

160 AUST covered metal tradesmen, boilermakers, electricians and plumbers, among other skilled workers. St Anne, above n 44, 72.

161 St Anne, above n 44, 44.

162 These were raised to 15% for the first $50,000, with the remainder taxed at 30%. Previously, only 5% of a lump sum benefit had been included in assessable income. St Anne, above n 44, 50.

163 Pha, Anna (2004) *How Super Is Super?* (24 February 2004) Communist Party of Australia www.cpa.org.au/resources/australian-politics/how-super-is-super.pdf.

were issued, which included preservation of vested benefits before age 55. The *Occupational Superannuation Standards Act* was passed in 1987 and in 1988 tax on lump sums up to a limit was reduced to zero, with 15% tax above the limit, and a 15% tax on contributions. *Reasonable Benefit Limits* were also introduced in 1988.

The Accord (Mark 2) between the unions and the Labor government of 1986 agreed that remuneration for employees should increase by 6% per annum, to keep pace with inflation, and that half the increase would be paid into individual accounts in industry funds.[164] In June 1986, the *Industrial Arbitration Commission* awarded a 3% superannuation payment instead of the 4% cost-of-living increase claimed by the ACTU.[165] This was challenged, unsuccessfully, in the High Court by the CAI.[166]

In October 1986, the combined steel unions agreed with BHP that all employees would be paid 3% superannuation contributions into a substantially improved company fund.[167] In December 1986, workers in the clothing, textile and footwear industries were provided with a superannuation fund, the benefits from which included resumption of payments following maternity leave.[168] John Howard, then opposition leader, opposed the extension of industry superannuation, saying that it "represented everything that was rotten with industrial relations in Australia" and that it owed more to a "Chicago-style racket than it does to a proper and logical extension of superannuation".[169]

Nevertheless, for the next three years, union leaders argued for and achieved large extensions to occupational superannuation through the industrial award system.[170] The *Retail Employees Superannuation Trust* (REST), for example, was established in 1988.[171] By the end of 1990, about 64% of the workforce was covered by superannuation schemes, the assets of which were $123 billion.[172]

The payment of 3% superannuation contributions as a norm had been established with the Arbitration Commission during the 1980s. In early 1991, the ACTU requested that the *Industrial Relations Commission* (IRC) approve a further 3%, taking the total to 6%.[173] The Commission rejected the ACTU claim and

164 Bateman and Piggott, above n 61, 5.

165 *National Wage Case – June 1986* (1986) 301 CAR 611.

166 The High Court, in ruling against the CAI, stated that superannuation was an 'industrial matter' and within the Arbitration Commission's jurisdiction. This judgement was important as it reinforced union determination to push for universal superannuation. St Anne, above n 44, 61.

167 This fund was first established in the mid-1960s after a long campaign by the Federated Ironworkers Association (FIA). St Anne, above n 44, 64.

168 St Anne, above n 44, 67.

169 St Anne, above n 44, 45.

170 Olsberg, Diana (1997) *Ageing and Money* (Allen and Unwin).

171 See Rest Industry Super, *About REST*, www.rest.com.au/About-REST.aspx.

172 Nielson, Leslie (2010) 'Chronology of Superannuation and Retirement Income in Australia' (Background Note, Parliamentary Library, Parliament of Australia); Insurance and Superannuation Commission (ISC), *Annual Report 1990–91*.

173 The IRC was established in 1988, taking over from the *Arbitration Commission*, and ceased operation on 31 December 2009. See Australian Industrial Relations Commission, *Our History*, www.airc.gov.au/about/ourhistory.htm.

instead called for a national conference on superannuation.[174] This decision led to the idea that the superannuation increase should be legislated, rather than be achieved through the industrial relations arrangements.[175] Keating continued to campaign on superannuation during the period after he had resigned as Treasurer in June 1991, and canvassed the idea of increasing the compulsory component to 9% during speeches from the backbench.[176] It was, however, Treasurer John Kerin who finally announced the introduction of the *Superannuation Guarantee Charge* (SGC), beginning at 3% and rising to 9% by 2002.[177]

3.8 Handing over strategy and management to the private sector

There are many pivotal moments when key policy decisions were made, including decisions to outsource administration and management of the industry funds, the privatisation of the state-owned banks and insurers, deregulation of the financial services industry, and the development (and repeated variation) of tax concessions for superannuation. Subsequently, policy responses to the various inquiries into the system, in the face of persistent lobbying by an increasingly influential industry, reinforced these early decisions. The wholehearted acceptance of market-driven approaches under the Clinton and Blair administrations in the US and UK during the 1990s also provided justification, albeit misguided, for Australian policymakers.[178]

The decision not to establish a national superannuation scheme, but rather to encourage private provision, was formalised in a 1989 policy statement.[179] The decision had already effectively been made by previous rejection of the Whitlam proposals, first by the Senate and then explicitly by the Fraser government in 1976, and by the failure of the Hawke government to follow up on the ALPs call

174 St Anne, above n 44, 177.

175 The idea came from a meeting between Kelty, Ian Ross and Keating on the day after the Commission decision. Keating subsequently undertook that the government would legislate to ensure for the first 3%. St Anne, above n 44, 178; An AFR article reported the change: Kitney, Geoff (1991) 'Government May Legislate to Implement Super', *Australian Financial Review* (Sydney), 26 April 1991.

176 For example, a speech at the Australian Graduate School of Management (AGSM) on 25 July 1991. In fact, Keating wanted to eventually phase in a higher percentage, believing that 15% (with 3% of this provided by workers) was necessary to make the system sustainable. St Anne, above n 44, 196.

177 This was subsequently increased to 9.5% in July 2014.

178 For further discussion of how misguided beliefs in efficient markets misled policymakers, see Greenspan, Alan (2008) *Evidence to the House Committee on Oversight and Government Reform*, (Washington, DC, 23 October 2008); Borio, Claudio (2009) 'The Financial Crisis of 2007 – Macroeconomic and Policy Lessons' (Speech delivered at the G20 Workshop on the Global Economy, Mumbai, 24–26 May 2009), 13; Rajan, Raghuram (2010) *Faultines: How Hidden Fractures Still Threaten the World Economy* (Princeton University Press), 3.

179 Howe, Brian (1989) 'Better Incomes: Retirement Income Policy into the Next Century' (Press Statement by the Minister for Social Security, August 1989).

in 1984 for a national superannuation scheme. The 1989 policy statement established that retirement income policy be based upon the 'twin pillars' of the age pension and private superannuation, explicitly rejecting the option of a national superannuation scheme.

The choice of how to manage the rapidly growing funds was hotly debated between left-wing unions, who wanted to retain control, and the ACTU leadership who wanted to "sustain legitimacy in the eyes of the employers, the government and the public".[180] Because the ACTU leaders did not want to give any excuse to their opponents to criticise the superannuation movement, they adopted a conservative stance on investment strategy, on board selection, and in using AMP, Colonial Mutual and National Mutual (among others) as their investment managers.

The Australian Chamber of Manufacturers, concerned over the growing importance of the union funds, set up the Australian Retirement Fund (ARF) in 1987 and offered membership to employees of their 6,000 members.[181] AMP was initially appointed as administrator and investment manager.[182] Corporate superannuation funds were converted to industry funds, for example the Civil Aviation Authority Staff Superannuation Fund became AvSuper.[183]

The challenge of setting up big schemes quickly required both skilled people and suitable computer systems, neither of which the unions felt they could assemble quickly enough, hence reinforcing the decision to outsource.[184] The ACTU and the building unions also chose to unbundle service providers: for example, in setting up the Building Unions Superannuation Scheme (BUS) separate contracts were awarded for the administrative, insurance and investment functions.[185] REST had initially been started under the Retail Traders Association, and included an agreement with National Mutual to act as its administrator.[186] The foundations of today's complex, multi-layered system had been laid, and the ongoing importance of the insurance and banking industries established.[187]

180 Olsberg, Diana (1997) *Ageing and Money* (Allen and Unwin).

181 Bill Kelty was appointed to the original ARF Board.

182 Subsequently, JANA Investment Advisers took over the investment management role as ARF Trustees found AMP to be too conservative. St Anne, above n 44.

183 AvSuper adopted the representative trustee model, and was established as a DB scheme. The latter created conflict with the ACTU, who wanted it to follow the accumulation model. St Anne, above n 44, 90. AvSuper also developed a reputation for aggressive investment strategies, including 40% allocation to emerging bond markets and 20% in corporate debt with a BBB or below rating. AvSuper was one of the first funds to invest in hedge funds. St Anne, above n 44, 156, 160.

184 St Anne, above n 44, 85.

185 BUS and AUST merged in 1992 to form Construction and Building Unions Superannuation (CBus). See Cbus (2017), *Cbus' Story* www.cbussuper.com.au/about-cbus/the-cbus-story.

186 St Anne, above n 44, 85.

187 St Anne, above n 44, 84, 95. REST transferred its administration to AAS, a subsidiary of AMP, in 1991 following an attempted fee increase by Nexis, National Mutual's administration subsidiary. REST also paid advice specialist Money Solutions to provide advice to members.

3.9 Legal and regulatory framework

The 1997 *Wallis Committee* reported on the Australian Financial System, including superannuation arrangements.[188] The inquiry considered, *inter alia*, changing customer needs, technology driven innovation, regulation as a driver of change, the changing financial landscape, cost and efficiency, conduct and disclosure, financial safety, stability, co-ordination and accountability, and deregulation.

The Wallis Committee cited compulsory superannuation as one of the major factors driving change in the Australian system, expecting superannuation assets to grow to between $1,494 and $1,825 billion by 2020.[189] They recognised that the nature of these investments meant that households would bear a greater proportion of risk directly than they had done in the past. The Committee recommended greater encouragement of member choice in superannuation as a solution.[190]

The Wallis Committee recommendations led to the *Financial Services Reform Act 2001* (FSRA). This introduced new licensing provisions and mandatory product disclosure rules in an attempt to introduce consistency across different types of financial product.[191] The result was that regulation of the products and operations of fund managers became more aligned with wealth management products (insurance, investments and superannuation) than with that of securities and securities dealers. The FSRA also replaced the provisions of the *Insurance (Agents and Brokers) Act 1984* to impose stricter disclosure requirements on life insurance companies.[192]

The Wallis Inquiry also proposed the establishment of an *Australian Prudential Regulation Commission* (APRC) and a *Corporations and Financial Services Commission* (CFSC) which would be responsible for market integrity and consumer protection.[193] Under the proposed new system the *Reserve Bank of Australia* (RBA) would remain responsible for systemic stability, monetary policy and payments systems regulation.[194] The APRC was to take over the superannuation responsibilities of the existing *Insurance and Superannuation Commission*, and to be the regulator charged with prudential regulation of financial institutions.[195]

188 Commonwealth, Ken Wallis (Chair), above n 37.

189 Ibid. 295. In fact, assets have already grown to above the top of their projected range.

190 The Commonwealth Government had previously announced a policy of choice of fund in 1996 and introduced a detailed proposal in the 1997 Budget. The relevant Bill was defeated in the Senate in August 2001 but reintroduced in 2002. Select Committee on Superannuation, Parliament of Australia, *Provisions of the Superannuation Legislation Amendment (Choice of Superannuation Funds) Bill 2002 (Cth)* (2002).

191 Explanatory Memorandum, *Financial Services Reform Bill 2001 (Cth).*

192 This reinforced the provisions of the *Insurance Act 1973* (Cth) and the *Life Insurance Act 1995* (Cth), which require a registration system and also provide for basic supervision of insurers, brokers and agents.

193 A version of the CFSC in due course was established as ASIC.

194 These recommendations are discussed in detail in Harper, Ian R. (1997) 'The Wallis Report: An Overview' 30 *Australian Economic Review* 288.

195 The APRC proposed by Wallis became the Australian Prudential Regulatory Authority (APRA) before it was established.

The legislation that followed the Wallis Inquiry set up the current regulatory structure, which consists of five regulatory agencies: *ASIC, APRA, the ATO, the Reserve Bank of Australia (RBA) and the Australian Competition and Consumer Commission (ACCC)*.[196] The ATO has responsibility for smaller funds, with fewer than four members, the RBA is responsible for financial system stability and for the regulation of the payments system,[197] and the ACCC has various powers to protect competition in the financial system (although it has no direct remit for consumer protection). Responsibility for SMSFs was transferred from APRA to the ATO in 1999.[198]

ASIC was given additional responsibility in 1998 to regulate the market for financial products and services.[199] It now enforces legislative provisions relating to investments, insurance, superannuation and deposit-taking activities (but not lending); is responsible for the registration of companies, auditors and liquidators; supervises futures markets; implements the provisions of the FSRA; monitors and assesses compliance with a variety of codes of practice;[200] and has a range of market integrity and consumer protection responsibilities.[201] ASIC is funded by the Commonwealth Government, although it also receives fees and charges from companies.

APRA commenced operations on 1 July 1998, as a result of the *Australian Prudential Authority Act 1998*.[202] APRA is largely funded by industry levies, and is supervised by a full-time executive group of between three and five members appointed by the Governor General. APRA is responsible for the prudential regulation of *Authorised Deposit-taking Institutions* (ADIs) (banks, building societies and credit unions)[203] as well as friendly societies, life and general insurance companies, and superannuation funds. It has powers to revoke licences, issue enforceable directions and in extreme cases to intervene in management. APRA's powers bring together those previously held by the RBA (in respect of banks),[204] the ISC (for insurance companies and superannuation funds), and the Australian Institutions Commission (AIC) (for building societies and credit unions). APRA has a wider role as a data collection agency, for example *Registered Financial Corporations* (RFCs, including finance companies) and *Discretionary Mutual*

196 The RBA is the only agency able to provide emergency liquidity support in the event of a threat to the stability of the financial system. In addition, the Department of Human Services is responsible for assessing applications for early release of superannuation funds on compassionate grounds. See www.humanservices.gov.au/customer/services/centrelink/early-release-superannuation.

197 Through the Payments System Board under new legislation, the *Payment Systems (Regulation) Act 1998* (Cth) and the *Payment Systems and Netting Act 1998* (Cth).

198 St Anne, above n 44, 221.

199 This is the role that the *Wallis Inquiry* envisaged for the CFSC.

200 Including the *Code of Banking Practice, the Credit Union Code of Practice, the Building Society Code of Practice* and the *Electronic Funds Transfer Code of Practice*.

201 ASIC took over these roles from the ISC and from the ACCC.

202 APRA was intended to carry out the role that the *Wallis Inquiry* envisaged for the APRC.

203 Under the depositor protection provisions of the *Banking Act 1959* (Cth). All ADIs are required to hold assets in Australia at least equal to their deposit liabilities in Australia.

204 APRA took over the banking supervision role from the RBA on 1 July 1998.

Funds (DMFs) are required to provide statistics to APRA even though they are not prudentially supervised by APRA.[205]

Trust law does provide some protection to members, though this is constrained in various ways. In the Australian superannuation industry, enforcement of the provisions of the SIS Act mostly concern breaches relating to malfeasance by individuals, which can give rise to a civil penalty order or criminal liability.[206] Other breaches can in principle result in the superannuation fund losing its complying fund status, and hence its privileged tax status.[207] The main effect of the latter could be that members transfer assets to another, complying fund. Individuals may also be barred from acting as directors.[208]

Nevertheless, Scott Donald has emphasised how "the protection [trust law] offers to the members of a superannuation fund is far more nuanced than the rhetoric of trust law implies", because trust law's substantive contribution is negated by "opportunistic contractual eclipse" and by the requirement that superannuation trustees be corporate entities.[209] He cites cases where judges have "expressed reservations about the wisdom of applying traditional trust principles to superannuation funds".[210]

Donald concludes, however, that "trust law does contribute directly to the calibration of the regulatory scheme in respect of the member protection objective, but perhaps not in the way sometimes simplistically assumed. Specifically, by according recognition to certain causes of action and by privileging certain decision criteria, trust law helps to bring about an allocation of accountability between the actors in the system."[211]

3.10 The emergence of the modern superannuation industry

The industry that ended up managing the superannuation funds evolved from the wider financial services industry, including the rapidly growing mutual fund and insurance sectors. Initially corporate funds and public sector funds were developed

205 Australian Prudential Regulation Authority (2017)*Protecting Australia's Depositors, Insurance Policyholders and Superannuation Fund Members*, available at www.apra.gov.au/AboutAPRA/Publications/Pages/APRA-Brochure.aspx.

206 Donald, M. Scott (2013) *Trusting in Trust: The Role of Trust Law in the Regulatory Scheme Applied to Superannuation in Australia* (PhD Thesis, University of New South Wales); *SIS Act* pt 21.

207 *Income Tax Assessment Act 1993* (Cth) pt IX.

208 *Corporations Act 2001* (Cth).

209 A consequence of the distribution of legislative powers effected by the Australian Constitution. Donald notes that this requirement "complicates the matrix of accountability, especially in regards to issues such as conflicts of interest, by introducing an additional layer". Donald, *Trusting in Trust*, above n 206, 6.

210 *Dillon v Burns Philp Finance Ltd* (Unreported, Supreme Court of New South Wales, Bryson J, 20 July 1988); *Sayseng v Kellogg Superannuation Pty Ltd* [2007] NSWSC 1009 (12 September 2007); *Vidovic v Email Superannuation* (Unreported, Supreme Court of New South Wales, Bryson J, 3 March 1995).

211 Donald, *Trusting in Trust*, above n 206, 9.

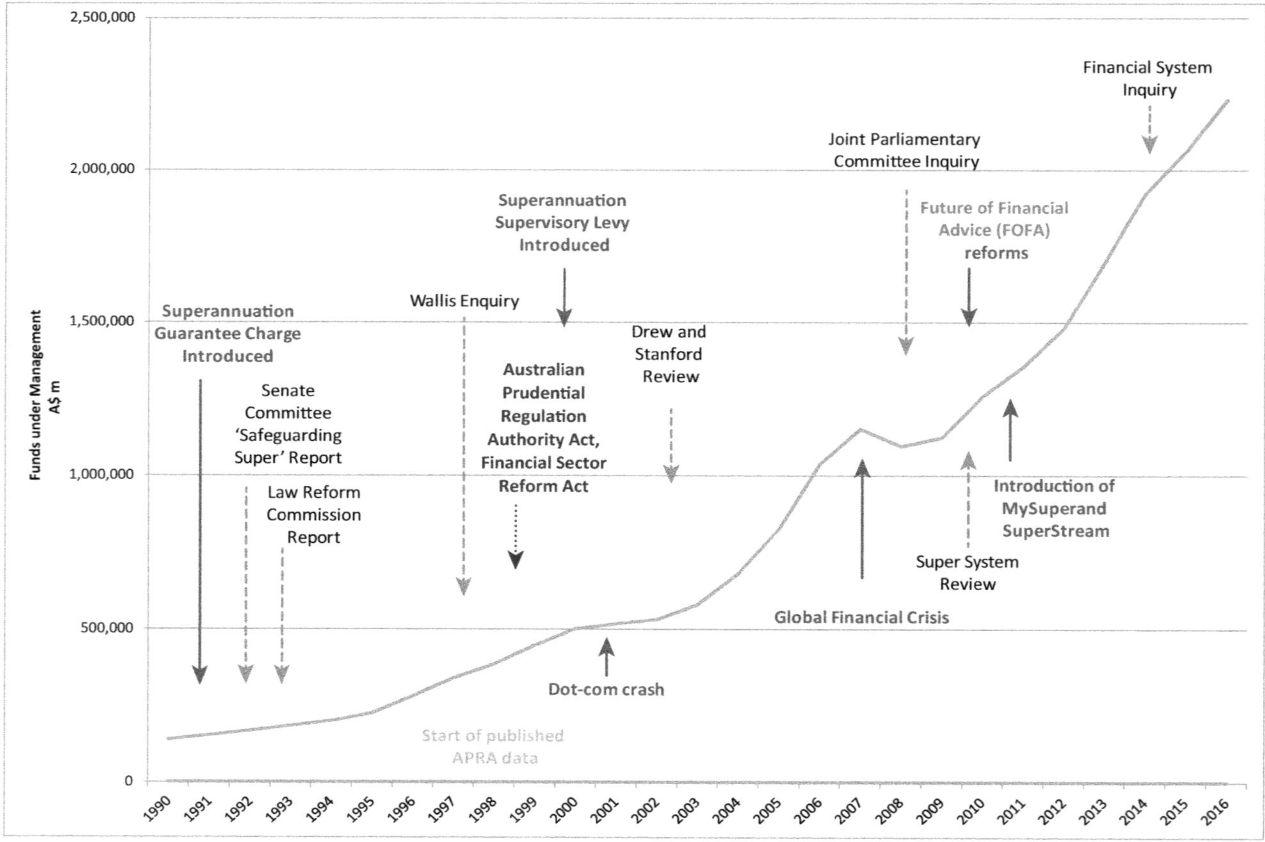

Figure 3.1 Major events in the development of Australian superannuation since 1991

during the nineteenth century. Retail funds emerged from the early 1900s after the introduction of tax concessions, with industry funds mainly developing as a result of productivity award super in the 1980s. The dominance of Australian financial markets by large banks and financial conglomerates led to them playing a substantial role. UK, US and global institutions took an increasing interest as assets grew, and brought with them marketing and technical expertise developed in a deregulated market environment.

The history presented above highlights how the choice of decentralised pension administration, funded by compulsory superannuation contributions, with the resulting funds managed by a lightly-regulated private sector, was the result of numerous different influences which converged in the 1980s. These influences created complexity that has increased cost, embedded market power and reduced transparency.

Figure 3.1 below shows the recent growth of superannuation assets in Australia, and a selection of the various relevant policy initiatives, events and inquiries during the last 25 years.

Table 3.1 shows that between 1 July 1991 and 30 June 2016,[212] a total of around \$2 trillion of contributions and rollover from other funds were made into superannuation funds, net of contribution taxes and surcharges.[213] After benefit payments of \$999 billion, investment earnings of \$1.17 trillion,[214] and net of reported expenses and other charges of \$278 billion, total funds under management grew by just over \$1.9 trillion.[215]

Figure 3.2 shows how the assets managed by different types of entity have evolved during the last two decades. The pronounced rise in the holdings of small funds (mostly SMSFs) was in part driven by tax changes in 2007 and 2008,

Table 3.1 Development of Australian superannuation fund assets 1991 to 2016

A\$million	*1991–2016*
Contributions net of tax and surcharge	1,840,336
Net benefit transfers and rollover	224,962
Benefit payments	(1,100,543)
Net investment income after tax	1,231,730
Total reported operating expenses	(112,204)
Net insurance flows and other charges	(23,795)
Change in the balance of life office statutory funds	(7,910)
Balancing item (unreported costs, adjustments etc)	(150,598)
Net growth in assets	**1,901,979**

Source: Own calculations based on APRA data

212 APRA data to 30 June 2016 was released on 1 February 2013.

213 Data on contributions taxes and surcharges before 2004 is not available. This conservative estimate is based on the author's computations assuming average tax rates in periods before the data is available.

214 Investment earnings are net of undisclosed fees deducted by third-party managers etc.

215 These estimates include some from the period 1991 to 1997 for which the available data is weak.

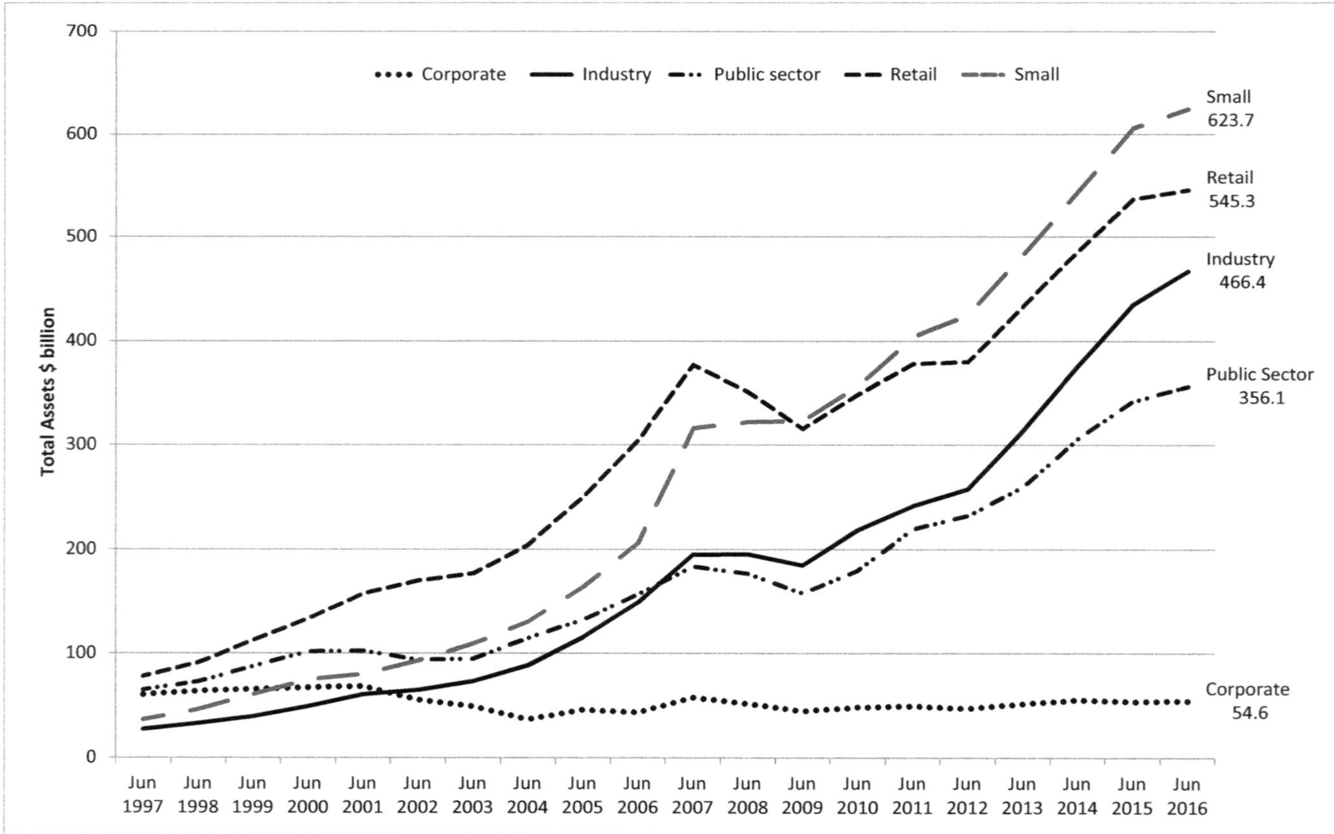

Figure 3.2 Superannuation assets by fund type, 1997 to 2016

Source: Australian Prudential Regulatory Authority, 'Statistics: Revised Annual Superannuation Bulletin June 2013' (APRA, revised ed., 5 February 2014) Table 9, updated using 'Statistics: Annual Superannuation Bulletin June 2016' (APRA, 1 February 2017) Table 8a.

Note: 'Small' funds are self-managed superannuation funds (SMSFs) and small APRA funds, including single member approved deposit funds.

but also reflects member perceptions of the high costs and low performance of the larger funds.[216] From 2009, small funds have held more assets than any other class, followed by retail. The share of industry funds has grown particularly steeply since 2012.

The introduction of compulsory superannuation in 1991 triggered large changes to the industry, as Australian and overseas companies recognised the opportunities ahead. AMP, MLC and Mercantile grew rapidly, acquiring a number of smaller players. Foreign firms such as County Natwest moved into the retail market, the St George building society entered into a management arrangement for investment funds with BT,[217] and Potter Warburg led a resurgence of equities specialists. Wholesale funds were developed by the leading management companies, and large master trusts emerged[218] as did fund-of-funds products.[219] American companies entered the market, including State Street and Vanguard (which developed passively managed funds). By the late 1990s, State Street Global was managing $50 billion of superannuation funds.[220]

Third-party marketing firms representing overseas clients emerged, the first being Super Communications. Merrill Lynch bought Mercury Asset Management in the UK, thus also acquiring an Australian subsidiary. Tower Life acquired Adriatic Life in 1991 and subsequently the funds management arm of FAI, while Colonial First State took over Legal and General, and Prudential. Master trusts increased ten-fold between 1994 and 2001, from $9.6 billion to $90 billion.[221] Further mergers have led to substantial recent consolidation. The Australian Retirement Fund (ARF) merged with the Superannuation Trust of Australia (STA) in 2005 to form Australian Super, which then merged with WestScheme; First State Superannuation (FST) merged with Health Super in 2011; and Care Super merged with Asset Super.

Between 1990 and 1998, four major life offices demutualised: Capita through acquisition by MLC Life; National Mutual Life through sale to former members and foreign interests; and Colonial Mutual and Australian Mutual Provident Society through sale to former members. At the time of demutualisation, they held $20 billion of net assets and controlled $164 billion in total assets.[222]

216 The rapid growth of SMSFs in 2006/7 was partly driven by transitional arrangements leading up to the 'Simplified Superannuation' legislation that came into effect in July 2007. The legislation introduced a cap on after-tax superannuation contributions, but allowed up to $1 million contributions to be made between May 2006 and July 2007: Reserve Bank of Australia (2013) 'Financial Stability Review September 2013' (24 September 2013), 54.

217 And subsequently became a bank, acquiring ASGARD and Advance in 1997.

218 For example, those run by Norwich Union, ASGARD and MLC.

219 For example, that developed by Bain and Co, now a subsidiary of Deutsche Bank.

220 St Anne, above n 44, 154.

221 ASSIRT estimates, reported in Personal Investor (January 2002), 45.

222 Reserve Bank of Australia (1999) 'Demutualisation in Australia' (Bulletin, January 1999). Just under half of National Mutual's eligible shareholders, 77% of Colonial's and 88% of AMP's elected to retain their share allocation instead of taking cash in lieu, thus increasing the proportion of Australians with share ownership.

The demutualisation of these life offices left only one mutually owned life office.[223] Industry assets held by mutuals fell from 58% in 1985 to under 1% by 1998. These demutualisations were mostly triggered by management (which argued that they were necessary in order to improve access to financial markets). A similar trend occurred in Building Societies, Credit Unions and Friendly Societies, as well as at the Australian Stock Exchange.[224]

In 1999 Bankers Trust Co in the US was acquired by Deutsche Bank AG, and BT Australia was subsequently sold to Westpac, which also bought Rothschilds Funds Management.[225] In 2001 the Commonwealth Bank acquired Colonial Mutual First State and NAB bought MLC from Lend Lease.[226] The ANZ entered into joint venture with ING Australia. By 2002 over 60% of the retail funds management industry (at least in terms of administration and distribution) had come under the auspices of the four major banks, AMP and AXA.[227]

Aggressive marketing by distributors such as ING, and by the operators of investor-directed portfolio service (IDPS) platforms such as Macquarie, led to rapid growth in assets under management. Unit trust structures (which had typically involved a manager and a custodian) gave way to a three-tiered scheme, in which manufacturing, administration and distribution were typically run by different entities. The providers of administration and distribution services were often no longer ‘responsible entities’, and custodial duties (which had previously been carried out by Trustees) were increasingly outsourced.[228]

A combination of the increasing wealth of Australian households and advances in technology spawned substantial growth in financial advice. Computers became important tools for the industry from the 1980s onwards and by the early 1990s instant access to financial data was also available to retail investors. Fund managers established advisory centres, and large commissions were paid to advisers to recommend investment products. Investment advisers expanded their branch networks into the suburbs in order to support the rapidly growing number of smaller investors.[229]

In the late 1980s, the industry funds appointed asset consultants to advise them on their strategies. REST and ARF appointed Jana Investment Services, while HESTA and Hostplus appointed Frontier Investment Consulting. Both Jana and

223 See Keneley, Monica (2004) ‘Adaptation and Change in the Australian Life Insurance Industry: An Historical Perspective’ (School of Economics, Deakin University, Melbourne, Australia), available at www.deakin.edu.au/__data/assets/pdf_file/0007/402586/swp2003-08.pdf.

224 Ibid., provides details of these demutualisations as well.

225 The BT Australia transaction was finally completed in 2002.

226 Colonial Mutual had itself absorbed several smaller players including the State Bank of NSW’s First State in 1994.

227 Mees, Wehner and Hanrahan, above n 53. Paul Keating famously described these as the “six pillars”.

228 Ibid. 38.

229 Greenwood, R. (1985) ‘Advisers Branch out to Suburbs’ 3 *Personal Investment* 1, 50.

Frontier selected individual fund managers based on their ability to manage specific asset classes, and so sector specialists also began to thrive. HESTA and TISS (now FIRST Super) hired PIMCO as the only global bond manager in Australia. Sponsorship by the large industry funds permitted these advisory companies to grow rapidly. Other global equity and bond managers were attracted to Australia and began to build local businesses, for example Fidelity Worldwide Investment established an Australian equities team in 2003.

Industry Fund Services (IFS) was formed in 1994 by a group of industry funds to provide ancillary services.[230] The success of IFS in providing services to the industry funds led to the development of Industry Funds Management (IFM),[231] Members Equity and ME Bank,[232] the asset consulting business Frontier Investment Consulting (Frontier), Industry Fund Financial Planning (IFPP), arrears collection services (IFCC), IFS insurance broking, and the eligible rollover fund AUSFund.[233] The idea was that this family of companies would pool the costs and product development, and also that IFS would offer competing retail services, thus bringing down costs.[234] IFPP, in particular, operated on a fee-for-service basis, eschewing the commissions-based model used elsewhere in the industry.[235] In 1998, the IFS group formed a joint venture with Colonial to run the back office and membership functions of the funds.[236] In 2000, Frontier was separated from IFS because of concern over conflicts of interest between advice and investment practices.[237] In 2006, IFS and IFM merged with ME Bank to create the ME Group.[238]

The industry funds also sought to encourage the growth of boutique fund managers. UniSuper, for example, developed a separate incubation business. Many of the new private firms were spin-offs from larger firms, for example Integrity

230 Initial shareholders included Colonial (who sold its stake in 1996), STA, CBus, HESTA, Hostplus and the Australian Retirement Fund. St Anne, above n 44, 127.

231 IFM started as Development Australia Fund (DAF), which had originally been formed by AMP and the Australian Chamber of Manufacturers, but which was taken over by IFS in 2004. It has concentrated on innovative infrastructure investments including Citylink tollroad and the takeover of Pacific Hydro, as well as investing offshore, particularly in the US. St Anne, above n 44, 136–7.

232 In partnership with National Mutual. The business began in 1994 with the development of Super Members Home Loans (SMHLs), to provide low-cost home loans to Super Funds members, underwritten by AXA (AXA sold out in 2003).

233 AUSFund's main business is identifying 'lost' superannuation after members leave funds.

234 St Anne, above n 44, 128–9.

235 This proved popular among the funds, and IFPP tripled in size between 2004 and 2008.

236 Jacques Martin Industry Funds Administration (JMIFA). JMIFA became 100% owned by the industry funds when Commonwealth Bank took over Colonial in 2001. Today it is Australia's largest wholesale administrator, managing six million superannuation accounts, and has been rebranded Superpartners. St Anne, above n 44, 130.

237 St Anne, above n 44, 134.

238 The creation of ME Bank was an attempt by the Industry Funds to strengthen their capability to make large-scale investments without relying on established players such as Macquarie. However, the financial crisis caused problems because the majority of ME Bank's funding was from securitisation markets. ME Group was restructured in 2009, after injection of funds from the Industry Funds that own it.

Investment Management (IIM),[239] and Solaris Investment Management.[240] Some Industry Funds recruited in-house chief investment officers, often from the asset consultants, which improved their ability to interface with the external advisers and fund managers.[241]

IFS and Frontier Consulting, in consultation with the Industry Funds,[242] argued that a move into alternative investments, such as infrastructure, private equity and hedge funds, would yield better returns. A number of pooled funds were set up by IFS from 1990 onwards, and by 2010 IFM was managing $30 billion, including large-scale investments in infrastructure assets in the US, UK and Eastern Europe. Cbus also established a property unit to invest directly, often in partnership with AMP and other firms.[243] In the search for innovation, firms such as Frontier and Jana monitored what US funds were doing and then sought to replicate these ideas in Australia.[244]

Financial advisers are required by ASIC to demonstrate they have adequately researched the investments they recommend. This is often satisfied by only permitting products that have achieved specified research ratings or third party endorsements from research houses. A survey of the funds management industry illustrated the resulting dominance of asset consultants and research houses in Australia:

> These specialists have become so influential in Australia that it is estimated that more than 90 per cent of superannuation funds under management [are] heavily influenced by asset consultants while research houses advise on the majority of managed funds that are selected for placement on retail platforms.[245]

239 IIM was set up by the head of equities at UBS Asset Management, who took his entire team and persuaded Care Super, Asset Super and the Australian Catholic Superannuation Retirement Fund to become early clients. St Anne, above n 44, 162.

240 Solaris was formed from the entire equities team at Suncorp, and also persuaded a number of industry funds to switch managers within the first months of operation. St Anne, above n 44, 162.

241 For example, Sunsuper recruited David Hartley from Russell Investment Group, and UniSuper David St John from Mercer. St Anne, above n 44.

242 Garry Weaven, Bill Kelty and Elana Rubin all believed that the move into alternative investments would yield better returns. Weaven wrote a paper entitled 'Super Investment: Where to from Here?' which argued that as superannuation funds grew to dominance in Australia it became necessary for them to invest directly (for example in property), in small caps and development capital, overseas and in alternatives. St Anne, above n 44, 158; Weaven, now Chairman of Industry Funds Management, argues in a similar way today, see Garry Weaven, 'Developing Infrastructure Investment Models for Super Funds' (Industry Super Australia, 29 March 2012) www.industry-supernetwork.com/tag/garry-weaven.

243 Cbus Property now includes a portfolio of commercial buildings in Sydney and Melbourne and has $1.5 billion in assets under management. St Anne, above n 44, 160.

244 St Anne, above n 44, 162.

245 Dunnin, Alex (2011) *Fund Management in Australia: Market Entry Report* (Rainmaker Information), 5.

The advice of the asset consultants has not always been beneficial. For example, from 2005 onwards, MTAA Super took advice to invest heavily in unlisted infrastructure and property assets, following a strategy called 'Target Return Portfolio'.[246] Unfortunately, these assets performed particularly poorly during the Global Financial Crisis, causing heavy losses for MTAA's members. There has also been concern about possible conflicts of interest where asset consultants also move into 'implemented consulting', earning fees on the acquisition of assets on which they have previously advised their clients. The case of MTAA and complicated arrangements over the sale of a stake in South Australian Flinders Ports Group once again brought the role of advisers into high relief late in 2011, following suggestions that ASIC investigate conflicts of interest.[247]

Industry associations played an important role in representing the evolving industry. At the beginning of the 1980s, the Association of Superannuation Funds of Australia (ASFA) was the primary body representing superannuation funds. The Unit Trust Association of Australia (UTAA) was re-founded, and in 1983 the Australian Investment Planner's Association (AIPA) was formed.[248] *Personal Investment* magazine was launched in 1983, as was the UTAA's *Unit Trust News*.[249] ASFA re-introduced its magazine, *Superfunds*, in 1988, and initiated education programmes in collaboration with Macquarie University.[250] By the end of the 1980s firms such as ASSIRT and Independent Funds Research had begun ranking retail funds. The Conference of Major Superannuation Funds (CMSF) held its first annual conference in 1990.[251] AIPA re-emerged as the Financial Planning Association (FPA) in 1992.[252] The Investment and Financial Services Association (IFSA) was created in 1991 through merger of the Life, Investment and Superannuation Association, the Investment Funds Association and the Australian Investment Managers Association. In 1992, the Australian Institute of Superannuation Trustees (AIST) was created as the peak body for not-for-profit funds, and pioneered training courses for trustees.[253] The Australian Council of Superannuation Investors (ACSI) was established in 2001, with membership

246 St Anne, above n 44, 170–171.

247 Ferguson, Adele (2011) 'Ports Sales Spotlights Super Conflict' *Business Day* (The Sydney Morning Herald (Sydney) 30 November 2011); Durie, John (2011) 'Asset Consultants Face Scrutiny from Regulator' (The Australian (Sydney), 10 June 2011).

248 The Unit Trust Association of Australia had closed during the managed funds trough of the early 1970s.

249 Personal Investment (1983–99); Unit Trust News (UTAA, 1983–9).

250 St Anne, above n 44, 229.

251 The conference was held in Wollongong, NSW. Ibid. 230.

252 It became the Australian Society of Investment and Financial Advisors as an intermediate step towards the foundation of the FPA.

253 See www.aist.asn.au/about/about-aist.aspx. AIST merged with the CMSF and the Training and Compliance department of IFS in 2007. St Anne, above n 44, 232.

from the industry superannuation funds.[254] Industry Super Network (ISN), an advocacy body, was formed in 2008.

By 30 June 2016, total superannuation assets were $2.045 trillion, of which $1,292 billion was held by APRA-regulated superannuation entities and trusts.[255] A further $132.2 billion was held in exempt public sector schemes, $53.3 billion in life office statutory funds, and $621.7 billion in 577,236 self-managed superannuation funds (SMSFs) regulated by the Australian Taxation Office (ATO).[256] In total, 75.8% of assets for entities with more than four members were allocated to defined contribution (DC) funds (covering 95.5% of member accounts), with only 18.2% allocated to defined benefit (DB) schemes (covering 3.3% of member funds).[257]

In the 1950s and 1960s, annual management fees had been rare, and firms such as AFT typically relied on upfront fees (of as much as 8%).[258] Some provisions were made for skimming from dividends, but these tended only to be used when unusual costs were incurred. So industry profitability was dependent on the regular winding-up of closed-ended trusts and the transfer of unit-holders to new trusts. By the mid-1980s, increased competition for investors caused entry fees to fall to around 6%, but this was compensated for by ongoing service fees, typically 1%. Following the growth in retail master trusts, management expense ratios (MERs) became a focus of attention by the early 1990s.

Partly because of concerns over fees and charges in the APRA-regulated funds, and partly as a result of tax incentives, many chose to place their contributions into SMSFs. SMSFs became particularly popular following changes in legislation in late 1990s – which split so-called 'excluded' funds into 'small APRA' and 'SMSFs'. The SMSF sector has grown by an average of around 20% per annum since 1999, and today manages around one third of superannuation assets in Australia. The *Super System Review* included a review of this subsector, which revealed that SMSFs received 41% of all contributions in the year to 30 June 2007.[259] Over the five-year period to 30 June 2008, member contributions to SMSFs were greater than employer contributions by a factor of approximately

254 ACSI's mission is described as assisting members to 'manage environmental, social and corporate governance (ESG) investment risk'. ASCI, Home www.acsi.org.au. ACSI has taken leadership positions internationally on major issues, for example in 2011 leading the campaign to vote against the re-election of the News Corp Board. St Anne, above n 44, 234.

255 Australian Prudential Regulatory Authority (2017) Statistics: Annual Superannuation Bulletin June 2016 (1 February 2017) Tables 1 and 3. As at 30 June 2016, there were 144 Regulated Superannuation Entities (RSE) licencees, with another 225 RSEs under trusteeship, with a total of 27.04 million members. Of these entities, 195 were for-profit and 174 not-for-profit.

256 Ibid., Table 3.

257 Ibid., Table 11. 6% of member benefits were allocated to funds with both defined benefits and defined contribution benefits interest. Of the total of 28 million member accounts, 7.5 million were 'inactive' and 0.5 million 'lost'.

258 Mees, Wehner and Hanrahan, above n 53, 43.

259 This was the year in which the abolition of the former Reasonable Benefit Limit was abolished, and a temporarily high one-off annual contribution limit of $1 million was available.

three to one.[260] As at 30 June 2016 there were over 577,000 SMSFs, with over $621 billion FUM or 29.6% of all superannuation funds.[261]

The result of the last 25 years' evolution is a financial sector in Australia which has grown to a size which the Bank for International Settlements (BIS) regards as too large.[262] A BIS report has noted that the finance sector in Australia accounted for 11.5% of industry value added in 2012, compared with the 2008 peak of 7.7% in the US and 10.4% in Ireland.[263] Australia's finance sector employs 3.7% of the Australian workforce, more than Britain's 3.5%, despite Britain's much larger role as an international financial centre.[264]

3.11 Recent attempts at reform

Concern over the management of Australian superannuation has been a repeated theme during the last 25 years. ASIC Chairman, David Knott, defined the challenge in 2002:

> The gradual evolution of the industry from a relatively obscure ancillary of employment to centre stage of household savings carries with it requirements for transparency, market competitive performance, and risk management.[265]

The *Super System Review* summarised the problems thus:

> It has to be said that the original superannuation architecture was somewhat optimistic in that it relied on notions of market forces, disclosure and competition (along with trust concepts) to resolve consumer issues surrounding complex products, structures and conflicts.[266]

260 Commonwealth (2009) *Review into the Governance, Efficiency, Structure and Operation of Australia's Superannuation System: A Statistical Summary of Self-Managed Superannuation Funds*. The year 2008 saw particularly large flows, triggered by a large increase in the limit on contributions.

261 Australian Prudential Regulatory Authority (2016) *Statistics: Annual Superannuation Bulletin June 2016*, Table 3.

262 Cecchetti, Stephen G. and Enisse Kharroubi (2012) 'Reassessing the Impact of Finance on Growth' (Working Paper No. 381, Bank for International Settlements, July 2012); for discussion of the implications of this report for Australia see Uren, David (2012) 'BIS Warns Australia's Finance Sector is Too Big for our Economy' (The Australian (Sydney), 20 August 2012).

263 A share that has doubled since the mid-1980s. In the BIS analysis, only Canada, Switzerland, Ireland and the US had financial sector shares in total employment that exceeded that of Australia in 2005–2009. Cecchetti and Kharroubi show that "[t]he faster the financial sector grows, the slower the economy as a whole grows" (Cecchetti and Kharroubi, above n 262, 12).

264 Figures provided by Stephen Cecchetti, Chief Economist at the BIS Annual Conference, Switzerland, August 2012: Cecchetti and Kharroubi, above n 262.

265 Knott, David (2002) 'Changing Dynamics of the Australian Superannuation Industry' (Speech delivered at the ASFA Luncheon, Sydney, 25 September 2002).

266 Super System Review Panel (2010) *Review into the Governance, Efficiency, Structure and Operation of Australia's Superannuation System: Final Report ('Super System Review'), Part Two: Recommendation Packages.*

Recent inquiries have suggested that the financial and superannuation systems need to be made more efficient and accountable and have suggested reforms. These include the *Ripoll Inquiry* into corporate scandals and failures (following the GFC)[267] and the *Super System Review*.[268] The relevant outcomes of these inquiries are discussed briefly below: more detail on their findings is provided in Annex B.

The *Future of Financial Advice* reforms followed the *Ripoll Inquiry* and were announced in April 2011.[269] They included a ban on conflicted remuneration structures including commissions, the introduction of a statutory fiduciary duty for financial advisers to act in the best interests of their clients, the introduction of a two-yearly opt-in arrangement and annual fee disclosure statements for financial advisers, limitations on the percentage-based fees that can be charged, increased availability of low-cost 'simple advice', strengthening the powers of ASIC, and development of an improved compensation scheme.[270] These proposals were implemented from 1 July 2012. Compliance with the new measures was intended to be voluntary until 1 July 2013 and mandatory from then on. However, the initial recommendations were watered down following lobbying and consultation, including reduction in the scope of conflicted remuneration, removal of the 'opt in' requirement for financial planners, amending grandfathering arrangements and changes to the specification of 'best interests'.[271]

267 Parliamentary Joint Committee on Corporations and Financial Services (2009) Parliament of Australia, Inquiry into Financial Products and Services in Australia: Final Report (Cth).

268 Ibid.

269 The reforms were legislated through the *Corporations Amendment (Future of Financial Advice) Act 2012* (Cth) and the *Corporations Amendment (Further Future of Financial Advice Measures) Act 2012* (Cth) ('FOFA Acts'), with compliance voluntary until 1 July 2013 and compulsory thereafter. Supporting regulations include the *Corporations Amendment Regulation 2012 (No. 4)* (Cth); the *Corporations Amendment Regulation 2012 (No. 8)* (Cth); the *Corporations Amendment Regulation 2012 (No. 10)* (Cth); the *Corporations Amendment (Intra-fund Advice Fees) Regulation 2013* (Cth); the *Corporations Amendment Regulation 2013 (No. 2)* (Cth); the *Corporations Amendment Regulation 2013 (No. 3)* (Cth); the *Corporations Amendment Regulation 2013 (No. 4)* (Cth); and the *Corporations Amendment Regulation 2013 (No. 5)* (Cth).

270 Australia operates a Securities Exchanges Guarantee Corporation (SEGC), which provides a "clearing guarantee for ASX markets, a guarantee of contract completion for clients and a fidelity fund against which clients of member brokers can claim compensation for the default of a broker". See Securities Exchanges Guarantee Corporation Limited (1994) *Submission to the Financial System Inquiry*, available at https://fsi.treasury.gov.au/content/downloads/PubSubs/000192.pdf and details of current operations at http://www.segc.com.au/. Similar arrangements are common in most developed countries (for example, the FSCS in the UK and the SIPC in the US) and also exist in China (through the Securities Investor Protection Fund (SIPF)). The Australian government has left open for 'future consideration' the possibility of an industry-funded last resort scheme to compensate consumers impacted by a financial collapse.

271 Although the initial recommendations have been watered down following lobbying and consultation, including reduction in the scope of conflicted remuneration, removal of the 'opt in' requirement for financial planners, amending grandfathering arrangements and changes to the specification of 'best interests'. See Spits, Jason (2014) 'Federal Government Announces FOFA Changes' (Money Management, 6 January 2014). www.moneymanagement.com.au/news/fofa/federal-government-announces-fofa-changes; King and Wood Mallesons (2014) 'Reforming the Reforms — Government Releases Draft FoFA Amending Legislation' (30 January 2014) www.mallesons.com/publications/marketAlerts/2014/Pages/Reforming-the-reforms-Government-releases-draft-FoFA-amending-legislation.aspx.

Reports commissioned subsequent to the FOFA legislation have recommended changes to strengthen professional indemnity insurance, to enhance communications about risks to consumers, and to improve the governance of managed investment schemes. Implementation of the reforms was co-ordinated by a Superannuation Regulators Working Group, composed of representatives from Treasury, APRA, ASIC and the ATO.[272] Following the collapse of Trio Capital,[273] the Government has referred the issue of investment fraud to the Heads of Commonwealth Operational Law Enforcement Agencies (HOCOLEA).[274]

Substantial changes were subsequently announced to the implementation of the FOFA reforms by the incoming Coalition government in 2013. These included easing the requirement for financial advisers to always act in the interest of clients, changing the 'opt in' arrangements, and changes to disclosure requirements. These changes were argued by the Assistant Treasurer to reduce compliance costs and regulatory burden.[275]

The *Super System Review* led to a number of changes, still being implemented, including the strengthening of default options, through a process named 'My Super' and the modernisation of administrative processes through 'Super Stream' reforms. The Review also recommended an increased mandate for APRA,[276] a new code of trustee governance, and changes to industry fund boards. The 'MySuper' reforms are also seeking to encourage the wider use of simpler standardised products. APRA has been given significant new powers to introduce prudential standards for RSE licencees,[277] and some risk management requirements have been repealed from the SIS Act in order to make way for APRA's new arrangements.[278] APRA was required to define four prudential standards: for risk management, operational risk financial requirements, conflicts of interest and the regulation of defined benefit procedures. APRA has subsequently published numerous prudential practice guides (PPGs) covering risk management, outsourcing, business continuity management, pandemic planning, information technology security and data risk, insurance, accrual and payment standards, the

272 For more detail of the government's response and actions, see Shorten, Bill (2013) 'Comprehensive Response to Combating Superannuation Investment Fraud' (Media Release No. 28, Treasury, 26 April 2013).

273 Department of Treasury (2013) *Review of the Trio Capital Fraud and Assessment of the Regulatory Framework* (Cth). The report states that "Trustees, directors and investors alike were continuously deceived throughout the operation of the managed investment scheme, in respect of the actual existence of underlying assets and the supposed rates of return on investments".

274 The membership of HOCOLEA includes the Australian Federal Police, the Australian Crime Commission and the Attorney General's Department.

275 Sinodinos, Arthur (2013) 'Delivering Affordable and Accessible Financial Advice' (Media Release, 20 December 2013), available at http://axs.ministers.treasury.gov.au/media-release/011-2013/.

276 The recent development of Prudential Practice Guides (PPGs) by APRA formed part of the implementation of the Super System reforms.

277 The *Superannuation Legislation Amendment (Trustee Obligations and Prudential Standards) Act 2012* (Cth) amended the SIS Act to introduce new legislative covenants for RSE licensees.

278 SIS Act ss 29H, 29P; See Australian Prudential Regulation Authority (2013) *Superannuation Prudential Standards* (Regulation Impact Statement, OBRD ID 14155, 2013).

MySuper transition, governance, 'fit and proper' and conflicts of interest.[279] The PPGs are prescriptive, and, for example, the SPG 521 requires RSEs to establish a conflicts management framework.[280]

The Gillard government implemented many of the *Super System Review* recommendations under a reform programme called '*Stronger Super*'.[281] All superannuation funds are required to provide a MySuper product, with full disclosure to APRA, publication of fees, and articulation of the target risk and return.[282] The technological overhaul envisaged in SuperStream, combined with improved regulatory oversight, was expected to reduce costs substantially.[283] The *Super System Review* recommendations about improving the representative trustee model (particularly by introducing independent directors) were not implemented, however, with the government opting instead to introduce trustee standards, requirements for operational risk reserves and improved valuation information. The *Stronger Super* reforms also include improved regulation of SMSFs, with proposed rules on auditor registration and independence, and restrictions on transactions involving third parties.[284] Additional powers were provided to the ATO to regulate SMSFs, effective from 1 July 2013.[285]

APRA has also taken action to improve its ability to supervise risk. The *Probability and Impact Rating System* (PAIRS) and the *Supervisory Oversight and Response System* (SOARS) were both implemented in October 2012.[286] Both are expected to improve APRA's ability to intervene when excessive risks emerge. APRA also released 35 proposed new reporting standards in March 2013, of which 32 were implemented in June 2013.[287] Three further reporting standards were released for consultation in July 2013.[288] APRA also intends

279 These are organised into three series, SPG (Superannuation Practice Guide), CPG (Compliance Practice Guide) and CPS (Compliance with Prudential Standards). Many previous versions have now been archived, see www.apra.gov.au/Super/Pages/Archived-Superannuation-Guidance.aspx. There are currently 23 active PPGs, see www.apra.gov.au/Super/PrudentialFramework/Pages/superannuation-ppgs.aspx.

280 Australian Prudential Regulation Authority (2013), *Prudential Practice Guide SPG 521 – Conflicts of Interest* (July 2013).

281 For a detailed summary of the Stronger Super reforms, see Australian Government: The Treasury, *Overview of Reforms*, available at http://strongersuper.treasury.gov.au/content/Content.aspx?doc=reforms.htm.

282 See Commonwealth of Australia (2011) *Stronger Super — Information Pack* (Cth).

283 Shorten, Bill (2011) 'A Better Deal for Superfund Members' (Press Release No. 131, Treasury, 21 September 2011) includes that "[o]nce fully implemented, the reforms could reduce the fees paid by members by up to 40%".

284 Commonwealth, *Stronger Super – Information Pack*, above n 282, 17–18.

285 See Australian Government: The Treasury, *Self Managed Superannuation Funds (SMSF)*, available at http://strongersuper.treasury.gov.au/content/Content.aspx?doc=reforms/delayed_measures.htm.

286 See Australian Prudential Regulation Authority (2012) *Probability and Impact Rating System (June 2012)*; Australian Prudential Regulation Authority (2012) *Supervisory Oversight and Response System (June 2012)*.

287 Australian Prudential Regulation Authority (2013) *Annual Regulatory Plan, 2013–2014* (July 2013).

288 Relating to MySuper product dashboards and product disclosure requirements in the Corporations Act 2001 (Cth) and the Corporations Regulations 2001 (Cth).

further consultation on disclosure requirements for insurers.[289] Consultations announced in 2017 included on strengthening operational guidance of RSE licensees, and on compliance for margin requirements.[290]

In February 2017, ASIC issued a new version of Regulatory Guide 97 (RG97) with the title 'Disclosing fees and costs in PDSs and periodic statements'. RG97 applies to issuers of superannuation products but not to annuities.[291] RG97.48 requires the disclosure of the "difference between the price paid for acquiring an asset and the price that would be payable if it were disposed of as part of transactional and operational costs". However, this partial solution, imposed at the retail level, does not address the issue of full disclosure of costs at the wholesale level.[292] ASIC has recently participated in a cross-agency group streamlining the development of retirement income stream products.[293]

The Australian Productivity Commission has been undertaking a study of the competitiveness and efficiency of Australian superannuation since 2016.[294] Stage 1 of this study developed criteria for how to assess competiveness and efficiency,[295] while Stage 2 examined alternative models for allocating fund members to products. Stage 3, which began in July 2017, is expected to be completed during 2018, with the government to consider the outcomes of the study in 2020.

In November 2016, the Australian Government introduced the Superannuation (Objective) Bill 2016, which sets out the objective for the superannuation system "to provide income in retirement to substitute or supplement the Age Pension".[296] The Australian Treasury was also intending to introduce a bill in 2017 to ensure that employee salary sacrifice contributions are not used to reduce employer payments of the superannuation guarantee. This follows the report of the Superannuation Guarantee Cross-Agency Working Group, which includes senior representatives from the ATO, the Treasury, the Department

289 APRA released reporting requirements for a variety of subsectors of the financial services industry on 6 June 2013 and at that time announced its intention to consult further with the industry about the refinement of these disclosure requirements.

290 See www.apra.gov.au/Super/Pages/superannuation-consultation-packages.aspx for a list of recent consultations.

291 Available at http://asic.gov.au/regulatory-resources/find-a-document/regulatory-guides/rg-97-disclosing-fees-and-costs-in-pdss-and-periodic-statements/.

292 For discussion of this issue, see Morris, Nicholas and Rob Nicholls (2017) 'Do it once, get it right: Wholesale regulatory intervention in price and cost disclosure' 11 *Law and Financial Markets Review* 2–3, 1–7.

293 See http://asic.gov.au/regulatory-resources/superannuation-funds/further-resources-on-superannuation/cross-agency-process-for-retirement-income-stream-products/.

294 Details of this study may be found at https://www.pc.gov.au/inquiries/current/superannuation.

295 Productivity Commission (2016) 'How to Assess the Competitiveness and Efficiency of the Superannuation System' (Research Report, November 2016), available at www.pc.gov.au/inquiries/current/superannuation/competitiveness-efficiency/report/superannuation-competitiveness-efficiency.pdf. The Commission's assessment framework comprises five system-level objectives, twenty-two corresponding assessment criteria, and a suite of supporting performance indicators.

296 See https://treasury.gov.au/superannuation-reforms/ for a summary of the reforms, most of which were implemented on 1 July 2017. They include revised targeting of tax concessions, introduction of a *Low Income Superannuation Tax Offset* (LISTO), adjustments to transition to retirement rules and some streamlining of administrative processes.

of Employment, ASIC and APRA and was set up in December 2016.[297] In the 2017–2018 Budget, the government also announced a package to establish a *First Home Super Saver Scheme*, and to allow a special 'downsizing' contribution into superannuation.[298]

The evolution of Australia's superannuation system has led to political choices that have placed Australia at one end of the spectrum with regard to savings choices – now heavily prescribed for the majority of workers – and at the other end of the spectrum in terms of the management of the assets required to fund retirement income – which is left largely to the individual, acting through various agents. A by-product of the political and regulatory evolution of the system has been the withdrawal of many employers from pension provision for their employees, thus removing one element of the protection from exploitation that employees previously enjoyed.[299]

During the last decade the Australian industry has undergone significant consolidation, leading to many fewer funds. Although in principle this should have led to significant cost savings and hence better net-of-cost performance, there is limited evidence that costs have fallen to any great extent. It seems, instead, that increased market power and reduced competition continue to permit providers to charge high fees.[300]

297 See http://kmo.ministers.treasury.gov.au/media-release/060-2017/.

298 The draft legislation for the downsizing measure would "allow individuals aged 65 years or over to make non-concessional contributions of up to $300,000 from the proceeds of selling their main residences to their superannuation accounts". See https://treasury.gov.au/consultation/c2017-t200724/ for details.

299 As employers typically, with some glaring exceptions, operated their pension schemes to the benefit of workers whose well-being they sought to enhance.

300 In the Terms of Reference for the Productivity Commission 2017 report, the Commission observed: "The Financial System Inquiry noted that fees have not fallen by as much as would be expected given the substantial increase in the scale of the superannuation system, a major reason for this being the absence of consumer-driven competition, particularly in the default fund market." Productivity Commission (2017) *Superannuation: Alternative Default Models* (Draft Report, March 2017), iv.

4 Empirical evidence on costs and performance

This chapter explores empirical evidence on the costs and performance of Australian superannuation funds during the last 20 years. After highlighting key findings, the available data is described, as is detailed micro-simulation work that compares fund performance, in aggregate and by type of fund, with a synthetic benchmark that calculates the financial outcome should alternative policy choices have been made. Then the costs and performance relative to benchmark of Australian funds are compared with international funds, using an international database of US, Canadian and European funds. Finally, the empirical work done by others is summarised, providing further evidence which reinforces the empirical findings.

The results highlight the negative impact of excessive fees and charges on returns to investment. These impacts are explored for different types of fund and in different time periods. Lessons learned are discussed at the end of the chapter.

4.1 Key findings

Simulation modelling, based on published APRA data, shows that a single (competently managed and non-corrupt) public agency could have generated considerably more wealth for Australian retirees than the industry achieved during the 20 years from July 1996 to June 2016. If the available funds had been invested entirely in a fairly typical balanced portfolio, on a passive basis, aggregate fund assets would now be some \$700–900 billion larger.[1] Sensitivity tests show this general finding to persist across various alternative benchmark portfolios and time periods (including the years prior to the Global Financial Crisis (GFC)). Doing this would also have resulted in a simpler and less costly industry structure.

1 This calculation also assumes annual management costs – including the costs of member liaison, benefit administration, custody and regulatory compliance – of 100 basis points (bps) and commissions on newly invested assets of 50 bps. This, very conservative, assumption almost certainly overstates the necessary costs: actual funds management fees for a large passively invested portfolio are likely to be around 20–30 bps, while trading costs should also be achievable for a similar amount. It is unlikely that remaining costs would require 70–80 basis points: however, this rather generous allocation was made in order to be sure that the calculations did not overstate the shortfall. Assuming lower costs would, obviously, increase the estimated gap between benchmark and actual performance.

Detailed analysis of the Australian funds provides further insights. The largest retail funds are shown to be the least efficient and most costly, while the most efficient are non-public-offer corporate and public sector funds. There is strong evidence that the most expensive funds also have the poorest net-of-costs performance. All of this suggests that the greater the degree of separation between fund managers and members, the poorer the likely outcome will be for members.

International comparison suggests that Australian funds have performed less well than US, Canadian and European funds. Most Australian funds underperformed their benchmark in the period 2004 to 2012 (the period for which comparable data exists).[2] In contrast, many of the international funds examined outperformed their benchmarks.[3] That performance in Australia appears to have been worse than in the three other jurisdictions is consistent with the greater degree of separation between principals and agents that exists in Australia than in other countries. This has permitted the Australian industry to extract higher fees and charges, which is the primary reason for its lower performance. The best performing Australian funds are those that are operated for the benefit of the employees of the sponsoring organisation, providing some preliminary evidence of implicit cross-subsidy.

In the US, there is stronger competition between fund managers, in Canada there is closer public sector supervision, and in Europe there is greater linkage to societal controls, all of which can be expected to exert some downward pressure on costs and encourage improvement in performance. Further, the fact that the other countries' funds are mostly operated on a DB basis means that there is likely to be more scrutiny of fund performance by fund sponsors than in the predominately DC environment in Australia.[4]

The empirical work reported below also provides support for the contention that more passive management would be in members' interest. Although only anecdotal indications of the impact of the high degree of active management employed by Australian funds are available, international funds employing a higher degree of passive management are shown to have outperformed those relying principally on active management during the period.[5]

2 In the absence of accurate data on the actual asset allocations of the funds, the benchmark chosen for each fund was the stated allocation of its most typical default fund.

3 For the international funds, data on asset allocation is provided, so these funds' benchmark was the average asset allocation across all their activities during the period considered.

4 Smith Freehills, Herbert (2014) 'Financial System Inquiry: Costs in Superannuation' (Report by M. Scott Donald, Michael Vrisakis and Fiona Smedley, 14 August 2014), however, makes the point that the implicit guarantee provided by fund sponsors in DB schemes is not included in their recorded costs.

5 However, there is, arguably, a downside to widespread adoption of passive management in that the price signals generated by active managers would then be weakened. See Costanzo, Gian Luigi (2011) 'The Contribution of the Asset Management Industry to Long-term Growth' *OECD Journal: Financial Market Trends* 1, 69–78, for a discussion of the wider contribution to economic growth made by the asset management industry.

These empirical findings are consistent with the Australian and international empirical literature. Australian costs and charges have been shown by several studies to be higher than international benchmarks. Although increased size of fund has exerted some downward pressure on costs, there is little evidence, either in Australia or overseas, that the full economies of scale that should accompany larger fund size have been passed on to members. Investment performance has been shown in many studies to be negatively correlated with fees and charges. For-profit funds have been shown to perform less well after costs than their not-for-profit counterparts. Outsourcing does not seem to generate sufficient improvement in performance to justify its additional cost. Complexity and active management, and their associated costs, appear to reduce, rather than improve, net returns to investors.

4.2 Available data on Australian superannuation funds

APRA publishes aggregate data for all Australian superannuation funds, and has done so since 1994 (although a full series of data is not available until 1997).[6] The APRA data is based on detailed annual returns prepared for regulatory purposes, which are audited and signed off by fund trustees. These data provide estimates of the total assets of all funds at the end of each financial year, as well as contributions made (net of contribution taxes and surcharges), benefits received, net rollovers (from other funds), and changes in balances held by life funds. The data include self-reported estimates of administrative costs and other expenses incurred directly by the funds. APRA also report the net earnings of Australian superannuation funds and their tax liabilities.[7]

These data are used by APRA to produce estimates of increases in the net value of all funds in aggregate, and disaggregated to the main classes of fund, year-by-year. Asset value estimates in the APRA data are generally accepted to be reasonably robust, because they are subject to audit.[8] However, the data is recognised to under-report fees and charges, partly because the annual return responses fail to disclose some items, but mainly because external investment management fees are previously deducted from reported earnings. The under-reporting of expenses sometimes leads to a mismatch between implied and actual

6 The most recent version is the Australian Prudential Regulation Authority (2017), *Statistics: Annual Superannuation Bulletin June 2016* (APRA, 01 February 2017). Available at http://www.apra.gov.au/Super/Publications/Documents/2017ASBEXCEL201606%20-%20PDF.pdf.

7 Although tax liability data is not published for some earlier years.

8 APRA puts much effort into encouraging institutions that are responsible for superannuation funds to comply with its auditing requirements, and has done so throughout the period considered. See, for example, the letter written by APRA Head of Statistics: Davies, Steve (2003) 'Quality of APRA Statistical Returns – Superannuation' (APRA, 9 September 2003), available at www.apra.gov.au/Super/ReportingFramework/Documents/Letter-to-Auditors-Accuracy-of-Annual-Returns-080903.pdf.

growth in assets, and this is dealt with in the APRA data by 'balancing items'.[9] In some years, there is also a mismatch between reported earnings and costs and the resulting movement in assets.[10]

A consistent series for some of the main aggregates from financial year (FY) 2004 to FY 2016 was provided in APRA's *Annual Superannuation Bulletin 2016*, which also contains detailed financial information for FY 2016. Further detail for earlier years is given in each year's *Superannuation Bulletin*. However, the Bulletins for the years 2004 to 2008 inclusive have now been withdrawn from circulation by APRA on the grounds that they have not been sufficiently validated, and issues prior to 2016 are no longer available online. Examining these data and comparing them to the series that are published in the 2016 Bulletin does reveal some discrepancies.

A further series for FY 1997 to FY 2006 was provided in 'Celebrating Ten Years of Superannuation Data Collection' (special edition of APRA's 'Insight' publication, July 2007).[11] Comparing the two series there are some revisions for 2006 in the later set of data, but otherwise they are consistent for the three years of overlap. There is less detail, for example, of tax payments, in the data prior to 2000.

The database used for the micro-simulation model was constructed from the data described above. Where there were discrepancies between two sets of data, the most recent estimates were taken. Consistency checks and sensitivity analysis have been used wherever possible to ensure that data deficiencies did not invalidate the conclusions of our analysis. A number of commentators have criticised APRA data, although such criticisms are usually levelled at computations made by APRA of specific aspects of fund performance, rather than at the underlying asset data itself.[12] Concern over the accuracy of the data, especially in the earlier years, means that some care needs to be taken in interpreting precise estimates, especially of costs, but despite these caveats it is helpful to use analysis of the only comprehensive dataset available to explore the important matters covered in this book.

9 These balancing items are mostly unreported costs, which means that net-of-cost assets are reduced further, but may also contain payments by employer sponsors, although the available data does not permit these to be separately identified.

10 This is particularly prevalent in the earlier years when APRA's systems were less developed. There also may be some subsidisation of costs by employer sponsors in the not for profit sector.

11 Australian Prudential Regulation Authority (2007) 'APRA Releases 10 Years of Superannuation Data: 1996–2006' (Media Release, 26 July 2007), available at www.apra.gov.au/MediaReleases/Pages/07_28.aspx.

12 In 2008, the Investment and Financial Services Association (IFSA), commissioned the International Centre for Financial Services (ICFS) to review APRA's superannuation statistics publications: Cheong, Chee Seng and Ralf Zurbruegg (2008) 'Review of APRA's Investment Performance Statistics of the Australian Superannuation Industry' (Review, ICFS). This review was critical of a number of APRA's methodologies, and in particular APRA's calculation of return on assets and its characterisation of retail funds as high cost. APRA responded to this report: Australian Prudential Regulation Authority (2008), 'A Response to: Review of APRA's Investment Performance Statistics of the Australian Superannuation Industry' (30 September 2008), available at www.apra.gov.au/Super/Publications/Documents/APRA_RRPS_092008_ex.pdf.

The APRA data described above is also used for the empirical work later in this Chapter, and for the detailed fund data (from 2004 to 2012) which is compared with US, Canadian and European funds below. These data have also been used by other researchers during the past 15 years, and a selection of their results is reported later in this chapter.

4.3 Comparison of outcomes with a synthetic benchmark

This section describes micro-simulation modelling using published APRA data for the period 1 July 1997 to 30 June 2016, a 20-year period, and the development of a synthetic benchmark using accumulation indexes for the main asset classes.[13]

4.3.1 Construction of the benchmark model

The benchmark model uses detailed APRA data to explore an alternative strategy in which fund assets were invested in a passively managed balanced portfolio (with reasonable fees and industry-standard commissions on entry). The model covers contributions, rollovers, benefit payments, transfers to life funds and expenses on a year-by-year basis. The model also contains routines, which are discussed in more detail below, which seek to estimate the tax liability of the benchmark fund as it evolves over time, including inter-period carry-forward of franking credits. The model was constructed such that it can use any portfolio allocation as a benchmark, however what follows focuses on that which could have been achieved using the *Australian Super Balanced Default Portfolio* allocation between asset classes.[14] The detailed working of the model is summarised algebraically in Annex D.

In order to create the benchmark, the model assumes that the accumulated funds had been invested in a passively managed fund since 1 July 1996. Justification for this choice of benchmark may be found in Malkiel, who has shown that passive investment strategies perform well in all markets, for "small capitalisation stocks as well as large-capitalisation equities, markets as well as international markets, and bonds as well as stocks".[15] The use of such a benchmark requires that the movement of key indices that might have been used in such an investment strategy are tracked,[16] and also the costs and taxes that would

13 The period has been chosen to coincide with data availability, and covers the main period of growth of Australian superannuation (overall assets at 1 July 1996 were $245 billion, by 30 June 2016 they had grown to $2.045 trillion). Limited data is available prior to 1996, but this is not available in sufficient detail for the modelling.

14 See www.australiansuper.com/investments-and-performance/what-we-invest-in/retirement-income-premixed-investment-options/balanced.aspx.

15 Malkiel, Burton G. (2003) 'Passive Investment Strategies and Efficient Markets' 9 *European Financial Management* 1, provides an evaluation of the situations in which passive investment may be a better strategy than active.

16 The accumulation indices used for this purpose were sourced from Vanguard, 'Interactive Index Chart', https://tool.vanguardinvestments.com.au/indexchart/ui/app.html. They are listed in Annex G.

be paid are defined. Annual management fees of 1.0%[17] and commissions of 0.5% on newly invested assets[18] are assumed. As discussed above, this probably overstates the necessary costs for a passively managed portfolio, so that the estimates of shortfall generated by the model should be regarded as a lower bound.

The tax routines require detail of the Australian tax system, as described in more detail in Annex D, including the operation of franking credits.[19] These credits are carried forward if not offset in the current year. For international equities, the tax rate on earned income is simply 15%, with tax losses carried forward indefinitely. Interest is also taxed at 15%.

For property holdings, it is assumed that rental income is offset by expenses, with the remaining return taken as capital gains and hence not taxed (as assets are held indefinitely). Assuming the tax position is suitably optimised, an average tax rate of 5% is assumed. Similarly for private equity the assumption is made that the tax position is optimised, and again an average tax rate of 5% is used.

4.3.2 Growth in assets

Table 4.1 summarises the APRA data provided in various years *Superannuation Bulletins* on how the contributions made, net of benefit payments, operating expenses and other charges, led to actual growth in funds under management (FUM) over the 20-year period 1 July 1996 to 30 June 2016.[20] A proportion of the growth in funds occurred because of transfers and 'rollover' from other and previous funds.[21]

17 This is a generous estimate of the charges needed to support administrative costs of a passively managed, large-scale and long-term fund, as well as necessary insurances, benefit administration, custody and member liaison. As detailed below, the Deloitte survey of Australian fund management costs estimated total annual percentage costs for passive, balanced MySuper funds of 0.32% for the larger funds (with FUM greater than $20 billion). The overall expense ratio of Vanguard funds in the US in the 1990s was around 0.31%, which includes actively managed as well as passively managed funds, see Slater, Robert (1997) *John Bogle and the Vanguard Experiment: One Man's Quest to Transform the Mutual Fund Industry* (McGraw-Hill), Appendix II, 253. More recent evidence suggests that this has declined further, to 0.2% in 2008, see Vanguard (2009) Vanguard Expense Ratios (29 May 2009) https://institutional.vanguard.com/iam/pdf/IAMERPDF.pdf.

18 This is also a generous estimate, and reflects typical commissions charged by stockbrokers in the Australian market for smaller private transactions. Major transactions are often negotiated to a much lower percentage.

19 Franking Credits (also known as imputation credits) allow Australian companies to pass on tax paid at the company level to shareholders, thus 'grossing up' the dividend they have received net of tax. Franking credits can be set off against other taxation, or received as a tax refund. See http://frankingcredits.com.au/ for more explanation.

20 This breakdown of how the net growth in assets occurred is provided to assist the reader in understanding the detail of how superannuation assets have grown over the period. Only the overall growth in assets is required for the comparison made in the benchmark model, so that concerns over the size of the APRA 'balancing item', for example, do not invalidate the final results.

21 'Rollover' is that element of the benefits payments recorded in the APRA reporting system that involve transfers from one fund to another, and which have not already been netted off by the reporting entities.

Table 4.1 Net growth in superannuation fund assets 1996–2016

A$million	*1996–2016*
Contributions net of tax and surcharge	1,723,499
Net benefit transfers and rollover	224,319
Benefit payments	(1,013,247)
Net investment income after tax	1,148,386
Total reported operating expenses	(103,801)
Net insurance flows and other charges	(19,755)
Change in the balance of life office statutory funds	(7,910)
Balancing item (unreported costs, adjustments etc)	(150,598)
Net growth in assets	*1,800,893*

Source: Own calculations based on APRA data

During the period, fund assets grew by $1.8 trillion, to $2.044 trillion,[22] an amount slightly smaller than the total contributions and rollover made into the funds of $1.95 trillion.[23] Investment earnings were $1.15 trillion, after undisclosed investment management and other costs, and reported operating expenses were $104 billion.[24] The industry made benefit payments of just over $1 trillion. The APRA 'balancing item' is mostly unreported costs, but also includes adjustments to data in the earlier years, partly as a result of the reclassification of funds.

One important feature of the Australian superannuation system is the impact of taxation. Choices made by fund managers are influenced by tax minimisation considerations, although the extent to which tax and funds management are effectively co-ordinated is a matter of dispute.[25] Many, but not all, Australian equities carry franking credits that may be offset against other taxes. After the large losses made in 2008 and 2009, many funds accumulated tax losses and franking credits that they were able to carry forward into later years, thus contributing to better net-of-tax performances in those years.

Throughout the period, the corporate tax rate was 30% and the tax on superannuation fund earnings was 15%. Tax losses can be carried forward indefinitely. As an example of the tax liabilities that have actually occurred, over the 16 years for which relevant data is available (2001 to 2016 inclusive) total reported tax expense on earnings of the Australian superannuation funds with more than four members was $12.2 billion, on taxable income of $244.6 billion, or around 5%.[26]

22 This was 81% of one year's Australian GDP in 2015/16. Australian Bureau of Statistics (2017) *1345.0 Key Economic Indicators*.

23 Because benefit payments greater than the net investment return were made out of the funds.

24 Including life insurance premiums, and other balancing items.

25 In his submission to the Super System Review, Gordon MacKenzie argued that Australian superannuation funds do not in fact take full advantage of tax minimisation opportunities. If they did, the impact would be greater. Mackenzie, Gordon D. (2009) 'Tax Governance of Superannuation Funds' (Submission to The Review into the Governance, Efficiency, Structure and Operation of Australia's Superannuation System).

26 Australian Prudential Regulation Authority (2017) Statistics: Annual Superannuation Bulletin June 2016 (1 February 2017), Tables 1 and 3.

For the case where the benchmark is based on the Australian Super default portfolio allocation, the synthetic benchmark is estimated by the model to pay total tax of 5% of total net earnings, a figure consistent with these reported outcomes. Timing patterns mean that corporate and public sector funds pay a slightly higher proportion, while industry funds pay less. The similarity of these estimates to outturn tax rates reported in the APRA data provides some comfort that the tax routines reflect reality.

The intention of the empirical analysis is to explore whether the growth in assets, after taxation, represents a good or bad outcome relative to alternative benchmarks. The synthetic benchmark alternative used to do this is one which could have been chosen by policymakers, and would have involved the creation of a single fund, or small number of funds, with a passive investment strategy. The literature discussed in Chapter 2 and summarised below suggests that the combination of centralised administration and passive management has potential to reduce costs substantially relative to the present system.

4.3.3 Key findings

A key finding from the benchmark modelling is that if these funds had been invested entirely in the Australian stock market,[27] they would now be in excess of $776 billion larger (or 38% of 1 July 2016 funds under management).[28] If they had been invested passively with an investment strategy that matched Australian Super's 'Balanced Default' portfolio allocation,[29] then the value of superannuation funds by 30 June 2016 could have been $901 billion (44% of funds under management) greater. A significant proportion of this shortfall comprises disclosed and undisclosed fees, and charges levied by funds managers. This is clearly a very significant amount, which could have made a large difference to the living standards of the next generation of retirees.

4.3.4 Robustness of findings: alternative benchmark portfolios

The simulation model has also been used to explore the shortfall relative to holding the assets in a single asset class,[30] and to a variety of alternative benchmarks. These results are consistent with other studies that have sought to compare fund performance with benchmarks, including those reported below.

The conclusion that Australian superannuation funds in aggregate have underperformed what could have been achieved through passive management of the

27 With returns matching the All Ordinaries S&P/ASX index.

28 After allowing for the effects of the dot-com collapse and the Global Financial Crisis in both scenarios.

29 Australian Super 'Balanced Default' portfolio allocation for 2017 is 24% ASX, 31% International Shares, 9% Property, 10% Infrastructure Assets (proxied by a mix of Australian and overseas commercial property), 3% cash, 17% credit and fixed interest and 4% private equity.

30 The administrative costs and commissions have been assumed to be the same as with the balanced portfolio, although in some cases – for example, cash – the appropriate costs could be lower.

Table 4.2 Estimates of shortfall using alternative benchmark portfolios

Possible alternative asset holdings	*Estimated shortfall*	*As % 2016 FUM*	*ASX (local shares)*	*Int Shares*	*Australian Comm/Res Property*	*Aus/Int Commercial Property*	*Cash*	*Fixed and credit*	*Private equity*
Single asset class									
All fixed and credit	(744,858)	36.4%						100%	
All ordinaries (S&P/ASX)	(776,308)	37.9%	100%						
All Australian property (50% res/comm)	(673,276)	32.9%			100%				
All international (non Australian) equities	(739,374)	36.1%		100%					
Alternative portfolios									
Australian super balanced default	(901,406)	44.1%	24%	31%	9%	10%	5%	17%	4%
Australian super balanced conservative	(782,847)	38.3%	17%	22%	8%	6%	12%	34%	1.0%
Australian super high growth	(883,851)	43.2%	30%	39%	7%	8%	5%	6%	5%
European investment funds	(732,843)	35.8%	20%	13%	12%	6%	15%	32%	2%
European discretionary mandates	(813,916)	39.8%	17%	12%	7%	3%	6%	54%	1%
UK – EFAMA estimates	(806,870)	39.4%	27%	18%	6%	3%	9%	36%	1%
Canadian pension fund (ave 2006–2011)	(899,663)	44.0%	20%	39%	6%	4%	2%	29%	
Index used			*AS&P ASX*	*S&P 500*	*ABS constructed*	*Commercial Property*	*UBS Bank Bill*	*Barclays Treasury*	*Thompson Reuters*

Source: Own calculations based on APRA data

funds seems robust to the choice of alternative portfolio, all of which generate 'shortfall' estimates of broadly similar magnitudes. Table 4.2 reports a selection of those which have been explored. Investing entirely in a mix of residential and commercial Australian property – which of course no pension fund would do, so that these estimates are merely provided for comparative purposes – would have generated around $670 billion (33%) more than outturn, while investing entirely in non-Australian equities could have generated $740 billion (36%) more.

Of course, investing in a single asset class would not meet the risk management objectives of most superannuation fund members. It is generally accepted that a balanced portfolio is more likely to meet most members' preferences in the medium term. So the benchmark model was also used to test the industry outcome against a range of alternative portfolio allocations for the passively invested benchmark. *Australian Super*, as well as being the largest fund in Australia, offers a fairly typical range of portfolio allocation options.[31] Three have been chosen for this analysis: the 'balanced default' (reported above), 'balanced conservative' and 'high growth'. Investing passively in a portfolio that matched these allocation schemes would have resulted in funds, over a 20-year period, between $780 billion (38%) and $900 billion (44%) greater than those in fact achieved by the Australian superannuation industry.

Overseas portfolio allocation practice is different from that employed in Australia, typically using fewer equities, and more cash and fixed interest. Four overseas portfolio allocation schemes have been tested against Australian outcomes. European and UK allocation schemes, passively invested, would have performed better than the Australian industry actually achieved, by between $730 billion (36%) and $814 billion (40%). Canadian pension fund allocations would have performed particularly well, mainly because of the much higher weight of international equities in their portfolios, and would have outperformed the Australian industry outcome by around $900 billion (44%).[32]

4.3.5 Market movements in the benchmark period

To understand how these results emerge, a short description of the external environment in which the funds have been managed is provided below. This is important because these indices drive the benchmarks against which the performance of the Australian industry is compared.

The last 20 years have, of course, been turbulent, with rapid growth created by a credit boom followed by the recent financial crisis, and some recovery since. The 20 years for which aggregate performance data is available is thus a particular period in history, with unique market settings. It contains three growth periods (1998–2001, 2004–2007 and 2009 onwards) and two major collapses in asset values (2002–2003 following the Enron/Worldcom problems in the US, and the 2008–2009 financial crisis).

31 See www.australiansuper.com/investments-and-performance/what-we-invest-in.aspx.

32 This is true both for the average 2006–2011 allocation, and for the 2013 plans.

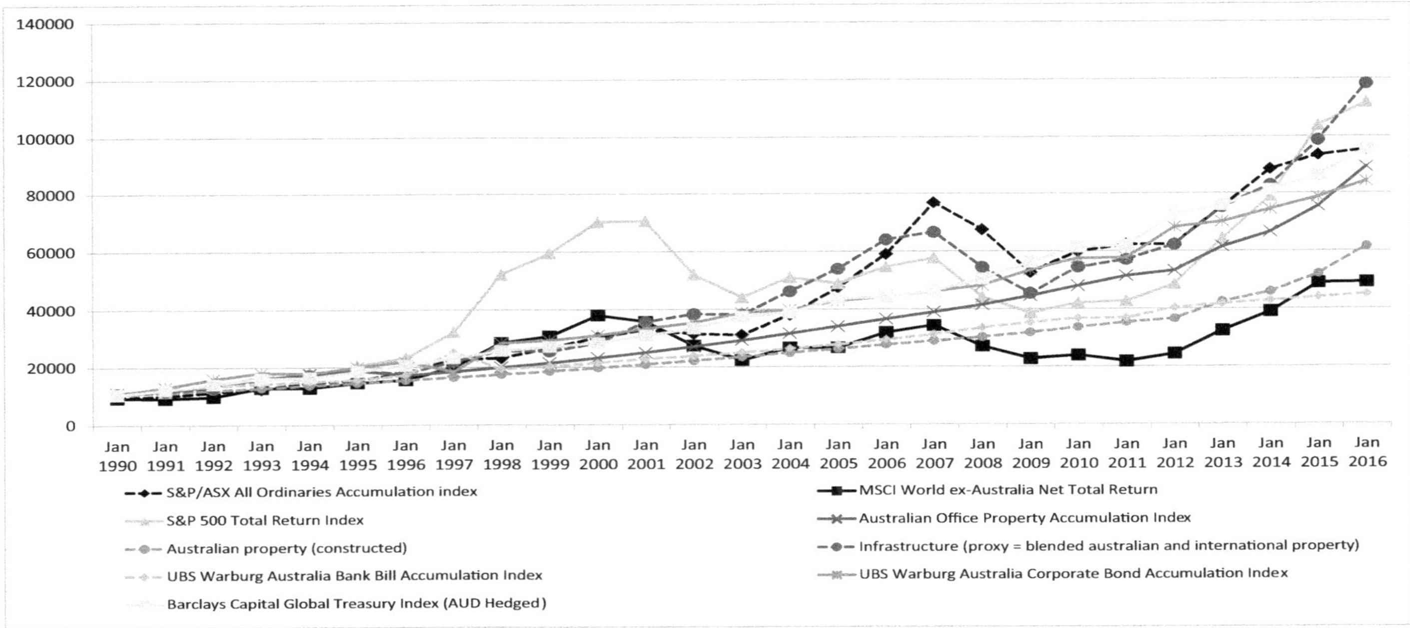

Figure 4.1 Movement of Benchmark Indices 1997 to 2016

Source: Own calculations based on data sourced from Vanguard 'Interactive Index Chart', https://tool.vanguardinvestments.com.au/indexchart/ui/app.html.

Figure 4.1 below shows the movement of a selection of indices during the period under consideration.

The S&P 500 index was the most volatile during the period, rising steeply in the late 1990s but falling steeply as a result of the dot-com crash. It then recovered, but fell again, though less, following the global financial crisis. By 2016 it had recovered again, outperforming all indices except a blended proxy for infrastructure investments in Australia and worldwide. The S&P/ASX all ordinaries index broadly tracked the other indexes until 2000, outperforming property and fixed interest securities, but underperforming global equities. Between 2001 and 2007, the Australian resources boom led to steep rises in Australian property prices, but these fell steeply in 2008 and 2009, recovering from 2010 onwards to end up with a similar overall performance to treasuries.

International equities, including in developing countries, performed poorly from 2000 to 2003, recovered to 2007 and then fell from 2008 to 2011, recovering strongly in recent years but still ending up some way below the US and Australian equity markets. Fixed interest securities tracked steadily, but grew less fast towards the end of the period as interest rates were reduced. The UBS Warburg Australia bank bill accumulation index, the proxy used for cash holdings with variable interest rates, grew steadily throughout the period.

4.3.6 Period-by-period results

Table 4.3 looks at how the performance of the Australian superannuation industry, in aggregate, developed during selected sub-periods. These are the first eight years for which adequate data exists (July 1996- June 2004), the period immediately before the financial crisis (2004–2007), the financial crisis period (2008–9), and the recent period from July 2009 to June 2016.

As noted above, in the 20-year period considered (1996 to 2016), the assets of the Australian superannuation industry overall grew from $245 billion to $2.046 trillion, a growth of $1.8 trillion. This growth in assets is the result both of cash inflows (from contributions and rollover from other funds) and outflows (principally benefit payments), as well as the net-of-costs returns from investment of the assets. The table provides detail of how these inflows and outflows developed over time, which in earlier years separates out changes to the balance of life office statutory funds and net insurance flows.[33]

33 It also includes a 'balancing item' which accounts for the difference between the items reported in APRA statistics and the eventual change in assets. These include unreported costs, and differences caused by the amalgamation or change in classification of individual funds. As noted above, concern over the detailed components of the APRA data which lead to growth in assets does not invalidate the comparison with benchmark made by the model (which merely requires the growth of assets itself). Cash movements – contributions in, rollovers and benefits out – are used in both calculations.

Table 4.3 Period-by-period analysis

A$million	*1996–2016*	*1996–2004*	*2004–7*	*2007–9*	*2009–16*
Average FUM	849,104	404,645	661,843	1,053,958	1,378,782
Total FUM-year	16,982,075	3,237,160	1,985,530	2,107,915	9,651,471
Contributions net of tax and surcharge	1,723,499	394,801	372,815	200,386	755,497
Net benefit transfers and rollover	224,319	77,835	82,670	19,466	44,348
Benefit payments	(1,013,247)	(215,584)	(123,413)	(122,969)	(551,281)
Net investment income after tax	1,148,386	190,211	340,493	(193,262)	810,944
Total reported operating expenses	(103,801)	(25,201)	(15,981)	(10,602)	(52,017)
Net insurance flows and other charges	(19,755)	(19,755)	–	–	–
Change in the balance of life office statutory funds	(7,910)	(7,910)	–	–	–
Balancing item (unreported costs, adjustments etc)	(150,598)	**(65,394)**	**(101,250)**	**2,973**	**13,073**
Net growth in assets	**1,800,893**	**329,003**	**555,334**	**(104,008)**	**1,020,564**
	20 years	**8 years**	**3 years**	**2 years**	**7 years**
Net return from industry activities (net growth less net contributions and rollover plus benefits)	**866,322**	**71,951**	**223,262**	**(200,891)**	**772,000**
Net return/year	43,316	8,994	74,421	(100,446)	110,286
Net return/FUM	5.1%	2.2%	11.2%	–9.5%	8.0%
Internal rate of return during period	4.5%	6.1%	8.4%	–3.2%	7.6%

Source: Own calculations based on APRA data

Table 4.4 Period-by-period comparison with benchmark

A$million	*1996–2016*	*1996–2004*	*2004–7*	*2007–9*	*2009–16*
Selected benchmark:	*Australian super balanced default 2017*				
Average FUM	1,167,125	518,254	1,050,724	1,457,547	1,875,601
Total FUM-year	23,342,505	4,146,032	3,152,173	2,915,094	13,129,206
Net growth	2,702,299	559,234	675,970	(198,277)	1,665,372
Shortfall	**(901,406)**	**(230,231)**	**(120,636)**	**94,269**	**(644,808)**
Net investment income	2,001,153	343,642	375,420	(266,009)	1,548,100
Net return using benchmark strategy (net growth less net contributions and rollover plus benefits)	**1,767,728**	**302,182**	**343,898**	**(295,160)**	**1,416,808**
Net return/year	88,386	37,773	114,633	(147,580)	202,401
Net return/FUM	**7.6%**	**7.3%**	**10.9%**	**–10.1%**	**10.8%**
Benchmark internal rate of return during period	**7.2%**	**11.6%**	**14.8%**	**–4.5%**	**9.5%**
Actual internal rate of return during period	**4.5%**	**6.1%**	**8.4%**	**–3.2%**	**7.6%**
Difference	**–2.7%**	**–5.5%**	**–6.5%**	**1.3%**	**–1.9%**

Source: Own calculations based on APRA data

In order to provide a comparable measure of performance between periods, an internal rate of return has been calculated for each sub-period. This uses as inputs the initial overall assets at the beginning of the period, net cash flows (contributions and rollover less benefits) during the period, and the final assets at the end of the period.[34] Over the whole 20-year period, the IRR was 4.5%, with better performance in the period 2004–7 and after the global financial crisis.

Table 4.4 shows the investment income, and therefore the growth in assets, which could have been achieved under the benchmark strategy, using the *Australian Super Balanced Portfolio* asset allocation. Over the whole period, such a strategy would have achieved an IRR of 7.2%, or 2.7% better than the industry actually achieved. This difference, of 2.7% of the relevant funds in each year over a 20-year period, had a substantial effect on how the assets in fact accumulated. To understand how important this difference is, consider an investment of $100 which earned 4.5% per annum, with the returns reinvested in the fund. Compounding the 4.5% over 20 years would yield $100*(1.045^20) or $241 by the end of the period. If instead returns were compounded at 7.2%, the resulting assets would be worth $100*(1.072^20) or $401, a difference of $160 or some 66% of the $241 achieved at the lower rate of return.

In fact, the story is a little more complicated than in this simple example, as the funds have flows in and out, and as net contributions are made the assets to be invested grow over time. In addition, the various asset classes that comprise the portfolio being invested have different potential returns in different periods, as seen in Table 4.3 above. Nevertheless, these findings are important, as they provide a clear indication of the large impact apparently small differences in net-of-costs returns can have on outcome fund asset values. In a world where the risk free rate is less than 3%,[35] costs approaching that level can all but wipe out investment returns.

Figure 4.2 compares the year-by-year performance of the industry overall with what could have been achieved by the benchmark. The measure of return for each year is the net growth in assets less cash inflows, divided by average funds under management in that year.

Broadly, this pattern shows the Australian industry mostly failing to match the benchmark after expenses, sometimes by a wide margin, but doing slightly better in 2007 and 2008, and again in 2011. Looking in detail at the sub-periods, the industry underperformed the benchmark in all periods except 2007–2008, during the GFC, in which it performed slightly less badly than the benchmark (minus 3.2% compared with minus 4.5%).[36] Overall, as noted above, the industry achieved a growth in assets about $900 billion less than could have been

34 Computed using the Excel function XIRR, see Annex D for an algebraic explanation.

35 In late 2017, ten-year government bonds in Australia traded at around 2.8%, see https://tradingeconomics.com/australia/government-bond-yield.

36 This finding, that actively managed funds perhaps performed better in response to a crisis than a previously chosen passive portfolio would have, is worthy of further investigation, but is beyond the scope of this book.

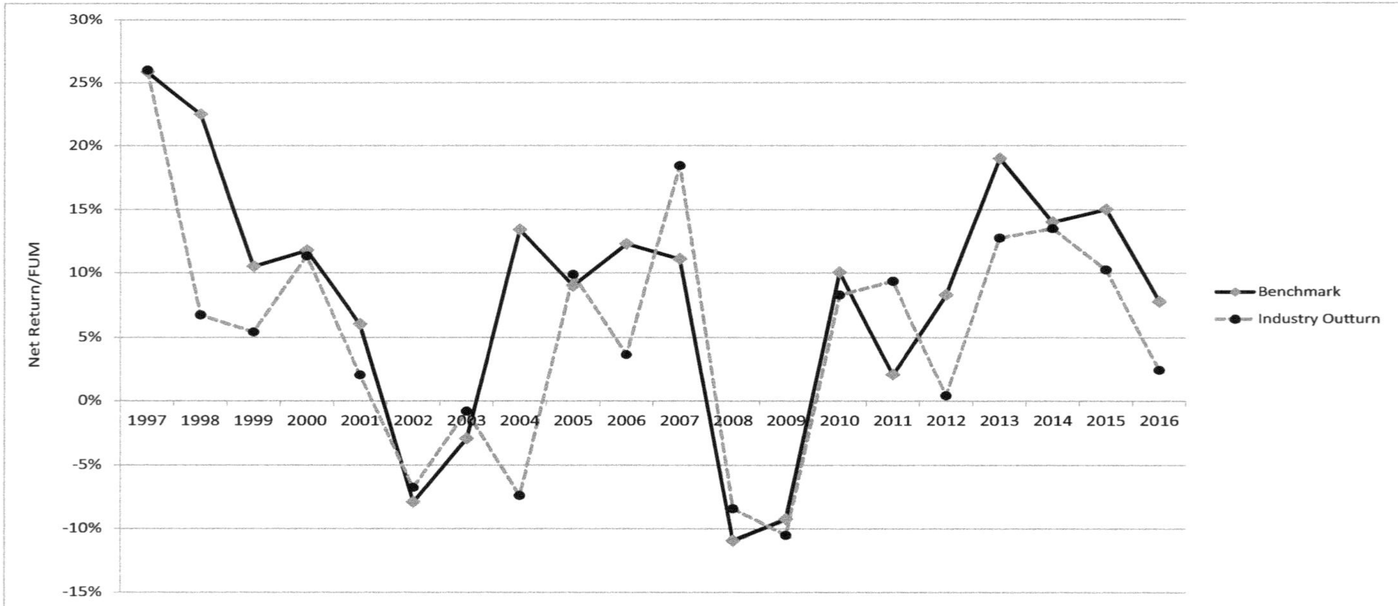

Figure 4.2 Comparison of industry outturn with benchmark 1996–2016

Source: Own calculations based on APRA data

achieved with the benchmark strategy. The majority of this shortfall ($645 billion) occurred in the period since 2009, because the funds were by then much larger. On a positive note, however, the proportional gap between the industry's performance and the benchmark, which was quite large in the earlier years, seems to have narrowed somewhat, although the difference in IRRs is still some 1.9%.[37]

4.3.7 Focus on different types of fund

The micro-simulation model permits disaggregation of the overall return made by the synthetic benchmark to different types of funds.[38] This utilises data on the financial results for each type of fund published by APRA annually.[39]

APRA have recently published a consistent summary of financial data for the period 2004 to 2016 for four types of fund with 'greater than four members', namely corporate, industry, public sector and retail funds, as well as for smaller APRA-regulated funds and SMSFs.[40] For each of these six types of fund, a year-by-year dataset has been constructed that includes data on contributions, rollover, benefits paid, expenses, life insurance payments and balancing items. Some care has been put into ensuring consistency between the sectoral data and the aggregate, and the internal consistency of the sectoral data.

Table 4.5 below summarises results for each type of fund, including IRRs computed on the same basis as used for the period-by-period analysis above.

The disaggregated results show that there is a significant difference between the performances of different types of fund. Corporate and public sector funds have done better relative to benchmark, while retail and SMSFs have done badly,[41] with industry funds between the two extremes.

A particular feature of the period was the withdrawal of assets from the (better performing) corporate funds and the transfer of these assets to industry and (less well performing) retail funds. Small APRA funds have been declining in share, with cash outflows through most of the period, while the share of SMSFs has grown. Reported operating expenses for the retail funds are proportionately higher than for the other classes. This is in part due to the retail funds following asset management strategies which are more actively managed, and have a different portfolio allocation, than those followed by the predecessor DB funds.

37 This, encouraging, finding may reflect success in rationalising the industry and the impact of the 'Cooper' reforms in seeking to reduce excessive costs. However, the shortfall remains large.

38 Corporate, Industry, Public Sector, Retail and Small Self-Managed Funds (SMSFs).

39 Published in each year's Superannuation Bulletin for the period from 2004 onwards, and in 'Celebrating Ten Years of Superannuation Data Collection' (special edition of APRA's *Insight* publication, July 2007) for the period from 1 July 1996 to 30 June 2006.

40 APRA (2017) *Annual Superannuation Bulletin June 2016* (Issued 1 February 2017). The year-by-year data (Table 4a) is only available in the Excel file that accompanies the annual bulletin, and not published in the pdf version. SMSFs are regulated by the Australian Taxation Office (ATO), but the ATO data has been incorporated in the APRA dataset for this purpose.

41 Although this is partly because a higher proportion of SMSF funds are in a decumulation phase, and rollover from other funds is particularly pronounced in the last years before retirement.

Table 4.5 Performance relative to benchmark for different types of fund

A$ million, 2004–2016	*Corporate A$million*	*Industry A$million*	*Public sector A$million*	*Retail A$million*	*Small APRA plus SP ADFs A$million*	*SMSFs A$million*	*Whole industry A$million*
Contributions, net of taxes and surcharge	32,040	264,043	271,545	343,329	1,359	416,440	417,799
Net benefit transfers (inc. rollover)	(31,211)	13,893	(2,142)	55,166	(497)	111,566	111,069
Benefit payments	(14,803)	(86,923)	(196,706)	(256,265)	(1,929)	(241,036)	(242,965)
Contributions net of benefits and transfers	**(13,974)**	**191,013**	**72,697**	**142,230**	**(1,067)**	**286,970**	**285,903**
Investment income, net of expenses	38,518	203,321	172,989	240,239	1,790	301,314	303,104
Total reported operating expenses	(1,630)	(12,476)	(6,185)	(34,794)	(255)	(23,257)	(23,512)
Other changes, including charges and expenses	(5,844)	(4,101)	11,703	(15,223)	(1,212)	(70,819)	(72,031)
Balancing items (movements in funds etc.)	1,657	(226)	(9,605)	8,176	(59)	1	(58)
Net growth	**18,727**	**377,531**	**241,599**	**340,628**	**(803)**	**494,209**	**493,406**
Comparison with benchmark							
A$ million, 2004–2016	*Corporate A$million*	*Industry A$million*	*Public sector A$million*	*Retail A$million*	*Small APRA plus SP ADFs A$million*	*SMSFs A$million*	*Whole industry A$million*
Net return from industry activities (net growth LESS benefits, net contributions and rollover)	**32,701**	**186,518**	**168,902**	**198,398**	**264**	**207,239**	**794,022**

Average funds under management	49,679	246,611	214,349	378,482	2,439	374,551	1,266,111
							–
Net return using benchmark strategy (net growth LESS benefits, net contributions and rollover)	**97,385**	**225,611**	**174,631**	**406,903**	**2,860**	**396,697**	**1,304,087**
Average funds under management	120,679	273,120	210,116	500,868	3,582	493,944	1,602,310
Passive balanced							
SHORTFALL	(64,684)	(39,093)	(5,729)	(208,505)	(2,596)	(189,458)	(510,065)
Actual internal rate of return during period	**6.1%**	**6.2%**	**6.5%**	**4.4%**	**0.9%**	**4.2%**	**5.1%**
Benchmark internal rate of return during period	**7.3%**	**8.6%**	**8.0%**	**7.7%**	**6.9%**	**7.8%**	**6.9%**
Difference	**–1.2%**	**–2.4%**	**–1.5%**	**–3.3%**	**–6.0%**	**–3.6%**	**–1.8%**

Source: Own calculations based on APRA data

These findings are consistent with the literature described below. That literature highlights the impact of administrative costs on fund returns, and shows that employer-sponsored funds are the least costly and that retail trustees generated significantly lower returns than their not-for-profit counterparts.[42] Despite substantial increases in the size of funds, expense ratios have not declined significantly over time, and there remains significant scope to improve scale economies.[43]

4.3.8 Exploring 'leakage'

The empirical work reported above suggests that, relative to a passively managed balanced portfolio, the Australian superannuation industry extracted, or lost through mismanagement, some $900 billion over a 20-year period. Put in another way, the industry achieved an IRR of 4.5% when they could have achieved an IRR 7.2% by adopting a different strategy. This 'leakage' from the returns which could otherwise have accrued to members, on average funds under management of $845 billion-$1,170 billion,[44] amounts to some 400–527 basis points (bps) per annum.[45]

In an important article written in 2009, Ron Bird and Jack Gray sought to pin down some of this leakage, focusing on the impact of particular policy choices that had been made in the Australian system.[46] They identified what they called a "troika of leaks", which include:

1 Reliance on momentum and other non-information-based strategies, in order to compete with other funds on a short-term basis (this was estimated to cost 100 bps).
2 Direct and indirect agency costs, encouraged by the "ready availability of money", in excess of what is strictly necessary (100 bps).
3 Excessive choice, with members bearing the direct and indirect costs "for no substantive benefit" (50 bps) and an excessive number of funds (50 basis points).[47]

42 These findings are summarised in Bateman, Hazel and Olivia S. Mitchell (2004) 'New evidence on Pension Plan Design and Administrative Expenses: the Australian Experience' 3 *Journal of Pension Economics and Finance* 1, 63; These findings are reinforced by Ellis, K., A. Tobin and B. Tracey (2008) 'Investment Performance, Asset Allocation and Expenses of Large Superannuation Funds' 3 *Insight* 2; Coleman, A.D.F., N. Esho and M. Wong (2006) 'The Impact of Agency Costs on the Investment Performance of Australian Pension Funds' 5 *Journal of Pension Economics and Finance* 3, 299.

43 Bonarius, Nathan (2014) 'Superannuation Fees: Financial System Inquiry' (Rice Warner, 1 July 2014). Rice Warner, in a report prepared for the Financial System Inquiry, estimated that in the ten-year period from June 2004 to June 2013, when funds under management grew from $625 billion to $1,617 billion, fees (excluding SMSFs and small APRA funds) only fell from 1.4% to 1.2% of FUM. For discussion of this problem in previous time periods see Galagedera, Don U.A. and Param Silvapulle (2002) 'Australian Mutual Fund Performance Appraisal Using Data Envelopment Analysis' 28 *Managerial Finance* 9, 60.

44 Average FUM under actual and benchmark conditions.

45 Calculated as shortfall/FUM/20.

46 Bird, Ron and Jack Gray (2009) 'Improving Pension Management and Delivery: An (Im)Modest and Likely (Un)Popular Proposal' 2 *Rotman International Journal of Pension Management* 2, 36–40.

47 These observations have recently been echoed by the Productivity Commission (2016) 'How to Assess the Competitiveness and Efficiency of the Superannuation System' (Research Report).

The fact that these leakage estimates, which only cover a subset of the 'leakages' in the system, suggest numbers of a similar order of magnitude to the empirical findings outlined above provides some broad validation of the substantial size of the problem.[48] Bird and Gray arrived at these conclusions by undertaking detailed simulations based on representative data. They also made suggestions about how to "plug the leaks" through incentives to rationalise the industry and through provision of less choice.

John Bogle has provided further insights into other aspects of leakage in an article published in 2014, which attempts to estimate the drag on mutual funds in the US created by 'all-in' investment expenses. On top of conventional expense ratios, he argues, net-of-costs returns are also reduced by transactions costs, sales loads and cash drag. Over time he estimates that "compared with costly actively managed funds, over time, low-cost index funds create extra wealth of 65% for retirement plan investors."[49]

Bogle observes that transactions costs have risen over time, and has estimated that aggregate portfolio turnover has increased in the US from 30% in the 1960s to around 140%.[50] He also argues that actively managed funds suffer a cash drag relative to index funds, because actively managed funds typically carry a cash position of about 5%, whereas index funds are fully invested at all times. Finally, he notes that actively managed funds are relatively tax inefficient because they generate additional capital gains.[51]

In order to quantify the overall drag created by trading costs, Bogle cites studies of brokerage commissions paid by equity mutual funds[52] and expenditures by domestic equity funds,[53] which report trading costs of 60 and 144 basis points respectively, to provide a conservative estimate of 50 bps. Cash drag on actively managed funds is estimated to add 15 bps. Direct and indirect sales loads add another 50 bps in the Bogle analysis.[54]

4.4 International benchmarking of Australian fund performance

In this section the performance of the Australian funds is compared with funds in the US, Canada and Europe during an eight year period from 2004 to 2012.

48 The relationship between empirical and simulated results for the size of the shortfall in returns and these leakages is also worthy of further investigation.

49 Bogle, John C. (2014) 'The Arithmetic of "All-In" Investment Expenses', 70 *Financial Analysts Journal* 1, 13–21.

50 Bogle, John C. (2013) 'Big Money in Boston – The Commercialisation of the 'Mutual' Fund Industry', available at www.johncbogle.com.

51 Although this is of less concern to investors in tax-deferred retirement plans. Bogle estimates that, for taxable investors, this tax inefficiency costs some 75 bps. The lower capital gains liability occurs because stocks are held for longer periods of time under a passive strategy.

52 Haslem, John A. (2010) 'Mutual Funds and the New Total Expense Ratio' 19.2 *Journal of Investing* 22–26.

53 Edelen, Roger M., Richard B. Evans, and Gregory B. Kadlec (2013) 'Disclosure and Agency Conflict: Evidence from Mutual Fund Commission Bundling' 103 *Journal of Financial Economics* 308–326.

54 Extension of the Bogle analysis to Australia would also be helpful in pinning down how far these, different, aspects of potential leakage apply in the Australian case.

4.4.1 Data

Two datasets were utilised. For Australian superannuation funds fund-level data which is collected annually by the industry regulator, the Australian Prudential Regulatory Authority (APRA) data was used. For the non-Australian pension funds in the US, Canada and Europe, data from CEM Benchmarking Inc. were used.[55] The variables available in these two datasets are described in Annexes C and E.

For both datasets, only those pension and superannuation funds that have reasonably complete data for the relevant period were included. The starting point of 2004 was determined by the availability of fund-level APRA data for Australian superannuation funds, although CEM data for the US, Canadian and European funds are available for previous years (in some cases dating back to 1990). The CEM data were available for the period to 2012, however, so that this comparative analysis covers eight years.

Both sets of data provide detailed information on type of fund (DB or DC; corporate, public sector, industry) and on investment performance and costs. The CEM data (international pension funds) provides more detail on asset allocation, investment costs and investment style, while the APRA data (Australian superannuation funds) provides more detail on the characteristics of fund members.

As noted above, an important difference between the APRA and CEM data is that the CEM data reports all costs, including the costs of investment management, while the APRA data only reports costs which are disclosed to APRA for regulatory purposes. These latter are the costs that are incurred internally by the superannuation funds, and do not include the costs of investment management or other activities when management of the assets is outsourced to a third party (including companies within the same group as the corporate trustee).[56] To make the data comparable, a proxy for the undisclosed investment costs of investment managers to whom the Australian superannuation funds delegate was estimated. Further details are provided in Annex G.

4.4.2 Comparison of Australian and international funds

The APRA (Australian) and CEM (international) datasets were compared, containing a total of 256 superannuation and pension funds. Table 4.6 reports the average characteristics of the two samples during the period 2004–2012.[57]

55 Access to the CEM database was granted following a successful research grant application to ICPM, 'Comparative Risk Management Performance of Australian Superannuation Funds' April 2013. CEM Benchmarking, Inc. and the Rotman International Centre for Pension Management (ICPM), 151 Bloor Street West, Suite 702, Toronto ON M5S 1S4, Canada. The CEM sample exhibits possible self-selection bias, as the pension funds included are limited to those that are willing to reveal a full set of data about costs and asset allocation.

56 As illustrated in Annex F.

57 The CEM database reports pension fund performance data in a variety of currencies, consistent with the home country of each pension fund, while APRA data is reported in Australian dollars. For comparison between the datasets in this summary table, financial data was converted to US$. 2008 to 2012 data were converted using average exchange rates derived for the relevant period from weekly exchange rates shown in www.oanda.com/currency/historical-rates/. 2004 to 2007 data were converted using the mid-point of the relevant period taken from www.x-rates.com/historical/?from=USD&amount=1&date=2003-07-01.

Table 4.6 Comparison of APRA and CEM data, 2004–2012

Average annual (US$ million)	*APRA*	*CEM*
Number of funds	142	114
of which: defined benefit	4	86
defined contribution	84	1
hybrid/other/not defined	54	27
Total FUM (US$ million)	396,991	2,855,837
Total members	21,448,529	28,252,046
Estimated gross investment income (US$ million)	**21,203**	**178,472**
Reported fund administration costs	1,055	1,819
Estimated investment management costs	5,377	8,719
Total costs (US$ million)	**6,432**	**10,538**
Recorded net investment income (US$ million)	**14,772**	**167,934**
Gross investment income/FUM	5.34%	5.88%
Fund administration costs/FUM	0.27%	0.06%
Estimated investment management costs/FUM	1.35%	0.31%
Total cost/FUM	**1.62%**	**0.37%**
Net investment income/FUM	**3.72%**	**5.88%**
Average FUM per fund (US$ million)	2,796	25,051
Average members per fund	151,046	247,825
FUM/member (US$)	18,509	101,084
Cost/member (US$)	299.87	373.00

Note: For APRA superannuation funds costs are adjusted for 'drag', in order to allow for unreported funds management and other costs. For a description of this adjustment process see Annex G.

A number of differences between the samples are worthy of note. The most obvious difference is the considerably higher costs and lower net-of-costs performance of the Australian funds. This may partly be because the CEM (US, Canadian and European) pension funds are on average much larger than the Australian superannuation funds, with just under 250,000 members per fund and an average account balance of US$25 billion, compared with around 151,000 members and an average account balance of US$2.8 billion for the APRA funds. This difference is due to the immaturity of the Australian superannuation funds, as well as the mandatory nature of the Australian system, which has resulted in many small accounts (for low income and casual workers) and in many cases multiple accounts per member.

Australian funds are required by law to participate in the dataset as part of their regulatory compliance (in contrast to the CEM funds where participation is voluntary). While participation in a pension plan is not mandatory in most of the jurisdictions covered by the CEM data, most require benefits to be taken as lifetime pensions. Hence, the pension funds in that sample are more likely to include members on higher average incomes in the accumulation phase and higher balances in retirement than the Australian superannuation funds. Total reported costs as a proportion of investment income achieved are significantly higher in Australia.

A major difficulty with interpreting international comparisons is allowing for differences in the operating environment, mostly outside the control of the superannuation and pension funds. Australian equities and property markets did better during the Global Financial Crisis than international equities, for example. A second difficulty faced in this case is that the state of maturity of the superannuation and pension funds is different, with the Australian funds being younger, smaller and mostly in the accumulation phase, compared with the international funds, which tend to be older, larger and more balanced between the accumulation and decumulation phase. The third difficulty is that the US, European and Canadian funds are mostly DB while the Australian funds are mostly DC.

In order to explore international differences in more detail, the deviation of investment performance from a passively managed benchmark for each fund was used. This took actual asset allocation for the CEM pension funds, and the asset allocation of the default option for the APRA funds (as the best proxy available for the investment objectives of the Australian funds). A benchmark was then created that reflected the returns which could have been achieved if the assets of the superannuation/pension funds had invested in that portfolio during the period of analysis.[58] This was then compared with the actual net-of-costs investment return achieved by the CEM pension funds, and with the estimated net-of-costs investment return for the APRA superannuation funds sub-sample, after deducting recorded expenses and the investment costs proxy described above.

The next two sections explore the extent to which first Australian and second international funds matched a passively managed benchmark based on their chosen portfolio allocation. They therefore address the question of how far the management of the funds, *given choice of portfolio*, achieved the benchmark objective. The analysis does not explore whether the portfolio choice was in fact the right one to reflect the risk requirements of fund members.

4.4.3 Analysis of deviation from benchmark – Australian funds

A benchmark based on the Australian Super Balanced Default portfolio, passively managed, has been used to explore the performance of Australian funds in the period, with results reported in Table 4.7 below.

On average, the Australian superannuation funds underperformed their benchmarks by 1.65% of funds under management during the period 2004 to 2012.

58 After allowing for administration costs of 0.3% per annum, as a fairly typical investment management cost for a passively invested fund. This is higher than that required by Vanguard in the US, see Vanguard (2009) *Vanguard Expense Ratios* (29 May 2009) https://institutional.vanguard.com/iam/pdf/IAMERPDF.pdf.

Table 4.7 Analysis of deviation from benchmark – Australian funds

Fund characteristics	*Number of funds*	*Average deviation from benchmark*	*Recorded admin costs*	*Estimated investment costs*	*Average fund size (US$ million)*
APRA funds	**142**	**–1.65%**	**0.27%**	**1.35%**	**2,796**
Corporate	33	0.13%	0.12%	0.56%	955
Public sector	15	–0.37%	0.04%	0.39%	2,181
Industry	47	–1.02%	0.16%	0.89%	2,818
Retail	47	–2.55%	0.39%	1.94%	4,262
Outsourcing					
Custodian	81	–0.97%	0.15%	0.89%	2,714
Asset consultant fees	72	–0.87%	0.13%	0.86%	2,727
Public offer					
Yes	93	–1.98%	0.30%	1.54%	3,535
No	49	–0.01%	0.10%	0.48%	1,393

Source: Own calculations based on APRA data 2004–2012.

Note: Deviation from benchmark and costs are measured as a percentage of funds under management.

Among the Australian superannuation funds, retail funds performed least well (–2.55%), followed by industry funds (–1.02%), public sector funds (–0.37%) and lastly corporate (+0.13%), which confirms earlier analysis by Ellis et al.[59] This poor performance is strongly correlated with both administration and investment costs. On average, superannuation funds that outsourced specific activities did slightly better, but the effect is not large. Non-public-offer funds (that is, funds not open to the general public) performed considerably better relative to their benchmark than public offer funds, consistent with the hypothesis that the greater the degree of separation between beneficiaries and fund managers the worse the performance (and/or the higher the fees and charges).

The highest performing fund in the APRA sample, the Goldman Sachs and JB Were Superannuation Fund (a corporate fund for employees), reported low total costs, at only 0.24% of FUM, and it also has a high return, of an average of 7.53% after costs. It is hard to know how this exemplary performance is achieved with such low reported costs, but it may be that as a corporate superannuation fund for employees of Goldman Sachs and JB Were, the trustees and managers of this fund are able to take advantage of information and systems from their wider group which are not recorded or charged for explicitly.

59 Ellis K., A. Tobin and B. Tracey (2008) 'Investment Performance, Asset Allocation, and Expenses of Large Superannuation Funds' (APRA Working Paper, October 2008, and 3 *Insight* 2).

Table 4.8 Analysis of deviation from benchmark – CEM pension funds

Fund characteristics	*Number of funds*	*Average deviation from benchmark*	*Recorded admin costs*	*Recorded investment costs*	*Average fund size (US$ million)*
CEM funds	**114**	**–0.34%**	**0.064%**	**0.305%**	**25,051**
US	**65**	**–0.31%**	**0.069%**	**0.288%**	**25,135**
Corporate	24	2.22%	0.08%	0.41%	12,613
Public sector	26	–0.93%	0.06%	0.25%	46,340
Other	15	–0.40%	0.08%	0.35%	8,416
Canada	**37**	**–0.31%**	**0.055%**	**0.335%**	**28,798**
Corporate	15	1.68%	0.09%	0.44%	8,542
Public sector	16	–0.67%	0.04%	0.33%	51,368
Other	5	0.08%	0.09%	0.28%	23,105
Europe	**12**	**–0.94%**	**0.073%**	**0.287%**	**13,041**
Corporate	5	–0.54%	0.07%	0.25%	4,636
Public sector	8	–1.01%	0.07%	0.29%	16,664
Passive investment					
None	**19**	**–2.92%**	**0.04%**	**0.20%**	**36,764**
Less than 10%	52	0.74%	0.07%	0.37%	20,343
10% to 20%	23	0.18%	0.06%	0.35%	15,036
Greater than 20%	9	0.28%	0.08%	0.29%	37,683

Source: Own calculations based on CEM data 2004–2012

Note: Deviation from benchmark and costs are measured as a percentage of funds under management.

4.4.4 Analysis of deviation from benchmark – international funds

Table 4.8 provides a similar analysis for the US, Canadian and European ('international') funds in the CEM sub-sample to that provided for the APRA funds in Table 4.7 above. The tables differ in the analysis of indicators such as fund type, importance of the default strategy, extent of outsourcing, whether the superannuation/pension funds are public offer and use of passive investments, reflecting the differing information available in each dataset. On average, the international funds came closer to matching their benchmarks than did the Australian funds.

Among the international funds, Table 4.2 shows that the US and Canadian funds performed closer to their benchmarks than the European funds. In all three jurisdictions, corporate funds did better than public sector funds. Pension funds employing passive investment did better than those which relied entirely on active management.

4.5 Summary of previous findings

The findings reported above reflect previous findings by other researchers. The empirical work carried out by others in the past has focused on three main items: fees and charges; the performance of superannuation funds; and investigation of portfolio choice and of administrative and governance arrangements, including outsourcing. In what follows we relate these previous findings to the empirical results reported above.

4.5.1 Fees and charges

Despite substantial increases in the size of the Australian superannuation funds, expense ratios have not declined significantly over time, and potential economies of scale are often not reflected in lower fees and charges.[60] Those studies that make international comparison find costs in the Australian system to be higher than international benchmarks.[61] Previous studies of the performance of Australian superannuation funds have shown the impact of administrative costs on fund returns, and that high-cost retail funds generated significantly lower returns than their not-for-profit counterparts.[62] These results are consistent with the empirical findings reported in Section 4.4 above.

International studies have shown that cost increases associated with gains in market power tend to offset any benefits from increased economies of scale;[63] that sales costs and the use of affiliates (external advisers and managers) both reduce efficiency;[64] that larger fund size and less risky assets are associated with higher efficiency;[65] and that poor principal-agent relationships and lack of transparency are a cause of technical inefficiency.[66] International studies also indicate the inability of actively managed portfolios to outperform benchmark indices in Canada, US and Europe[67] and highlight large differences in

60 Galagedera, Don U.A. and Param Silvapulle (2002) 'Australian Mutual Fund Performance Appraisal Using Data Envelopment Analysis' 28 *Managerial Finance* 9, 60; Cummings, James Richard (2012) 'The Effect of Fund Size on the Performance of Australian Superannuation Funds' (Working Paper, Australian Prudential Regulation Authority, March 2012).

61 See OECD (2013) *Pensions at a Glance 2013: Retirement-Income Systems in OECD and G20 Countries*; www.oecd.org/pensions/pensionsataglance.htm.

62 Bateman and Mitchell, above n 42, 63; Coleman, Esho and Wong, above n 42; Ellis, Tobin and Tracey, above n 59.

63 Qu, Jason Zhiwei (2013) An Efficiency Study of the Australian Superannuation Industry (Unpublished Honours Thesis, University of New South Wales); Vidler, Sacha (2004) 'Superannuation: Choice, Competition and Administration Costs' 53 *Journal of Australian Political Economy* 27.

64 Barrientos, Armando and Aziz Boussofiane (2005) 'How Efficient Are Pension Fund Managers in Chile?' 9 *Revista de Economia Contemporânea* 289.

65 Sathye, Milind (2011) 'The Impact of Financial Crisis on the Efficiency of Superannuation Funds: Evidence from Australia' 10(2) *Journal of Law and Financial Management* 16.

66 Garcia, Maria Teresa Medeiros (2010) 'Efficiency Evaluation of the Portuguese Pension Funds Management Companies' 20 *Journal of International Financial Markets, Institutions and Money* 259.

67 Dyck, Alexander and Lukasz Pomorski (2011) 'Is Bigger Better? Size and Performance in Pension Plan Management' (Working Paper, ICPM, November 2011); Dyck, Alexander, Karl V. Lins and Lukasz Pomorski (2011) 'Does Active Management Pay? New International Evidence' (Working Paper, ICPM, October 2011).

costs internationally.[68] These results reinforce the empirical findings reported above, and result from the various problems set out in Chapter 2.

4.5.2 Performance of different types of fund

The findings of international studies show higher costs and lower performance in for-profit funds, where principal-agent and conflict of interest problems might be expected to be most severe.

Net returns in Australia during the last decade have been poor relative to benchmarks.[69] Bateman and Mitchell have estimated that employer-sponsored plans are the least costly, and retail the most costly.[70] They also found that the expense ratio in Australia was higher than that in US private sector plans. Sy and Liu found that investment performance of superannuation funds was negatively correlated with average costs.[71] Esho and Wong estimated that retail and industry funds had the lowest returns, and the highest expenses, while public sector and corporate funds had the highest returns, and lowest expenses.[72] Using the Sharpe Ratio as a measure of performance, many funds (particularly retail) were shown to underperform relative to a risk free investment in Treasury notes.[73] Ellis, Tobin and Tracey found that retail trustees on average generated significantly lower net returns than not-for-profit trustees.[74]

68 Bikker, Jacob A, Onno W Steenbeek and Federico Torracchi (2012) 'The Impact of Scale, Complexity, and Service Quality on the Administrative Costs of Pension Funds: A Cross-Country Comparison' 79 *Journal of Risk and Insurance* 2, 477.

69 Cummings, above n 60.

70 Bateman, Hazel and Olivia S. Mitchell (2004) 'New Evidence on Pension Plan Design and Administrative Expenses: the Australian Experience' 3(1) *Journal of Pension Economics and Finance* 63.

71 Sy, Wilson and Kevin Liu (2010) 'Investment Performance Ranking of Superannuation Firms' (Working Paper, Australian Prudential Regulation Authority, 23 June 2010).

72 Coleman, Esho and Wong, above n 42, 299.

73 The Sharpe Ratio was developed in 1966 by William F. Sharpe (who was awarded the Nobel Prize for his work developing the Capital Asset Pricing Model). It is calculated by deducting the risk free rate from the rate of return of a portfolio and then dividing the result by the standard deviation of portfolio returns. Sharpe argued that use of such a ratio permits returns that are simply the result of taking excess risk to be differentiated from those that result from clever investment management. Sharpe further developed the ratio in articles in 1975 and later in 1994. Sharpe, William F. (1966) 'Mutual Fund Performance' *Journal of Business* 119–138; Sharpe, William F. (1975) 'Adjusting for Risk in Portfolio Performance Measurement' *Journal of Portfolio Management* 29–34; Sharpe, William F. (1994) 'The Sharpe Ratio' *Journal of Portfolio Management*. A Sharpe ratio of greater than unity is usually considered acceptable, while a ratio of 2 or above is good. Formally, the Sharpe ratio for an asset class a may be represented as $(a) = \langle\langle rcomp\ (a) - rrisk\ free \rangle\rangle / \sigma vol.(a - rrisk\ free\ )$, where $rrisk\ free$ is the return from a risk free asset and $\sigma vol.(a - rrisk\ free\ )$ is the volatility of the aggregate asset class return less the return of the risk free asset.

74 Ellis, Tobin and Tracey, above n 59. The funds surveyed had total FUM of $210 billion.

They attributed this underperformance by retail funds to higher expenses, both explicit and embedded.

Cummings and Ellis found that not-for-profit funds allocated more of their portfolios to illiquid and less risky assets, on average, than retail funds, and as a result achieved higher risk-adjusted returns.[75] These allocations were more pronounced where there was significant in-house investment management, consistent with the hypothesis that a greater degree of separation reduces performance. Coleman, Esho and Wong found that the performance difference between for-profit and not-for-profit funds is caused by higher agency costs in for-profit funds (due to non-representative trustee board structures and potential board member conflicts of interest) than in not-for-profit funds (with representative trustee boards).[76]

Rice and McEwin explored risk-adjusted performance measures by fund type in Australian superannuation funds for the period 1995 to 2002.[77] They found that

> controlling for fund size, membership, benefit structure, and expenses, fund type is the primary determinant of the cross-Sectional variation in investment performance of Australian superannuation funds. This is consistent with the argument that agency costs in for-profit funds lead to significantly lower risk-adjusted performance.

Hallahan, Faff and Benson explored 'tournament behaviour' among Australian superannuation funds, and found evidence of the manipulation of strategies in order to achieve higher positions in performance tables, and hence higher market share.[78] They also found that managers that performed poorly in previous periods tended to take on more risk subsequently. They attributed this behaviour, which may not be in members' interest, to the desire to maximise fees. They also noted that fund manager compensation typically encourages such behaviour, as it usually has a component related to performance during the tournament period.

75 Cummings, James and Katrina Ellis (2011) 'Risk and Return of Illiquid Investments: A Trade-Off for Superannuation Funds Offering Transferable Accounts' (Working Paper, Australian Prudential Regulation Authority, 2011).

76 Coleman, Esho and Wong, above n 42.

77 Rice, Michael and Ian McEwin (2002) 'Superannuation Fees and Competition' (Report, Phillips Fox Actuaries and Consultants, 9 April 2002).

78 Hallahan, Terrence, Robert W. Faff and Karen L. Benson (2008) 'Fortune Favours the Bold? Exploring Tournament Behavior Among Australian Superannuation Funds' 33 *Journal of Financial Services Research* 3, 205.

These findings provide helpful detailed explanations for the poor performance we have identified by the Australian funds, and also provide evidence that the various problems identified in Chapter 2 do in fact occur in practice.

4.5.3 Governance and outsourcing

Many of the Australian studies attribute the high costs and poor performance of Australian funds to agency conflicts of interest and the impact of asymmetric information, reflecting experience in other countries. More specifically, attention has been drawn to poor fee negotiation, lack of direct investment, active management, lack of 'fund alignment with member interests', non-representative trustee board structures, and potential board member conflicts of interest.[79] The use of delegated management is shown to be extensive, to increase cost and not to improve performance significantly.[80] Retail funds tend to use related-parties for outsourcing, at higher fees than independent counterparts. The provision of choice by retail funds increases costs but does not provide a corresponding improvement in performance.

Bateman and Thorp analysed the delegation patterns of 198 not-for-profit funds.[81] They also reported Rainmaker data which showed that 93% of FUM in the Australian system was invested via delegated managers, noting that asset consultants play a crucial role. Funds employing as many as 13 external managers did no better than those with a single manager, while most trustees did not outperform randomly selected naïve portfolios.[82]

Liu and Arnold used APRA data to explore a variety of issues related to outsourcing. Using a sample of 115 funds compiled in 2006, they found widespread outsourcing of many functions including administration, asset allocation, and investment management.[83] All funds outsourced at least one function, and nearly two-thirds of the funds outsourced six or more. Not-for-profit funds were more likely to outsource, but when retail funds outsourced, they were more likely to use affiliated service providers. In a companion paper, Liu and Arnold found

79 Sy and Liu, above n 72.

80 This finding coincides with many previous findings internationally. The difficulty of screening agents for a delegated role is well known in the literature, in particular the problem of eliciting truthful information from those agents once they are employed. See Bhattacharya, Sudipto and Paul Pfleiderer (1985) 'Delegated Portfolio Management' 36 *Journal of Economic Theory*, 1–25.

81 Bateman, Hazel and Susan Thorp (2007) 'Decentralized Investment Management: An Analysis of Non-Profit Pension Funds' 6 *Journal of Pension Economics and Finance* 1, 21.

82 This finding as also consistent with their previous work, see Bateman and Thorp, ibid.

83 Liu, Kevin and Bruce R. Arnold (2010) 'Australian Superannuation Outsourcing: Fees, Related Parties and Concentrated Markets' (Working Paper, Australian Prudential Regulation Authority, 2 July 2010). Although useful, this survey has not been repeated subsequently.

that retail related-party service providers tended to charge higher fees than their independent counterparts, although there was no evidence of such higher costs for the not-for-profit funds.[84]

Over one third of the funds which provided information on this aspect used 11 or more providers, and around 90% of funds were managed by external parties. On average in 2006, only 5–8% of the retail and non-public offer funds were directly invested by the fund itself, compared with 20% for the public offer, not-for-profit funds.[85]

In 2012, Liu and Arnold also reported on the extent to which nomination of insurance companies to provide coverage to members affected performance, finding that the 'relatedness' of the insurance provider to the trustee tends to increase cost.[86] Langford, Faff and Marisetty used data for 257 retail funds that offered choice and for 47 limited choice funds in the period 1993 to 2001, in order to explore whether providing choice to investors is beneficial. They found that limited choice funds outperformed retail funds which offered choice, and that investors did not typically respond to differential fees and loads.[87]

Towers Watson have explored the relative benefits of active versus passive management, providing comparison of the 'gross alpha' achieved by Australian managers for the ten years to 31 March 2014 with global equity managers, and with movements in value of asset classes. Their broad conclusion was that:

> The overall impact of a widespread switch from active management to passive management would be to reduce the income of the asset management industry and increase overall net of fee returns for asset owners.[88]

This finding reinforces a 'thought experiment' and analysis carried out by Towers Watson's UK team, which shows that "the investment industry is sub-optimally structured from the perspective of the end saver" and concludes that the industry should have less active management.[89] The analysis was supported by surveys of investment managers which highlighted lack of trust in

84 Liu, Kevin and Bruce R. Arnold (2010) 'Australian Superannuation: The Outsourcing Landscape' (Working Paper, Australian Prudential Regulation Authority, July 2010).

85 Liu and Arnold, ibid. 16.

86 Liu, Kevin and Bruce R. Arnold (2012) 'Superannuation and Insurance: Related Parties and Member Cost' (Working Paper, Australian Prudential Regulation Authority, November 2012).

87 Langford, B.R., R.W. Faff and V.B. Marisetty (2006) 'On the Choice of Superannuation Funds in Australia' 29 *Journal of Financial Services Research* 3, 255.

88 Ibid. 30.

89 Hodgson, Tim (2014), 'There Are too Many Active Managers' (Towers Watson Perspectives, June 2014), 6.

the financial services industry, short-termism and the costs incurred through active management.[90]

These results highlight the importance of the degree of separation between agents and principals in leading to lower performance. Funds that are run for the benefit of those who manage them, or with whom these managers have a close relationship, tend to perform better. Where the degree of separation is large, governance and regulatory interventions are needed to seek to protect the interests of members. The literature suggests that these systems are not operating effectively enough to do so. In addition, the imposition of several layers of management inevitably adds cost which the literature above suggests does not yield sufficient improvement in outcomes to be justified.

90 Further evidence on the benefits of passive management is provided by the growth of Vanguard in the US, which achieved a substantial market share of the managed funds market by offering a low cost, passively managed option. See Slater, Robert (1997) *John Bogle and the Vanguard Experiment: One Man's Quest to Transform the Mutual Fund Industry* (McGraw-Hill, 1997). Sharpe, William F. (1991) 'The Arithmetic of Active Management' 47 *The Financial Analysts' Journal* 1, 7–9, has demonstrated that it is impossible for actively managed funds, on average, to outperform passively managed funds.

5 Lessons from Australia

This chapter uses the preceding analysis to draw out some of the lessons that may be learned from the Australian experience. Chapter 6 then provides suggestions on how to fix the problems we have identified.

The history presented in Chapter 3 above explains how tolerance of the emerging complexity of the industry, the main driver of high costs and lack of transparency, was encouraged by a misplaced belief in the ability of competitive markets to ensure efficiency. Governance arrangements, especially those highlighting the responsibilities of trustees and controlling the cost of outsourced management and advice, were allowed to remain inadequate. For most investors, there is now a large degree of separation between the fund members and those who make investment decisions on their behalf, created in part by extensive outsourcing of activities and responsibilities. This means that fiduciary duties, duties of care, responsibility for investment performance and recognition of the need to keep fees at reasonable levels are all diffused. Together, these have led to poor performance, as discussed below in Section 5.1.

A second reason for the problems the Australian system faces (discussed in Section 5.2) is ineffective legal and regulatory arrangements. Although in principle trust law places duties on trustees and others, extensive delegation of responsibility means that these duties are not in sharp focus. Legislation so far has been 'light handed', and regulatory responsibility is divided across multiple agencies. Disclosure of costs, particularly for funds management, is incomplete.

Section 5.3 examines Australia's performance in terms of managing risk, a necessary outcome of the choice of a predominately DC system. Section 5.4 explains the role played by tax subsidies, and difficulties with how they are targeted.

5.1 The reasons for poor performance

Chapter 4 has presented evidence that Australian superannuation funds perform poorly relative to passively managed benchmarks, and also relative to international benchmarks. Internal rates of return (net of costs) for the period 1996 to 2016 averaged around 4.5%, while investing in a simple, passively managed, balanced portfolio could have yielded some 7.2%. This poorer performance is estimated to have cost Australian retirees up to $900 billion in a 20-year period. In this section we explore some of the reasons for this outcome.

5.1.1 Complexity

The decisions taken as to how to develop superannuation in Australia have led to a multi-layered industry where many aspects of the management and administration of superannuation funds have been delegated to third parties. Although responsibility for the majority of funds is vested in trustees, who are in principle required by trust law to act as fiduciaries for the members they represent, these trustees often choose to pass on responsibility for investment strategy to advisers, management of fund assets to fund managers, and a variety of other activities to third parties.

Other agents, including insurance companies, stockbrokers, custodians, and the developers and managers of fund platforms, funds of funds, hedge funds and providers of derivative instruments also play important roles. Many of these agents belong to groups that are linked financially, operationally and socially.[1] Accountants, lawyers, credit rating agencies and research houses provide and analyse information on which these various agents rely. Politicians, regulators, the courts and the tax authorities intervene in various ways, not always to the benefit of members. All of this complexity leads to great potential for both principal-agent and conflict of interest problems to emerge, and for unfettered rent-seeking.[2]

Chapter 4 also provides evidence that poor principal-agent relationships, poor governance, and lack of transparency are a major cause of technical inefficiency in superannuation. Higher service quality and more complex investment strategies are shown to increase costs significantly, to a degree that is often not justified by the additional benefit to members. Providing greater choice to members also increases costs, and the literature suggests that the resulting benefit does not outweigh this cost.

5.1.2 Outsourcing and leakages

Delegation of management and outsourcing has been demonstrated to increase cost to an extent that cannot be justified by improvements in performance. In aggregate in 2006, for example, outsourced services added about 1% of FUM to annual costs for not-for-profit funds and 1.85% of FUM for retail funds.[3] Retail

1 These inter-relations have been explored, for example, in Donald, Scott, Hazel Bateman, Ross Buckley, Kevin Liu and Rob Nicholls (2016) 'Too Connected to Fail: The Regulation of Systemic Risk within Australia's Superannuation System', 2 *Journal of Financial Regulation* 1, 56–78, 11.

2 For analysis of some of the many places where conflicts arise, see Asher, Anthony (2008) 'Conflicted Super Structures: Are Australian Investors Being Short-changed?' in J. Evans, M. Orszag and J. Piggot (eds), *Pension Fund Governance* (Edward Elgar, 2008), Figure 1.

3 Although now dated, the 2006 APRA survey (reported in Liu, Kevin and Bruce R. Arnold (2012) 'Superannuation and Insurance: Related Parties and Member Cost' (Working Paper, Australian Prudential Regulation Authority, November 2012)) remains the most recent comprehensive survey of investment management costs. APRA has not repeated the survey. Liu and Arnold's work was discussed in Chapter 3. Although substantial, these figures understate the costs of outsourcing, namely those reflected in reduced net-of-cost returns provided by third parties.

funds are most likely to outsource, often to related-party affiliates (which often charge higher fees than independents). The various intermediaries and layers in the system add to costs. Higher costs drive a wedge between gross and net returns, a wedge that seems to be larger in the Australian case than in other jurisdictions.[4]

Figure 5.1 shows how the assets which were placed under investment managers rose steeply to around $500 billion by 2007 and have continued to rise since.

Since the GFC, and partly as a result of the increasing size of funds, there has been some reversal of the relativity between internal and external management, with more funds choosing to manage assets internally, but the dominance of outsourcing remains.[5]

In Chapter 4 we also noted 'leakages' created by the need to compete with other funds on a short-term basis, agency costs, excessive choice and the very large number of funds. Other factors contributing to reduced performance include

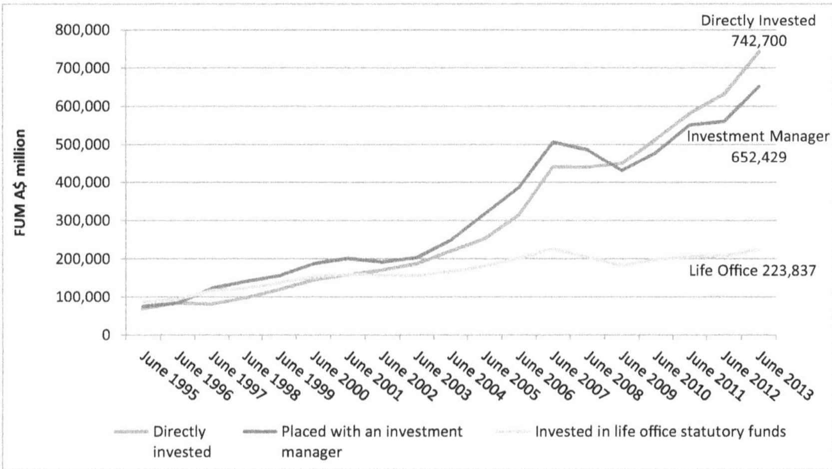

Figure 5.1 Methods of investment in all funds, including SMSFs

Source: Australian Prudential Regulatory Authority, 'Statistics: Annual Superannuation Bulletin June 2013' (Report, revised ed., 5 February 2014) Table 14, 47.

4 Liu and Arnold, above n 3; Ellis K., A. Tobin and B. Tracey (2008) 'Investment Performance, Asset Allocation, and Expenses of Large Superannuation Funds' (APRA Working Paper, October 2008, and 3 *Insight* 2); Coleman, A.D.F., N. Esho and M. Wong (2006) 'The Impact of Agency Costs on the Investment Performance of Australian Pension Funds' 5 *Journal of Pension Economics and Finance* 3, 299.

5 Subsequent APRA bulletins beyond 2014 have not contained this analysis, so June 2013 is the latest data available. Versions of the bulletin prior to 2016 have now been withdrawn from circulation. The available data on outsourcing are discussed in detail in Liu, Kevin Yi (2013), Australian Superannuation: Operational Structure, Investment Performance and Trustee Governance (DPhil Thesis, University of Sydney, June 2013).

poor fee negotiation, lack of direct investment, active management, and problems over a lack of "fund alignment with member interests".[6] Potential economies of scale have only been reflected to a limited extent in lower fees and charges.[7] Higher agency costs (caused by non-representative trustee board structures and potential board member conflicts of interest) are a further cause of the difference in performance between for-profit and not-for-profit funds.[8]

5.1.3 Degrees of separation

The difficulties created by the initial policy choice of moving towards a fully funded and defined contribution system, with the funds managed mostly by the private sector were highlighted in Chapter 2. In the Australian industry today, crucial decisions on asset allocation and management are taken by those with several degrees of separation from, and no direct relationship with, or responsibility to, fund members. Lack of requisite time, skills and knowledge on the part of trustees, and the delegation of authority to other entities, has weakened governance controls over delegated responsibilities. In addition, remuneration systems may give trustees, and those with delegated responsibility, the incentive to act in ways other than in the best interest of members, and governance systems rarely counteract this effectively.

Against this background, the rapid accumulation of funds has led to the development of a multi-layered industry, while pushing the risk down to members has led to the need for numerous risk management mechanisms including the provision of choice and the creation of large numbers of different funds.[9] The result is a substantial degree of separation between those who manage the funds and the fund members.

Taken as a whole, the empirical results presented in Chapter 4 suggest that a higher degree of separation between managers and beneficiaries leads to lower efficiency. This is partly because the greater the number of players to whom activities and responsibilities are delegated, the higher the cost;[10] partly because greater separation weakens the degree of scrutiny that beneficiaries and their agents are

6 Sy, Wilson and Kevin Liu (2010) 'Investment Performance Ranking of Superannuation Firms' (Working Paper, Australian Prudential Regulation Authority, 23 June 2010).

7 Cummings, James Richard (2012) 'The Effect of Fund Size on the Performance of Australian Superannuation Funds' (Working Paper, Australian Prudential Regulation Authority, March 2012).

8 Cummings, James and Katrina Ellis (2011) 'Risk and Return of Illiquid Investments: A Trade-Off for Superannuation Funds Offering Transferable Accounts' (Working Paper, Australian Prudential Regulation Authority, 2011).

9 The Productivity Commission have noted the "egregious systemic failure" of the system in that members end up with multiple accounts, and recommended that those who do not exercise choice should be allocated to a default product only once. Productivity Commission (2017) Superannuation: Alternative Default Models (Draft Report, March 2017), 2.

10 Morris, Nicholas (2014) The Cost of Complexity: Australian Superannuation (D. Phil Thesis, UNSW Law); Freeman, John P. and Stewart L. Brown (2001) 'Mutual Fund Advisory Fees: the Cost of Conflicts of Interest', 26 *Journal of Corporation Law* 609.

able to exert on the managers of their funds; and partly because responsibility is diffused the longer is the chain. Australia has widespread delegation of responsibility, with associated higher costs and lower performance for most of the funds examined. The funds that perform better in Australia seem to be those where the degree of separation is less, often those where the fund is run for the benefit of employees of the firm doing the management.

5.2 Ineffective legal and regulatory constraints

5.2.1 'Light handed' legal arrangements

The idea that competition and choice can control private sector rent-seeking, so that regulation can be 'light handed', lies at the heart of various decisions Australia made to rely on private sector provision and management, and continues to form the basis of many suggestions for reform. As noted in Chapter 3, the SIS Act set rules for selection of trustees, investments, management, fund accounts and administration, enquiries and complaints.[11] Part 6 of the Act, in particular, sets out the fiduciary duties of trustees and licensees.[12] However, the SIS Act stopped short of defining a formal code of conduct for trustees, and associated enforcement mechanisms, perhaps because the architects of the system believed that the general trust and common law would be sufficient. In addition, following extensive consultation and lobbying, the protections afforded by the general law against conflicts of interest have been watered down in various ways, including complicated provisions that permit in-house investments in related parties and investments made at a loosely defined 'arms length'.[13] We return to how the obligations of those who manage superannuation funds could be specified and enforced better in Chapter 6.

Arguably, the frequency with which it has been deemed necessary to change legislation, as outlined in Section 3.9, is a direct result of flawed initial design, and this has created difficulties for subsequent management of the system. Over the last 25 years, various governments have adjusted the legislative framework for superannuation on many occasions. A recent review of the system has expressed the view that a "major threat to the superannuation system is the federal government's own continued changes to the system's tax and regulatory settings",[14] while others have noted "continuing dissatisfaction with areas of governance and outcomes".[15]

11 Superannuation Industry (Supervision) Act 1993 (Cth) ('SIS'). SIS also regulates the operation of superannuation funds and sets penalties for trustees. The Superannuation Complaints Tribunal commenced operations in 1994.

12 Although Section 56B exempts funds from the conflict of interest provisions of the general law.

13 The SIS Act, however, reduced the allowable proportion of in-house investments.

14 KPMG (2017) *Super Insights Report 2017*, available at https://assets.kpmg.com/content/dam/kpmg/au/pdf/2017/super-insights-report-2017.pdf, 16.

15 Taylor, Sue, Anthony Asher and Julie Anne Tarr (2017) 'Accountability in Regulatory Reform: Australia's Superannuation Industry Paradox', 45 *Federal Law Review* 257–290.

5.2.2 Division of regulatory responsibility

A major problem in Australia is that there is no single agency charged with the effective development of a regulatory regime for superannuation. Instead, regulatory responsibility is divided up between numerous agencies, with each agency having a narrowly defined role. As a result, no one takes responsibility either for the performance of the industry as a whole, or for the development of a unified regime. Division of responsibility between regulators, albeit in a different part of the financial system, had disastrous consequences in the UK prior to the GFC, because no one took responsibility for key elements such as liquidity.[16]

The size and complexity of the industry has often swamped the limited resources of those with responsibility for its regulation. The regulatory system continues to be unable or unwilling to prevent rent extraction by financial services firms, and also has insufficient focus on the performance of the sector as a whole. A recent survey of superannuation trustees and licensees, for example, has "revealed that fund members are vulnerable to significant and expanding private-interest rents generated by the financial services sector. This may be explained by regulatory capture mechanisms variously described as statutory, agency, corrosive and intellectual capture".[17]

As noted in Chapter 3, decisions to divide responsibility for aspects of the governance and regulation of the industry between five agencies have reduced regulatory focus.[18] These decisions emerged from the Wallis Committee's view that a single agency might become excessively powerful, and that technical and other expertise for particular activities was best concentrated into individual agencies, irrespective of the market segment each agency was regulating.[19] As a result, no one agency is responsible for the efficient performance of the superannuation system as a whole.

There is nevertheless some overlap between the responsibilities of the various regulators. For example, APRA covers the prudential regulation and retirement income provisions of the *Superannuation Industry (Supervision) Act 1993*, while ASIC has responsibility for the other provisions, including aspects of consumer protection set out in the *Corporations Law*. The RBA regulates the payments system, as

16 For discussion of what went wrong in the UK regulatory system prior to the GFC, see Jaffer, Sue, Susana Knaudt and Nicholas Morris (2014) 'Failures of Regulation and Governance', in Nicholas Morris and David Vines (eds), *Capital Failure: Rebuilding Trust in Financial Services* (Oxford University Press, 2014), ch. 5.

17 Taylor et al. (2017), above n15, 257.

18 The five agencies are the Australian Prudential Regulatory Authority (APRA), the Australian Securities and Investment Commission (ASIC), the Australian Taxation Office (ATO), the Australian Competition (ACCC) and the Reserve Bank of Australia (RBA).

19 Cooper, Jeremy (2006) 'The Integration of Financial Regulatory Authorities – the Australian Experience' (Paper presented at Assessing the Present, Conceiving the Future, the 30th Anniversary Conference of the Comissão de Valores Mobiliários (Securities and Exchange Commission of Brazil), 4–5 September 2006).

well as being responsible for systemic stability. APRA and ATO share responsibility for smaller superannuation funds, with responsibility divided depending on whether there is deemed to be a need for prudential regulation. The regulatory philosophy of APRA has focused mostly on the monitoring of compliance with prudential standards.[20] In recent years, APRA has also concentrated on ensuring that the firms it regulates have suitable risk management systems, and on the licensing and prudential guidance of Registrable Superannuation Entities (RSEs). ACCC has overall responsibility for promoting competition and fair trading, including intervention in markets where there is deemed to be limited competition. ASIC is responsible for ensuring suitable disclosure by regulated entities. A *Council of Financial Regulators* (CFR) co-ordinates the activities of the RBA, APRA, ASIC and the Treasury, although its membership does not include either the ATO or ACCC.

5.2.3 Inadequate disclosure

A particular feature of the Australian system is inadequate disclosure of investment management costs. Although there are disclosure requirements at the fund level, for example to provide *Product Disclosure Statements* (PDSs), the information contained therein requires considerable expertise to interpret. Investment risks are particularly poorly reported.[21] There is no requirement for fund managers to disclose the costs of fund management, unless this is undertaken within an APRA-regulated entity. Entities that are not directly APRA-regulated can simply report a net of costs investment return, which makes it much harder for trustees and members to understand what they are being charged and for what services. Partly as a result, the majority of funds management activities are outsourced.

5.3 Risk management

When the decisions to set up the Australian superannuation system were made, the primary focus was the accumulation of funds. Little attention was given at the time to how risks would be managed in the retirement phase. This problem was highlighted during the *Cooper Inquiry*, and has been emphasised by Jeremy

20 For a description of APRA's research activities, see Australian Prudential Regulation Authority (2012) 'Insight into Superannuation Research' 1 *Insight* 46.

21 The Cooper Review recognised this problem, and made recommendations for changes to governance arrangements for trustees, both of MySuper products and more generally. In particular, the Panel was concerned that diversification be defined in a way that took risk explicitly into consideration, and that governance be improved to reduce unintended operational and investment risks: Super System Review Panel (2010) Review into the Governance, Efficiency, Structure and Operation of Australia's Superannuation System: Final Report ('Super System Review'), Part Two: Recommendation Packages, 9.6.1, 33, 44.

Cooper – who is now chairman of *Challenger*, the major provider of annuities in Australia – in a 2011 article where he said:

> The super industry needs to develop ways of making more concrete promises to ordinary Australians, particularly retirees, who should not be expected to embrace the volatility and uncertainty to which they are now exposed, with so few options to protect themselves.[22]

Now that many of those who began to accumulate their funds in the early 1990s are approaching retirement, there is a growing need to focus on how they will be able to manage the longevity and market risks they now face. The annuity market in Australia is in its infancy and, as discussed above, annuities are generally recognised to be overpriced, with competition between providers limited.[23] Asymmetric information and expertise in this market means that the principal-agent, rent-seeking and conflict of interest problems discussed above are all likely to emerge, unless appropriate regulation can be designed.

5.3.1 'My retirement' products

The Australian government has started to address the problem of how to help members with post-retirement risks, through a programme they have called 'MyRetirement'. Product offerings under this programme are intended to be "a 'balanced offering' that provides higher income (than [a] typical outcome in an account-based pension) and the peace of mind of an income for life, while retaining some flexibility".[24] The concept for this, voluntary, product, which is called a *Comprehensive Income Product for Retirement* (CIPR),[25] has been developed following an extensive investigation of member willingness to use such a product carried out by the *Behavioural Economics Team of the Australian Government* (BETA).[26]

The precise details of CIPR implementation are still the subject of consultation,[27] although some funds have started to offer products of this kind

22 Quoted in Wylie, Sam (2011) 'Not so Super' (Core Economics, 22 February 2011) available at http://economics.com.au/2011/02/22/not-so-super/.

23 The importance of annuity market imperfections, and implications for economic growth, is discussed in Heijdra, Ben J. and Jochen O. Mierau (2009) 'Annuity Market Imperfection, Retirement and Economic Growth' (CESifo Working Paper, No. 2717).

24 Wilkinson, Jenny (2017) 'Improving the Retirement Phase of Superannuation' (paper presented at the 25th CEPAR Superannuation Colloquium, UNSW, Sydney, 7 July 2017).

25 CIPRs were first suggested by the Financial System Inquiry in 2015.

26 This team is located within the Department of the Prime Minister and Cabinet (PMC). For a description of its mission and activities, see www.pmc.gov.au/domestic-policy/behavioural-economics.

27 The proposed MyRetirement framework is expected to be released in July 2018. See https://investmentmagazine.com.au/2017/04/get-a-jump-on-the-competition-in-the-cipr-market/. Further consultation is expected.

to their members.[28] Products are only to be sold to members that have received suitable advice. The Australian Government Actuary has developed a possible certification test for CIPRs, with three main components. These are (1) the expectation of a constant real income for life; (2) a minimum required income efficiency and (3) a minimum level of real income to be provided.[29]

There is not universal agreement that the government's initiative will work. David Bell, a leader of the team developing the *Members Default Utility Function* (MDUF) believes that the development of CIPRs, although a good idea in principle, "is still some distance away from [being] an implementable solution".[30] Three particular problems, which have been highlighted as creating significant welfare losses and moral hazard, are that CIPRs are risk agnostic, that residual benefits are not valued by the population, and that CIPRs are not yet integrated with the age pension.

5.4 Tax subsidies

The Australian superannuation system provides large tax concessions to encourage saving, with contributions, fund earnings and payouts all receiving concessional treatment.[31] A recent report by the Grattan Institute explored these tax concessions and their impact on Australia's fiscal position, noting that different tax treatments for different forms of saving introduces distortions to the savings market.[32] The authors estimated that the annual revenue foregone in superannuation tax breaks (on both earnings and contributions) was some $25 billion in 2014–2015, more than 10% of overall personal income tax collections, and that this would rise to $40 billion by 2017–2018.[33]

28 VicSuper launched a CIPR in June 2016 (see https://investmentmagazine.com.au/2016/02/vicsuper-learning-from-slow-take-up-of-cipr/), and Unisuper, the fund for employees in higher education, unveiled a CIPR product in late 2015 (see www.unisuper.com.au/news/2015/12/10/unisuper-unveils-innovative-cipr).

29 Australian Government Actuary (2017) Actuarial Certification Test for Comprehensive Income Products for Retirement. Available at www.treasury.gov.au/~/media/Treasury/Publications%20and%20Media/Publications/2017/Actuarial%20Certification%20Test/Downloads/PDF/CIPR_Certification_Test.ashx.

30 Bell, David (2017) 'Comprehensive Income Products for Retirement (CIPRs)' (paper presented at the 25th CEPAR Superannuation Colloquium, UNSW, Sydney, 7 July 2017).

31 Various arguments have been put forward for provision of such concessions, including compensating members for having to make mandatory contributions, incentivising private saving and overcoming inertia, financial myopia, loss aversion and other cognitive biases. For discussion of these arguments, and of the various ways in which taxation of pension systems can be structured, see Whitehouse, Edward (2001) 'The Tax Treatment of Funded Pensions', available at www.oecd.org/finance/private-pensions/2391559.pdf. Whitehouse also provides international comparison of pension tax regimes and some empirical estimates of the impact on personal savings.

32 Daley, John, Brendan Coates and Danielle Wood (2015) 'Super Tax Targeting' (Grattan Institute Report 2015–11, November 2015), 9.

33 These calculations drew on figures provided in APRA (2014) *Annual Superannuation Bulletin;* APRA (2015) *Quarterly Superannuation Performance June 2015;* and Treasury (2015) *Tax Expenditures Statement 2014.*

Choices made by fund managers are influenced by tax minimisation considerations, although the extent to which tax and funds management are effectively co-ordinated is a matter of dispute.[34] Australian superannuation funds are unusual by international standards in the share of portfolio allocated to equities.[35] This choice is partly driven by tax considerations, as most Australian equities carry franking credits which can be offset against other taxes. Repeated changes to the taxation of superannuation have distorted incentives and created rapid flows of funds into, and out of, particular parts of the system. The desire of members to minimise tax also led to increased reliance on advisers.[36] These influences have also led to lower performance and higher costs.

5.4.1 Targeting

These tax concessions are disproportionately targeted on the rich, and provide little benefit at the lower end of the income distribution.[37] The Grattan Institute noted that those earning less than $18,200 in 2015 paid 15% on superannuation contributions, compared with no tax on other income, while those earning between $180,000 and $300,000 enjoyed a 30% concession.[38] The Australian Treasury has estimated that in 2009–10, 37.8% of the combined tax concessions accrued to the top decile.[39]

As a result of concern over the unfair distribution of tax expenditures, a 'Division 293' surcharge was introduced in 2012 for those earning more than $300,000 per annum.[40] To prevent income manipulation to avoid the tax, this uses a modified

34 In his submission to the Super System Review, Gordon MacKenzie argued that Australian superannuation funds do not in fact take full advantage of tax minimisation opportunities. If they did, the impact would be greater. Mackenzie, Gordon D. (2009) 'Tax Governance of Superannuation Funds', submission to the Super System Review Panel, The Review into the Governance, Efficiency, Structure and Operation of Australia's Superannuation System.

35 Although this can be partly justified by the age of members and the fact that few superannuation funds provide benefits as lifetime pensions.

36 Advisers often emphasise this aspect of their service in advertising.

37 Ingles, David (2009) 'The Great Superannuation Tax Concession Rort' (Australia Institute Research Paper 61, February 2009). Ingles estimated in 2009 that 37% of concessional contributions went to the top 5% of individuals by earnings. Tax concessions provide substantially greater benefits for men than for women.

38 Daley et al. (2015), above n 32, Figure 4.2, 41.

39 Gallagher, Phil (2012) 'The Distribution of Government Support for Retirement Income – Point-in-Time and Lifecycle Estimates' (Presentation to Colloquium of Superannuation Researchers, UNSW, Friday 13 July 2012).

40 Division 293 tax was imposed on concessional contributions of high income earners whose income (and relevant concessionally taxed contributions) exceeded $300,000 in the financial years 2012–2013 to 2016–2017. The threshold was reduced to $250,000 in July 2017, see www.budget.gov.au/2016-17/content/bp2/html/bp2_revenue-10.htm. At the time, the opposition Labor party recommended that it should be $200,000, to more closely align with the top marginal tax bracket. An accessible summary of the tax is provided in www.dfrdb.gov.au/your-scheme/division-293-tax/ and more detail is provided in www.ato.gov.au/individuals/super/in-detail/withdrawing-and-paying-tax/division-293-tax---information-for-individuals/?page=3.

income for surcharge purposes.[41] The 2017 Federal Budget estimated that this surcharge would affect around 1% of taxpayers, and the Treasury estimated that the tax would collect $475 million in the 2015–2016 financial year.[42]

41 The definition is based on that used for Medicare levy surcharge purposes, see www.ato.gov.au/Individuals/Income-and-deductions/Income-tests/.

42 Hayden, Grant and Laura de Zwaan (2017) 'Assessing the threshold of the Div 293 Contributions Tax using a tax expenditures framework' (Queensland University Business School).

6 What can be done now

6.1 The challenge

The foregoing chapters provide evidence that Australia's superannuation system has not provided the returns on assets and incomes in retirement that could reasonably have been expected by the members of Australia's superannuation funds. This is because the major policy choices made in the 1990s – fully funded, defined contribution, run by the private sector – created the difficulties Australian members now face. The Australian superannuation industry is unnecessarily complex, expensive and inefficient, because it has focused on maximising profits and remuneration for those involved in the industry. This evolution has been at the expense of the Australian fund members, who now face retirement with smaller assets than they would have had if the industry had been managed differently. Disclosure of costs is insufficient to permit members and trustees to make informed judgements about long-term investments, conflicts of interest persist, and system design allows members and trustees to be inattentive.

It is clear that these problems present significant threats to the Australian superannuation system. Uncontrolled, they leave continued scope for rent extraction by those in the industry, to the detriment of Australia's fund members. Trust law in Australia, which ought to protect members' interests, provides insufficient guidance as to duties, is constrained by 'contractual eclipse' and has been weakened by the introduction of member choice. 'Light handed' legal and regulatory systems are not sufficient to control self-interested behaviour.

In forcing the Australian population to make substantial superannuation contributions during their working lives, successive Australian governments have attempted to avoid responsibility for the well-being of the majority of their citizens in retirement. They have passed the risk on to individuals, and thereby minimised the need for state pension provision, and denied citizens the benefits of risk pooling. However, there is little evidence that the majority of individuals are able to take the difficult decisions required to optimise the balance of risk and return in the management of their lifetime savings. This puts most people at the mercy of a financial services industry guided by self-interest.

Government response to this situation has, so far, been ineffective, despite the numerous reforms outlined in Chapter 3. I believe, however, that the government cannot get out of its responsibilities so easily. Many people retiring in the next 20 years will find that their funds are insufficient to provide a living standard close to that they enjoyed while in employment. This in turn could lead to a political backlash with people blaming the government for failure to protect their superannuation assets. At that point the various problems I have highlighted in this book will come into high relief.

The list of things that still need attention is, unfortunately, long, and the experience of the last 20 years shows that existing policy reform processes will continue to struggle to deliver sufficient change in behaviour. The present complexity of the industry, and of the product offerings it provides, needs curtailing further. In the short run, greater regulatory focus on outcomes, particularly costs and performance, is needed, while in the medium term attention needs to be given to increasing the trustworthiness of industry participants, enhancing competition, and improving the knowledge and motivation of trustees and members.

Improved legal and governance arrangements are also needed to enhance the ability and willingness of trustees to represent the interests of members effectively.[1] Creation of a single regulatory agency with a clear remit to improve the efficiency of the industry and a primary duty to promote competition, stronger use of trust law to define and enforce the fiduciary duties of trustees, enabling proper competitive pressures to emerge, and full disclosure of all investment management costs and conflicts of interest are discussed in the sections below. These are all necessary, but probably not in themselves sufficient.

In what follows, we explore what further can be done to fix these issues, a daunting task. Experience in other countries with similar initiatives (for example, the FSA's attempts to implement codes of practice in the UK) reveals that such initiatives are usually unsuccessful.[2] There remains a need to explore more fundamental changes in order to ensure that the reduction in potential asset values that has occurred since 1991 is not repeated for the (much larger) assets that will be accumulated in future.

The challenge, which we discuss at the end of this chapter, is to find further policy responses that are capable of making a significant difference, given that

1 Alexander, Kern (2004) 'Corporate Governance and Banking Regulation' (Working Paper No. 17, University of Cambridge, Cambridge Endowment for Research in Finance) 8; corporate governance can in particular be used to protect against abuse by insiders; see also Clarke, Thomas (2004) *Theories of Corporate Governance: The Philosophical Foundations of Corporate Governance* (Routledge, 2004); Farrar, John (2005) *Corporate Governance: Theories, Principles and Practice* (Oxford University Press, 2nd ed.).

2 See Parliamentary Banking Standards Commission (2013) *Changing Banking for Good* (HM Parliament, Westminster, June 2013, Vol 2, para 273).

well-meaning attempts at reform so far seem to have had little effect on industry behaviour. Creation of a publicly administered agency that offered a centrally administered, passively managed, fund could provide a genuine alternative to the high-cost options currently available.[3] Properly run, this could provide higher returns at lower fees than the majority of the options currently on the market. At a minimum, it would provide a benchmark against which existing fund performance could be judged. In addition, it could include risk-pooling arrangements which would overcome some of the problems of the present predominately DC environment.

6.2 Improving regulatory coherence

In principle, it should be possible to design a regulatory system that minimises the impact of principal-agent, conflict of interest and rent-seeking problems, notwithstanding the complexity of financial services. However, the Australian regulatory system lacks focus and effectiveness. Close interaction between regulators and those they regulate has led to the watering-down of many reform proposals, while 'revolving door' effects in a localised labour market put pressure on regulators to avoid controversy. In addition, misplaced belief in the efficacy of competitive processes to control rent-seeking has led to a 'light handed' approach by regulators.

While I agree with Wallis that creating a single regulator for superannuation would create a body that was too powerful is a serious danger, in my view this is outweighed by the importance of having an entity that is empowered to take responsibility for the development of the industry as a whole. This would mean combining the existing roles of APRA (prudential regulation and data collection), ASIC (disclosure and customer protection), ATO (SMSFs) and ACCC (competition) into a single entity.

Clearly, in order to respond to the Wallis concerns, such an agency would need a very clear mandate and, because of the importance of the industry to Australia's future, report directly and on a regular basis to Parliament. The new, or repurposed, agency should be responsible for effective development of the disclosure regime, for regular publication of benchmark performance indicators, for ensuring that trustees and those to whom they delegate responsibility are 'fit and proper', for defining the parameters of appropriate

3 As noted in Chapter 3, a variant of this idea was recently put forward by Peter Costello in a speech to the industry. He argued that where members do not make explicit choices about the allocation of their contributions to funds, they should automatically be placed in a publicly administered fund. Costello, Peter (2017) 'The Uncertain Path of Superannuation Reform' (speech to the SuperRatings & Lonsec 'Day of Confrontation 2017', Melbourne, 12 October 2017), available at www.petercostello.com.au/media/LonsecSpeech-12Oct2017-Uncertain-Path-of-Super-Reform.pdf.

retirement income products, and for the identification and policing of conflicts of interest.[4]

The regulator should also have a primary duty – perhaps in collaboration with the ACCC – to promote effective competition in the superannuation industry, a matter we discuss further in Section 6.4 below. The regulator needs to ensure genuine independence of trustees, further reduce the scope for privileged related-party transactions and cross-subsidies that benefit providers, make sure that fees and charges genuinely reflect costs, provide accessible benchmarks against which costs and performance may be judged, ensure that risks are fully understood, and develop mechanisms that punish transgressions of regulatory arrangements sufficiently to provide a genuine deterrent.

The success of the UK utilities regulators show that this can be achieved in a democracy, and the Australian energy regulator, established during the last decade, provides a precedent in Australia for introducing a unified regime.[5] The Ayres and Braithwaite idea of creating and empowering public interest groups (PIGs) that monitor the activities of the regulator may also be worth exploring.[6]

The new agency should in particular give attention to what type of regulatory system has the best chance of success in the particular context of Australian superannuation. The various forms that suitable pro-active regulation can take, with some commentary on international experience, are set out in Annex H. The least intrusive form of regulation is principles-based regulation, followed by rules-based regulation and finally outcomes-based regulation. Historically, codes of conduct have been developed in many countries, promulgated and enforced initially by self-regulatory organisations, and more recently by regulators, as part of a principles-based regulatory regime. There has been extensive debate about the effectiveness of each of these forms of regulation, which is also described briefly in Annex H.[7]

4 See Campbell, John Y., Howell E. Jackson, Brigitte C. Madrian and Peter Tufano (2010) 'The Regulation of Consumer Financial Products' (Working Paper No. RWP 10-040, Harvard Kennedy School) for helpful guidance on pro-active regulatory actions to improve superannuation products. Campbell et al. include regulation of the market for retirement savings products as a case study. They propose stronger regulations to ensure the appropriateness of products, but note the difficulties with the type of paternalism discussed by Thaler and Sunstein: Thaler, Richard H. and Cass Sunstein (2008) *Nudge: Improving Decisions about Health, Wealth, and Happiness* (Yale University Press).

5 See www.aer.gov.au/about-us.

6 Ayres, Ian and John Braithwaite (1992) *Responsive Regulation: Transcending the Deregulation Debate* (Oxford University Press). The idea is that PIGs can represent the interests of those who otherwise would be unrepresented in the regulatory process.

7 A general summary of regulatory problems in financial services may be found in Jaffer, Sue, Susana Knaudt and Nicholas Morris (2014) 'Failures of Regulation and Governance', in Morris and Vines (eds), *Capital Failure: Rebuilding Trust in Financial Services* (Oxford University Press), ch. 5.

Better stewardship by trustees is clearly crucial to the management of ever larger superannuation funds.[8] The selection of trustees needs to minimise potential conflicts of interest, while ensuring that those selected have sufficient experience and capabilities to protect members' interests effectively. Christopher Stone, for example, suggests the elimination of insider directors (in the superannuation case, those who have duties towards the supplier conglomerate); the appointment of publicly appointed directors and the provision of sufficient staff and resources for the directors to carry out their responsibilities, including dedicated and independent staff.[9] These are matters that the regulatory agency should orchestrate.

Enhancing the importance of reputation is particularly important, and this is an area on which the regulator should focus. Trustees need to be 'named and shamed' for poor performance, and praised if their funds do well. This needs to be done on an individual fund basis, otherwise the message will be diluted in wider corporate reporting and marketing. The separation of reporting arrangements is important, so that the performance of individual funds, even when subsumed into larger groups, can be monitored effectively. At present, it is impossible for even quite experienced researchers to extract such information. The importance of these measures is highlighted in recent OECD reports, which blame many of the excesses of the GFC on failures of corporate governance.[10]

The regulator should seek measurable outcomes in terms of improved trustworthiness of the relevant trustee firms and individuals.[11] Legal and regulatory penalties – such as removal of licences, meaningful financial penalties, or liability for the long-term consequences of actions – will be needed to enforce ethical standards. There is also a need to penalise externalities created by breaches of fiduciary duty.[12] The development of codes of practice will need to be agreed and accepted by those to whom they apply, through a

8 UK developments may provide useful guidance, for example the Walker Review suggestions for the introduction of a Stewardship Code, by separating the Combined Code into a corporate governance code and a stewardship code. United Kingdom, Walker, Stan (Chair) (2009) *A Review of Corporate Governance in UK Banks and Other Financial Industry Entities* (Final Recommendations).

9 Stone, Christopher (1975) *Where the Law Ends: The Social Control of Corporate Activities* (Harper and Row). UK reforms to corporate governance also provide helpful guidance – for example, limiting the number of directorships a director can hold and increasing time commitment; and paying greater attention to the expertise of board members.

10 Kirkpatrick, Grant (2009), 'Corporate Governance Lessons from the Financial Crisis' 1 *OECD Journal: Financial Market Trends* 61.

11 These matters have been discussed in detail, in the context of the wider financial services industry, in Morris and Vines (eds), above n 7.

12 See Armour, John and Jeffrey Gordon (2014) 'Systemic Harms and the Limits of Shareholder Value' in Morris and Vines (eds), above n 7, ch. 11.

well-informed negotiating process.[13] We return to discussion of how trust law could be enhanced to enable this in Section 6.5 below.

Both regulation and self-regulation have been made to work in other industries.[14] The utility industries, especially in the UK, have succeeded in establishing effective regulators that control both price and product quality, and which have succeeded in improving the efficiency of the industries for which they are responsible. Nuclear, chemical, clothing and advertising industries have established self-regulatory regimes that ensure the integrity of industrial processes, while industries as diverse as diamonds and forestry have arrangements that prevent individual self-interest from damaging long-term sustainability. Doctors and lawyers have established self-regulatory bodies that mostly ensure the professionalism of their members.[15] However, there are also cases where self-interested exploitation of regulatory loopholes persists in other industries and professions, for example in US accounting.[16]

This book contains compelling evidence that market failures abound in the Australian superannuation industry, and that these are not yet being suitably addressed by the regulatory system. Major issues are the charging of excessive fees for a variety of services and hiding anti-competitive behaviour in a complex value chain. Regulators in other industries have used price regulation to deal with the former, and insisted on unbundling and transparency

13 For discussion of the difficulties of achieving this, see Whiteside, Noel (2011) 'Creating Public Value: the Theory of the Convention' in John Benington and Mark H. Moore (eds), ***Public Value: Theory and Practice*** (Palgrave Macmillan).

14 The extent to which experience on self-regulation in other industries can be adapted for financial services is explored in Sue Jaffer, Nicholas Morris and David Vines, 'Restoring Trust' in Morris and Vines (eds), above n 7, ch. 16.

15 Short case studies of these regulatory systems, highlighting the relevance for financial services, are to be found in Jaffer, Sue, Nicholas Morris and David Vines (2014) 'Restoring Trust' in Morris and Vines (eds), above n7, ch. 16.

16 Sarbanes-Oxley, the Public Company Accounting and Investor Protection Act (2002) introduced (after the Enron and Worldcom scandals) a rules-based approach to regulation in the US. Rather than being seen as an early warning sign by the UK, the travails facing the US system were themselves arbitraged. The City of London exploited the unease of business, additional audit costs and litigation risk costs by suggesting an alternative framework based on the articulation of principles. Both practitioners and regulatory officials argued that the model could provide and did offer alternative and better oversight. The primary supporting evidence proffered for this derived from the absence of an accounting scandal in the United Kingdom, see Kershaw, David (2005) 'Evading Enron: Taking Principles Too Seriously in Accounting Regulation' 68 *Modern Law Review* 594; for wider discussion of these issues, see Keasey, Kevin, Helen Short and Michael Wright (2005) 'The Development of Corporate Governance Codes in the United Kingdom' in Kevin Keasey, Steve Thompson and Michael Wright (eds),*Corporate Governance: Accountability, Enterprise and International Comparisons* (Wiley) 21; Hill, Jennifer (2007) 'Evolving "Rules of the Game" in Corporate Governance Reform' in J. O'Brien (ed.), *Private Equity, Corporate Governance and the Dynamics of Capital Market Regulation* (Imperial College Press) 29.

to counter the latter. In a recent paper co-authored with Rob Nicholls, we described the various forms of price regulation that have been used in the utilities sector and recommended that a price cap be introduced for superannuation until effective competition can be established.[17] We also recommended that insurance provision (which currently costs members some $8.5 billion per year, with little clear rationale) be unbundled from the management of superannuation funds.[18] These are just two examples of helpful regulatory intervention: an agency charged with improving the efficiency of the superannuation industry would find many more.

6.3 Development of trust law

The control of rent-seeking behaviour requires that legal systems are developed that mitigate market power, moral hazard and asymmetric information and that enforce fiduciary duties, duties of care and duties of loyalty. In other countries, much effort is put into seeking to prevent such abuses through a combination of public and private law. Competition law seeks to prevent excessive abuse of market power,[19] tort law provides protection against damage to persons, property or the environment, contract law protects the parties to agreements, and criminal law protects individuals and society from theft, violence and murder.

We noted above that when the SIS Act was developed, its architects stopped short of including a mandatory code of conduct for those who manage superannuation funds. This may have been because they believed (or hoped) that a combination of competitive pressures and the other protections offered by trust law, or the more general common law, would be sufficient to prevent bad behaviour. Unfortunately, this was a misplaced belief. It is now clear that trust law in Australia, as it relates to superannuation, needs to be strengthened.

As discussed in Chapters 2 and 5, existing trust law places a duty on superannuation trustees to protect the interests of members and to avoid damaging conflicts of interest, and service providers have delegated duties in some cases. The formal responsibility (and the practical ability of the courts and regulators to

17 Morris, Nicholas and Rob Nicholls (2017) 'Do It Once, Get It Right: Wholesale Regulatory Intervention in Price and Cost Disclosure' (paper presented at the 25th Colloquium of Superannuation Researchers, UNSW Sydney, 6 July 2017).

18 Magnitude of insurance costs from Rainmaker Consulting (2017) *Superannuation Industry Review*. This report was prepared for Industry Super Australia and is the latest in a series of annual reports. Insurance requirements could be handled, at lower cost, by introducing a price-based allocation of the exclusive right to provide what would now be group insurance to Australians for a period.

19 See, e.g., European Commission Inquiry into Retail Banking (2007) *Report on the Retail Banking Sector Inquiry* (Commission Staff Working Document accompanying the Communication from the Commission – Sector Inquiry under *Art 17 of Regulation 1/2003 on retail banking (Final Report) [COM(2007) 33 final] SEC(2007) 106*, 31 January 2007).

enforce it) is, however, diluted the further down the chain one goes. In my view it is crucial that trustees are made, and enabled, to carry out their fiduciary obligations under trust law to protect members' interests. Their duty to decide what is, for example, the right balance of risk and reward for the members of the funds for which they are responsible must be emphasised and enforced. Amendments to legislation are needed to prevent 'opportunistic contractual eclipse' of trust law requirements, and to prevent the granting of member choice giving them an excuse to avoid these responsibilities. Member choice can then be achieved through switching funds (to a different set of trustees), and for those that remain dissatisfied with trustee performance, to self-management.

It would be possible to add to the SIS Act provisions similar to those applicable to companies in general. Section 20 (1) of the Australian Corporations Law (ACL),[20] for example, provides that "a person must not, in trade or commerce, engage in conduct that is unconscionable, within the meaning of the unwritten law from time to time". Section 21 of the ACL then creates a statutory version of what is meant by unconscionable conduct. A suitable amendment to the SIS Act would then say that trustees, and those who are responsible for the management of superannuation funds, "must act in the interests of trust beneficiaries within the meaning of the unwritten law from time to time" and then proceed to define what acting in the interest of beneficiaries means. The amendment would also need to specify that such action be consistent with regulations made by ASIC, APRA and the ATO, or the new regulatory agency, from time to time.

The revision to trust law would be most effective if there were general agreement in the industry as to what acting in the "interests of beneficiaries" comprised, and then all stakeholders recognised the practice. There is a successful precedent for such an approach, in the Australian telecommunications industry. In 2012, a *Telecommunications Consumer Protections Code* (TCP) was established. This covers all forms of consumer contact, advertising, contracts, billing, credit management, customer transfer and complaint handling.[21] It was developed by the industry, and the code is recognised by the industry regulator, the ACMA. Amendments to the code can be submitted by stakeholders when required.[22] The code is 'mandatory on breach', and the ACMA can issue a 'direction to comply' and, if necessary, apply to the Federal Court for a penalty to be imposed.[23]

20 Cth (2001), Corporations Act. The Corporations Act 2001 was subsequently modified by the Corporations Regulations 2001 (Statutory Rules 2001 No. 193 as amended) and the Corporations (Change of Incorporation) Regulations 2002 (Statutory Rules 2002 No. 168 as amended).

21 Grant, A. and H. Raiche (2012) 'Consumer Protection and Universal Service', ch. 7 in Alasdair Grant and David Howarth (2012) *Australian Telecommunications Regulation* (CCH Australian Ltd, 4th ed.), 381–386.

22 For example, the Communications Alliance submitted a revised version in October 2015, see www.tcpcode.com.au/comms-alliance-submits-revised-tcp-code/.

23 For an early example of the use of these powers, see www.tcpcode.com.au/acma-delivers-first-directions-to-comply-with-2012-tcp-code/.

6.4 Focused use of competitive pressures

In principle, market pressures in such a market should control self-seeking behaviour by agents, as hoped by Eugene Fama and many others.[24] If agents behave in a disloyal manner, which leads to low performance and high cost, then principals will switch, it is argued, to more loyal agents who offer better outcomes. If firms are unable to control their agency costs, then their competitors will gain market share by offering cheaper products. Management teams that fail to deliver the outcomes they promise will swiftly be replaced by those who are more faithful to those to whom they have duties.

Or so the story goes. But what has actually emerged, both in the case of Australian superannuation, and globally in the various excesses of the Global Financial Crisis, is almost the opposite. Short-term incentives to achieve personal or corporate gain at the expense of members and investors have dominated any concern over long-term market position or reputation. High-risk strategies are regularly pursued, even though the agents who pursue them know that they will be to the detriment of the principals they represent. How can this be?

The answer is that there is a fundamental asymmetry between the immediate and obvious financial gains that can be achieved by unscrupulous agents and the long-term, diffused, and poorly understood gains that could potentially be achieved for superannuation fund members. In practice, disengagement of members, short-termism, lack of trustee competence, information asymmetries, poor disclosure and exploitation of conflicts of interest all lead to an outcome where few agents who overcharge or who act against the interest of their clients are penalised. This contrasts with experience in some other industries, for example utilities and manufacturing, where anti-competitive pressures are mitigated by strong regulation, regulator-induced alterations to industry structure, and the effective implementation of competition law.

The large degree of separation between beneficiaries and those who make decisions on their behalf reduces pressures for switching, so that the market becomes 'sticky' and investor apathy (or lack of full understanding) permits rent-seeking to continue unabated. Remuneration systems, and asymmetries in the employment relationship, make it almost inevitable that those who design complex investment products will maximise short-term returns even if it is at the expense of unacceptable longer-term risk for members.[25]

24 See Fama, Eugene F. (1980) 'Agency Problems and the Theory of the Firm' 88(2) *Journal of Political Economy* 288.

25 For discussion of the incentives surrounding the creation of tail risk, see Noe, Thomas and H. Peyton Young (2014) 'The Limits of Compensation Strategies', in Morris and Vines (eds), above n 7, ch. 4.

In many other industries, competition law has been used successfully to prevent monopolistic or cartel-like behaviour. The UK,[26] the US,[27] and the European Union[28] all have well-developed anti-trust laws that are vigorously enforced. Ensuring competition is effective in controlling conflicts and the use of market power is, in these industries, an important method of ensuring that customers are well served and that charges are reasonable.

The post-GFC responses in the context of the wider financial services industry worldwide may provide guidance for how to make competition more effective, including requirements to break up dominant groups, improving switching mechanisms, reducing barriers to entry and, importantly, that regulators be given a clear primary duty to enhance competition. This means that a prime focus of their activity should be the introduction of measures to improve market discipline. The use of competitive tendering to be permitted to be a provider, as in Sweden and Chile, is a promising initiative that should put downward pressure on funds management costs. Competition law should be used to reduce collusion or anti-competitive cross-subsidy. Full disclosure of all costs, the development and publication of well-designed summary benchmarks, and a clear mandate for the regulator to prevent collusive behaviour, would all help to facilitate the competitive process. Perhaps the main message from this discussion is that if competition is to be used as a serious policy instrument, pro-competitive action needs to be taken by the relevant authorities.

The UK has made some progress in this regard, in the wider context of banking. The Independent Commission on Banking (ICB), for example, expressed concern that the financial crisis has weakened competition in banking in the UK due to the resultant increase in concentration.[29] The markets for personal customer and business accounts are particularly important because of the potential for cross-selling. In the past, switching rates have been low in the UK, with a significant proportion of customers believing that switching is difficult and risky.[30] Recommendations to increase competition by the ICB were: enhancing the

26 The *Competition Act 1998 (UK)* c 41 prohibits anti-competitive agreements and abuse of market dominance. The Enterprise Act 2002 (UK) c 40 also contains competition provisions regarding mergers, market investigations and participation in cartels.

27 A concise guide to the multiplicity of anti-trust laws in the US may be found at Washington State Office of the Attorney General, *Guide to Antitrust Laws*, available at www.atg.wa.gov/antitrust-guide.aspx.

28 See Ezrachi, Ariel (2012) *EU Competition Law – An Analytical Guide to the Leading Cases* (Hart Publishing, 3rd ed.).

29 Independent Commission on Banking (2011) *Interim Report: Consultation on Reform Options* (UK Government, April 2011).

30 Ibid. 33.

divestitures by Lloyds and the Royal Bank of Scotland (RBS),[31] assisting in the creation of new 'challenger' banks,[32] for improved means of switching between banks accounts to be introduced, reducing barriers to entry and improving customer choice, and for the Financial Conduct Authority (FCA) to be given a "clear primary duty to promote effective competition".[33]

One of the striking findings from the empirical analysis of Chapter 4 is that the funds that perform best are those that are run by the larger financial institutions for the benefit of their own managers and employees. These funds probably benefit from preferential access to information, and the ability to use systems and personnel from within the wider group on a basis that may imply an effective cross-subsidy. Certainly, their reported costs are far lower than their performance would imply was necessary. If this cross-subsidy is indeed occurring, then it is conferring a competitive advantage to such funds. Investigation of these issues, including the possible ring-fencing of such funds from the wider groups within which they are nested, would be helpful.

As discussed in Chapter 5 above, the complexity of the Australian superannuation industry hides considerable inter-relation between the various entities, and the 'insider' nature of Australian business practice means that the industry tends to act in concert rather than in competition.[34] Although difficult to track down, in my opinion this *de facto* collusion is worthy of further investigation by Australian competition authorities. This, in turn, means that either the ACCC needs to be given a greater role in ensuring that competition works, or, as in the UK, one of the other regulators, or the new agency, needs to be given a clear primary duty to promote effective competition. Consideration also needs to be given to whether the existing industrial structure, in which effective control over many aspects of the production chain is vested in a small number of banks and insurance companies, is too concentrated to permit effective competition.

In order to assist trustees and members in making decisions that facilitate competition and drive down fees and charges, it would be helpful for an 'official' set of benchmarks of fund performance to emerge. At present, several private organisations analyse product disclosure statements (PDSs) and seek to rank fund managers. However, each organisation that does this comes up with different

31 Which are already underway to meet the requirements of the European Commission.

32 Following its acquisition of HBOS, Lloyds has around 30% of UK current accounts.

33 United Kingdom, Independent Commission on Banking, above n29, 16.

34 Dignam and Galanis provide convincing evidence that Australia's listed market has many of the characteristics associated with insider systems. Dignam, Alan and Michael Galanis (2004) 'Australia Inside-Out: the Corporate Governance System of the Australian Listed Market' 28 *Melbourne University Law Review* 623. Insider systems can be made to work effectively, avoiding principal-agent and conflict of interest problems, if there is little separation of ownership and control. However, in the Australian superannuation system ownership (the members) and control (those who make operational decisions about the management of the funds) are quite widely separated.

rankings, depending on the particular aspect of fund operations they focus on.[35] A meaningful set of indicators would, at a minimum, cover administrative and funds management costs, risk profile, and net-of-costs returns. Developing such a set of benchmarks will require extensive consultation with the industry, a process that may lead to undue pressure being placed on those tasked with designing the benchmarks to adopt misleading indicators. However, it should be possible to develop a set of indicators that commanded widespread acceptance and the result would, in my opinion, be beneficial.[36]

6.5 Enhanced disclosure

Disclosure is a well-established method of seeking to prevent conflicts of interest and improve principal-agent relationships. In the US the *Securities Act* of 1933 codified disclosure practices that had previously been developed by J.P. Morgan and others.[37] The *Sarbanes-Oxley Act* and the *Global Legal Settlement* of 2002 increased supervisory oversight, established the *Public Company Accounting Oversight Board* (PCAOB) to supervise audits, and required investment banks to disclose their analysts' recommendations.[38] Most jurisdictions – including the US, the UK and Australia – now require public disclosure of specified information about financial products. However, the fundamental problem remains that the quality of service provided is not directly observable, the impact of investment decisions may take some time to become apparent, and market responses may be insufficient to prevent continued patronage of low performance managers and funds.[39]

There are several problems with the use of disclosure rules to ensure that trustees and members have sufficient information about the management of their superannuation funds. The first is that trustees and members have limited

35 For example, some focus on the personal characteristics of fund managers while others rely on simple measures of returns.

36 The creation of regulator-designed benchmarks, which now have wide industry recognition, has occurred in several UK utilities, notably water and transport.

37 Bahar, Rashid and Luc Thévenoz (2007) 'Conflicts of Interest: Disclosure, Incentives, and the Market' in Luc Thévenoz and Rashid Bahar (eds), *Conflicts of Interest: Corporate Governance and Financial Markets* (Kluwer Law International).

38 Crockett, Andrew, Trevor Harris, Frederic S. Mishkin and Eugene N. White (2003) 'Conflicts of Interest in the Financial Services Industry: What Should We Do About Them?' 4 *Geneva Reports on the World Economy* (Geneva and London: International Center for Monetary and Banking Studies and Centre for Economic Policy Research), 11. The Global Legal Settlement was an enforcement agreement with ten of the largest US investment firms by the SEC, the National Association of Securities Dealers (NASD) and NYSE.

39 See Ackerlof, George A. (1970) 'The Market for "Lemons": Quality Uncertainty and the Market Mechanism' 84 *Quarterly Journal of Economics* 488.

ability to understand complicated information. The second is that choice of what should be disclosed requires detailed understanding of the products being offered and the other matters of concern that need to be disclosed. The third is that often the things that need disclosure only become apparent after some catastrophic event, as for example in the aftermath of the Trio case discussed in Section 3.11 above.

In principle, superannuation funds in Australia are subject to a stringent disclosure regime, and regulatory authorities have relied on such disclosure, and the subsequent actions of well-informed investors and their agents, to prevent abuse. The disclosure requirements of the SIS Act are extensive, all funds are required to publish detailed PDSs, and APRA assembles much data that it publishes on a regular basis. As Chapter 3 describes, previous scandals in Australia led to calls from the 1970s onwards for mandatory disclosure,[40] and eventually to the *National Corporations Act* of 1991, which required disclosure of all relevant information to permit investors and their advisers to make informed decisions. These arrangements were strengthened following the Wallis Committee inquiry, leading to revised arrangements in the *Financial Services Reform Act* of 2001. An ASIC inquiry in 2002, a subsequent report in 2003, and regulations enacted in 2005 set out best practice arrangements for the disclosure of fees.[41] Every subsequent inquiry and most legislative changes have contained calls for actions to improve disclosure arrangements.

Yet problems over disclosure arrangements still persist. The Opes Prime and Trio frauds, and the Lehman judgment, all highlighted how investors were not provided with important relevant information. ASIC identified inadequate disclosure by financial advisers during its investigation into the Trio collapse in 2009.[42] The Parliamentary Joint Committee on Corporations and Financial Services found that nearly 6,090 Australians lost their money and concluded that most investors were not made aware of the risks.[43] Those who had invested in Trio through an SMSF had typically not been informed that they were ineligible to receive compensation under Pt 23 of the SIS Act, and adviser professional indemnity insurances were often inadequate. In its subsequent review of the fraud, the Treasury concluded that there was a lack of evidence to alert regulators

40 Including the Rae Committee of 1974.

41 Australian Securities and Investments Commission (2003) 'A Model for Fee Disclosure in Product Disclosure Statements for Investment Products' (Report No. 23, July 2003), available at www.asic.gov.au/asic/pdflib.nsf/LookupByFileName/Fees_disclosure_report.pdf/$file/Fees_disclosure_report.pdf. The fee disclosure model was subsequently updated in June 2004, and then superseded by the requirements of the Corporations Amendment Regulations 2005 (No. 1) (Cth). For detail on the 2005 regulations, see Australian Securities and Investments Commission, 'Disclosing Fees and Costs in PDSs and Periodic Statements' (Regulatory Guide No. 97, November 2011).

42 Australian Securities and Investments Commission (2013) 'Advice on Self-managed Superannuation Funds: Specific Disclosure Requirements and SMSF Costs' (Consultation Paper No. 216).

43 Parliamentary Joint Committee on Corporations and Financial Services (2012) *Parliament of Australia: Inquiry into the Collapse of Trio Capital.*

prior to the collapse, and an "expectations gap . . . about who is responsible for managing investment risks".[44]

It remains difficult to identify the majority of investment management costs for many funds. Embedded corporate funds that are probably benefitting from cross-subsidies within a larger group still report unbelievably low costs. Disclosure of conflicts of interest is still not universal. Most members, and many trustees, have difficulty understanding and analysing the information that is available. The *Super System Review* called for further improvements to disclosure rules, many of which have yet to be implemented, although in February 2017 ASIC issued a new version of Regulatory Guide 97 (RG97).[45]

Even with full disclosure it is hard for trustees and members to understand which managers provide the most cost-effective service. The collection and reporting, in a form that can be widely understood, of the full costs of investment management is essential.[46] Conflicts of interest need to be clearly identified and, where permitted, made clearer to all parties concerned. The provision of free market comparative data, and the development and regular dissemination of well-designed key performance indicators are important steps. The Trio and Lehman cases in Australia highlight how difficult it is, in a world of asymmetric information, to know in advance exactly what needs to be disclosed. Reducing complexity and simplifying fund management products are a necessary part of enabling trustees and members to understand what they are being sold. It is essential to make sure that the full costs of managing superannuation funds are disclosed, including the investment management and other costs of those to whom responsibility is delegated. This will require that third-party service providers introduce fair cost allocation processes, which in turn will need to be certified.

Collection and reporting of performance data has been proposed for different reasons, including the assessment of professional performance within a self-regulatory regime, the assessment of standards of service within a regulated regime, and for prudential monitoring. Benchmarking performance can provide credibility to self-regulation and improve its effectiveness. Diagnostic statistics of network resilience and stress testing based on systemic risk have been advocated for prudential supervision. Reporting of relative performance, using Key Performance Indicators (KPIs), has been used extensively in regulated industries, to ensure that standards of service and desired outcomes are not being diminished in the drive for improved efficiency. League tables are publicly reported in these industries to provide reputational incentives.

44 See Commonwealth (2013) *Review of the Trio Capital Fraud and Assessment of the Regulatory Framework* (Department of Treasury), 5.

45 ASIC (2017) *Disclosing Fees and Costs in PDSs and Periodic Statements* (Regulatory Guide 97, February 2017). As discussed below, this still has limited potential effect, as it excludes annuities and applies to retail level disclosure only.

46 APRA is currently considering the most appropriate way to achieve this. Hopefully, the consultation process will lead to the, much overdue, provision of such information.

In order to overcome the lack of ability, resources and willingness of members and trustees to understand the information that is provided, it is necessary to make this as simple as possible, and to make comparisons as easy as possible. Having an 'official' benchmark for funds, accepted by all stakeholders, on which they can rely would be very helpful. Simplifying products to a level that a simple set of metrics can describe attributes, performance and risk would also be valuable. Disclosure of conflicts of interest should become a matter of course, and any failure to do so should be penalised heavily once it becomes apparent.

6.6 Developing a viable alternative fund

We now turn to an approach that may help to cut through the labyrinthine difficulties discussed earlier in this chapter. This is the creation of a publicly administered, low cost and passively managed fund that is made available to all Australian superannuation fund members. Although the reforms we have discussed above are all both necessary and helpful, past experience suggests that reform in these areas will be slow and is likely to be incomplete. The policy option of setting up a new fund is aimed to short-circuit these problems by harnessing competition and choice in order to encourage improvement in the net-of-costs performance of the industry as a whole.

To create this alternative fund, it will be necessary for contributions to be paid into a single fund that had a mandate to invest them passively in a balanced portfolio.[47] This could be run by an entity that was directly responsible to Parliament. The combination of centralised administration and passive management would mean that costs could be considerably lower than those currently incurred through decentralised administration and predominately active management. As we have detailed in Section 4.5 above, passive management is likely to outperform the majority of existing funds, after costs, and so a significant number of people could be expected choose this option. The new fund would provide a benchmark against which other providers could be judged. In addition, many of the principal-agent and conflict of interest problems discussed above would not arise.

As with established practice in, for example, New Zealand Kiwisaver, participation in the new fund would not be compulsory, but would be the default where no other active choice was made. Employees starting new employment could be automatically enrolled unless they chose otherwise.[48] Existing employees could opt in to the new fund directly or through their employer, for all or part of their

47 The FSI interim report noted scope for fees to be driven down by all new members being placed in the same default fund, with management of the fund auctioned on the basis of fees, citing successful experience in Chile. Commonwealth (2014) *Financial System Inquiry: Interim Report* (July 2014), 2–112.

48 In New Zealand, new employees can opt out of Kiwisaver from week 2 to week 8 of their employment.

contributions and transfer funds from existing schemes through a 'rollover'.[49] People who are not employees, such as the self-employed and those currently seeking work, would be able to make contributions directly to the new fund.

Those who became members of the fund would have the ability to:

- choose between a limited number of schemes with different risk profiles (for example, balanced, conservative or growth), although those who made no explicit choice would be allocated to a default;
- transfer between options at any time;
- contribute up to 9.5% (or such higher rate as is determined in subsequent years); and
- make voluntary contributions directly to the fund;

In New Zealand, when Kiwisaver was established, the government contributed $1,000 to the fund on entry. Such an inducement should be considered to encourage use of the fund in, say, the first five years.

Establishment of the new fund would require an Act, both to set out the administrative arrangements for the fund administration, and to define the duties of employers with regard to the fund. The Act would need to, inter alia:

- require employers to provide name, tax file number and address of all employees subject to auto-enrolment;
- ensure that suitable information about the fund, including its performance and costs, was provided to all employees and others who became members, or who considered doing so; and
- set up the process for the transfer of contributions from employer payroll systems, and suitable interaction with ATO systems.

Employers would be allowed to set a suitable default risk allocation for their members who did not select their own, and permit employers to contract out where they chose, on behalf of their employees, and to use a recognised superannuation scheme instead. However, this choice should be subject to strict controls as to the provision of comparative cost and performance data to employees.

Ideally, administration and fund management should be independent of the existing financial services industry, carried out by suitably qualified public officials. However, and perhaps in a transition period, if this was felt to be impossible to achieve, a properly competitive tender process should be established to choose any commercial provider of these services.

49 'Rollover' between schemes is a well-established practice in Australia, part of the 'choice architecture' developed in the latest 'Stronger Super' proposals. See Cth (2010), *Stronger Super*, available at https://strongersuper.treasury.gov.au/content/publications/government_response/downloads/Stronger_Super.pdf, especially Recommendation 1.7 relating to rollovers to MYSuper products and Recommendation 10.15 relating to eligible rollover funds (ERFs).

Responsibility for the new fund should be entrusted to a new entity, with authority and funding provided directly from Parliament. Governance arrangements could include a role for the new regulatory agency. The entity would be responsible for:

- administering the fund and investing contributions;
- providing information about the fund to employers for distribution to employees;
- allocating new employees to a default scheme and sending the employee an investment statement for that scheme; and
- receiving contributions from employers and others.

Passive management is much less difficult and costly than active management, but some effort is still required to ensure that the portfolio of assets held does genuinely track the relevant indices. Vanguard and others offer such products, usually with fees some way below the market average. It may be that acquiring the necessary expertise will prove hard within a public sector environment, and that outsourcing of the (passive) management of the fund, or parts of the fund, may be more cost-effective. In this case, procurement using genuinely competitive tenders should ensure minimum cost.[50]

A major issue highlighted in various places in this book is the fact that DC schemes pass longevity and underperformance risks on to members, and thus do not provide the certainty about incomes in retirement that DB schemes do. A further advantage of setting up a new, publicly controlled, fund is that it could potentially offer a more 'DB-like' outcome to its members, by introducing risk pooling between members and tailoring asset allocation to their needs.[51] As discussed in Chapter 2, there are a number of ways of sharing risks, including collective DC schemes (CDC – as implemented in Denmark and the Netherlands) and lifecycle schemes (as marketed in the US).[52] Under a CDC plan, the employer pays a fixed contribution, and provides an expected or target benefit, but this is not guaranteed – actual pay-outs depend on the level of funding of the scheme in the year in question.

50 The idea of making funds tender for the right to run low-cost default funds has also been canvassed by Jim Minfie of the Grattan Institute: Minfie, Jim (2014) 'Super Sting: How to Stop Australians Paying Too Much for Superannuation' (Grattan Institute, April 2014), 34.

51 The potential benefits of public administration, provided suitable safeguards against political or bureaucratic interferences can be provided, include the provision of "social insurance that is either expensive or unavailable in private markets". Willmore, Larry (1999) 'Public versus Private Provision of Pensions' (Discussion Paper of the United Nations Department of Economic and Social Affairs, revised June 1999), available at www.un.org/esa/esa98dp1.pdf.

52 The various ways of making DC schemes more 'DB-like' are reviewed in Cooper, Jeremy R. (2014) 'Are Defined Contribution Pension Plans Fit for Purpose in Retirement?' 37 *Seattle University Law Review* 511–532, 525–527. Cooper argues that a "properly integrated retirement plan" needs to protect contributors from inflation, deviation from expected outcome and longevity risks.

Lifecycle schemes aim to tailor asset allocation based on the age of the member, thus delivering a better retirement outcome.[53]

The 2012 OECD Working Group on Private Pensions set out a ten-point roadmap for the good design of DC pension plans, which includes the establishment of default life-cycle investment options and the promotion of risk-hedging mechanisms against longevity risk.[54] These mechanisms are difficult and expensive for individuals to acquire on an individual basis, but can be developed on a group basis. Specialized products required to manage risk include insurance to protect against loss of capital or income,[55] an indexed income stream to deal expressly with inflation, and a lifetime annuity to deal with longevity risk. Acquisition of competitively priced insurance is much more feasible on a group basis, as is the development of an indexed income stream. If risk is pooled across the fund members, it can be invested in higher risk (and return) assets and earn an illiquidity premium, which individual members could not on their own.

In addition, the fund would be better placed to deal with longevity risk. As we have discussed in Chapter 2, the annuity market in Australia is in its infancy and annuities are not yet available to individuals at prices that make them a feasible risk management mechanism. The new fund would be of sufficient size that it could guarantee a minimum income stream to its members for their post-retirement lives, related to their contributions, on a cost effective basis. It would be possible for it to manage its balance sheet such that this guarantee was suitably insured, at preferential rates it would be able to negotiate with the major insurers. Alternatively, the guarantee could be provided by government, as in the Swiss and German examples outlined in Chapter 2.

There are three major difficulties with the implementation of such an approach today. The first is that substantial assets have already been contributed to the existing funds, and substantial expenditures have been incurred by the firms that manage them, including in IT systems. The second is that it may be difficult to protect a publicly administered fund from being influenced by political pressures, and to prevent the funds from being diverted to achieve short-term political objectives, against members' interests. The third is that costs of administration and funds management may not be as low as hoped if the activities are carried out within the public service.

53 See Basu, Anup, Alistair Byrnes and Michael E. Drew (2009) 'Dynamic Lifecycle Strategies for Target Date Retirement Funds' (Griffith Business School, Working Paper No. 2009-02), available at http://equella.rcs.griffith.edu.au/research/file/239b5535-4e45-804c-5b7c-0535764151bf/1/2009-02-dynamic-lifecycle-strategies-for-target-date-retirement-funds.pdf.

54 OECD (2013) 'Design and Delivery of Defined Contribution (DC) Pension Schemes – Policy Challenges and Recommendations', available at www.oecd.org/daf/fin/private-pensions/DCPensionDesignHighlights.pdf. See also OECD (2012), Pensions Outlook, available at www.oecd.org/finance/private-pensions/50560110.pdf.

55 Australia does not have a government guarantee protecting DC plan members in the event of failure of their superannuation fund, except that the government has discretion in the case of fraud to compensate a plan if it is "in the public interest". See Cth (1993), *Superannuation Industry (Supervision) Act 1993*, pt 23.

The second and third problems will require careful attention. Hopefully, the Australian political system is capable of establishing a protected regime, directly accountable to Parliament, which can resist the government of the day using the funds for its own political ends. As the new entity will be competing in the open market for member's funds, it will be in the interests of the public servants that run it to try to minimise costs and maximise performance. Their remuneration systems can be designed to seek to achieve such an end. Neither problem is insurmountable.

To gain widespread acceptance of the new fund, a gradualist approach will be necessary. The new entity would compete for members with existing funds. Or, as has been pioneered in New Zealand and in the UK, enrolment into the fund could become the default option (often termed 'auto-enrolment') where the member makes no explicit alternative choice. Its lower administrative costs and the lower costs of passive management should make it easily able to outperform the expensive actively managed funds that currently exist. Over time, it would grow in size and provide a benchmark against which other funds could be judged. This would have the dual benefit of providing a lower cost, higher performance alternative for future contributions and also putting pressure on the existing funds to improve performance and lower costs. Transfer of assets from existing funds would make the process faster, but would need to be controlled carefully to avoid unnecessary disruption to the wider financial services industry.

7 Conclusions

This book, and the research it summarises, provides evidence that all is not well in the Australian superannuation industry. Fees and costs are high and performance seems to be poor by international standards. With hindsight, the various decisions made during the evolution of the Australian superannuation industry were unfortunate. Incomes in retirement for a generation of Australians will be lower than could have been achieved if a different set of decisions had been made. The failures of the Australian system provide useful lessons for other systems worldwide.

Comparison with a hypothetical benchmark is a useful method of assessing fund performance. Such a benchmark can be constructed by exploring the returns that could have been expected if all Australian superannuation funds had been invested passively in a balanced portfolio, with reasonable fees and expenses. How the relative performance might have varied if alternative benchmarks had been chosen provides a test of the robustness of such an approach.

Using this technique, and based on a detailed micro-simulation model of financial outcomes, it was estimated that Australian funds, in aggregate, underperformed the 'balanced portfolio' benchmark by a total of $900 million over the 20-year period from 1 July 1996 to 30 June 2016. The actual performance of the Australian funds delivered an internal rate of return of 4.5%, when the benchmark strategy could have achieved 7.2%, a difference of 2.7 percentage points.

Sectoral disaggregation of the results confirms the findings of previous literature that corporate and public sector funds do better than other fund classes relative to the benchmark. This is consistent with the hypothesis developed in this book that a greater degree of separation between members and those who manage their funds leads to poorer net-of-costs performance. Retail funds perform particularly poorly, mostly because of their much higher fees and charges. SMSFs also perform poorly, perhaps partly because they do not have access to asset classes that are available to institutional investors and thus rely on retail products. Industry funds have a performance that is intermediate between the two extremes.

The recent *Financial System Inquiry* in Australia has triggered submissions and reports that show that the concerns expressed in this book are shared by many others. However, the accumulation of funds in Australia is only in its infancy: in 20 years' time the assets of superannuation funds will be at least three times what they are today. It is crucial that the mistakes made in the past are not compounded in the future, and that the next 20 years see the maximum possible accumulation of funds to support retirement. This means that fundamental reform is needed.

The *Super System Review* and the *Future of Financial Advice* (FOFA) reforms both represented steps in the right direction. Cooper's instincts that costs need to be driven down (through the *Stronger Super* reforms) and that simpler products provided part of the answer (through the introduction of *MySuper*) are both correct. However, subsequent implementation of their recommendations has illustrated how the power of industry lobbying can water down such proposals.[1] My view is that the endemic principal-agent and conflict of interest problems remain embedded in the system and that the complexity of the present industrial structure inevitably imposes unacceptable costs. Therefore, further solutions need to be investigated.

A single, well-resourced and empowered regulatory agency with a clear remit to improve the efficiency of the industry and a clear primary duty to promote competition should be created. Stronger use of trust law is needed to enforce the fiduciary duties of trustees, and removal of impediments to trustees taking full responsibility (such as member choice and 'contractual eclipse' through the trust deed). The stewardship of trustees should be enhanced, to include better selection processes and monitoring of performance.

Improving market discipline is also important, through the vigorous use of competition law to combat collusion and anti-competitive cross-subsidies, through effective disclosure and dissemination of suitable benchmarks, through the use of competitive tendering, and through the break-up of dominant groups, improving switching mechanisms and reducing barriers to entry.

Full disclosure of all investment management costs and conflicts of interest, combined with reduced complexity of products (to enable members and trustees to understand what they are being sold) is essential. Once this is available, the relationship between fees charged and costs incurred should be monitored carefully, by a well-resourced and empowered regulator, in order to ensure that super-normal profits are not being made.

Finally, a publicly administered agency that offers a centrally administered, passively managed, alternative fund to which anyone can contribute has potential to provide a performance benchmark, and to divert market share from higher cost alternatives. This, apparently simple, policy initiative could make a significant difference to the situation.

1 Minfie, Jim (2014) 'Super Sting: How to Stop Australians Paying Too Much for Superannuation' (Grattan Institute, April 2014) argues that *Stronger Super*, for example, is not likely to put significant downward pressure on fees.

Annex A

Timeline of key legislation and events

1849	Australian Mutual Provident (AMP) founded	
1884	Probate duty introduced on policies of British companies, worldwide	Increased competitive advantage of Australian companies
1889	Speculative investment 'bubble' burst, revealing massive frauds	
1901	*Commonwealth of Australia Constitution Act 1901* (Cth), S. 51(xxiii)	Gave government power to legislate for pensions
1908	*Invalid and Old Age Pensions Act 1908*	Introduced means-tested, flat rate, state pension from age 65
1910	Pension age for eligible women reduced to 60	
1915	*Income Tax Assessment Act*	
1927	Royal Commission on National Insurance	
1928	*National Insurance Bill*	Lapsed in 1929 when government defeated
1936	*Income Tax Assessment Act*	Formalised tax concessions for superannuation
1936, 1938	Australian Fixed Trusts (AFT), First Australian Unit Trust (FAUT) and Unit Trusts Ltd established	
1938	*National Health and Pensions Bill, Superannuation and Family Benefits Act*	Enabling legislation for establishing state-run superannuation scheme, never implemented because of war
1941	Introduction of bank licensing, regulated by Commonwealth Bank	
1945	Levy and payroll tax into National Welfare Fund	No direct link, National Welfare Fund abolished in 1985

(continued)

(continued)

1955	Universal Flexible Trusts (UFT) established	
1959	ANZ Public Retirement Fund and Australian Capital Fund (ACF) established	
1961, 1963	*Income Tax and Social Services Contribution Assessment Act*	Established tax concessions for superannuation
1965	*Fairfax v Commissioner of Taxation 114 CLR1*	Upholds Commonwealth's ability to control superannuation fund through taxation powers
1971	Collapse of Garretty Group and Mineral Securities Australia (MinSec)	
1973	*National Superannuation Committee of Inquiry*. Chairman Keith Hancock.	
1975	*Social Services Act (nos 34 and 110)*	Means test removed for those over 69, pension indexed to average wages
1976	Hancock Inquiry	Recommended partially contributory universal pension with earnings-related supplement
1977	*Cabinet Decision 3435 of 20 July 1977*	Rejected Hancock recommendations
1980	Hill Samuel cash management trust established	
1981	Campbell Committee of Inquiry into the Australian Financial System	Recommended deregulation of the financial services industry
1982	Bankers Trust enters retail market	
1983	*Statement of Accord (Prices and Incomes Accord)*	Between ALP and ACTU. Hawke/Keating government support for employee superannuation
1883	*Economy – Ministerial statement, P. Keating*	Began reform of taxation of superannuation
1984	CBUSS created (building industry)	First industry fund, with Board comprising employer and employee representatives
1986	Accord MkII includes 3% superannuation contribution in lieu of wage rise	Endorsed by the Conciliation and Arbitration Commission February 1986 and High Court in May 1986
1987	*Occupational Superannuation Standards Act 1987 (OSSA)*	Insurance and Superannuation Commission (ISC) established
1989	Better Incomes: Retirement Income Policy into the Next Century' published	'Twin pillars' of age pension and private superannuation, rejecting national superannuation scheme

1990	Conference of Major Superannuation Funds (CMSF) holds its first annual conference	
1991	Introduction of Superannuation Guarantee Charge	Implemented 1992
1991	Investment and Financial Services Association (IFSA) created	
1992	Senate Select Committee 'Safeguarding Super – The Regulation of Superannuation'	
1993	*Superannuation Industry (Supervision) Act 1993 (SIS Act).*	Fitzgerald Report advocates increasing household savings via superannuation
1995	Budget establishes principle of government co-contributions	'Saving for our future' statement accompanies budget
1997	Wallis Financial System Inquiry	Advocates superannuation choice
1997	*Income Tax Assessment Act 1997*	Basis of most current superannuation tax law
1998	Australian Prudential Regulation Authority (APRA) established on 1 July 1998	
1999	SIS Act amended to establish SMSFs	SMSFs to be regulated by the Australian Taxation Office
2001	*Financial Services Reform Act*	Creation of single licensing and disclosure approach
2004	*Superannuation Safety Amendment Act*	Introduced licensing for large eligible funds, and employee choice of fund
2005	Budget abolishes superannuation surcharge	*Transition to Retirement* introduced
2006	Budget introduces 'Simpler Super', mostly implemented 2007	Removes tax on lump sums and pensions, abolishes reasonable benefit limits
2008	Superannuation Advisory Group established by Minister Sherry	
2008	Henry Review into 'Australia's Future Tax System' commenced	Recommends Superannuation Guarantee rate increase to 12%
2009	*Schedule 2 Tax Laws Amendment (2009 Budget Measures No. 1) Act 2009*	Government co-contribution for low income members reduced temporarily (until 2014)
2009	*Social Security And Other Legislation Amendment (Pension Reform and Other 2009 Budget Measures) Act 2009*	Raises qualifying age for age pension by six months every two years from 2017
2009	Review into the governance, efficiency, structure and operation of Australia's superannuation system commenced (Cooper Review)	

(continued)

(continued)

2010	Report on 'Strategic Issues for the Retirement Income System' published	As part of Henry Review
2010	Cooper Review reports published	Recommends MySuper, optimising system (SuperStream) and reforms to self-managed superannuation
2010	Government accepts Henry Review recommendations	
2011	*Governance of Australian Government Superannuation Schemes Act*	Reforms to reporting standards, implementation of MySuper and SuperStream
2012	Government announces increases in tax on concessional contributions	
2013	Future of Financial Advice reforms implemented	But subsequently watered down by incoming Abbott government
2014	Financial System Inquiry	Focus on fees and costs of superannuation, active management

Annex B

Reviews of the superannuation system

Senate Select Committee 1995

In February 1995, the Senate Select Committee on Superannuation reviewed the early working of the SGC.[1] During its inquiry, it received submissions that claimed that the SGC had impacted employment levels and caused casualisation of the workforce. It observed that Australia was unique in that "the payment of compulsory superannuation is operated through private sector organisations rather than operating through a central fund or on a pay-as-you-go basis".[2] Concern was expressed that the *Occupational Superannuation Standards Act* (OSSA) was ineffective in controlling trustees.[3] Concern over lack of competition among funds also led to calls for greater employee choice.[4]

Drew and Stanford 2003

An academic review of the superannuation system carried out in 2003 concluded that "overall, we find that the New Superannuation System is inefficient, low return and high cost", and identified the "very substantial principal-and-agent problems that exist in the industry".[5] Drew and Stanford highlighted that the new system meant that members bore the investment risk, which they regarded as "high and increasing". They also devoted considerable effort to defining and exploring the role of the Trustees in the new system, and provided useful extracts from a 'Model Code' which set out their duties.[6]

1 Select Committee on Superannuation (1995) *Parliament of Australia, Super Guarantee – Its Track Record* (Cth). The Committee made a variety of reports on superannuation, beginning with *Safeguarding Super – The Regulation of Superannuation* in June 1992.
2 Select Committee on Superannuation 1995, above n 1, 2.15.
3 *Occupational Superannuation Standards Act 1987* (Cth); because the only available sanctions, withdrawal of complying status for tax concessions, was too draconian to be used. Ibid. 2.16.
4 Costello, Peter (1995) 'Address to Australian Superannuation Funds Association (ASFA)' (2 Nov 1995).
5 Drew, Michael E. and Jon D. Stanford (2003) 'A Review of Australia's Compulsory Superannuation Scheme after a Decade' (Discussion Paper No. 322, University of Queensland School of Economics, March 2003) 23, 2.

A particular issue Drew and Stanford raised was the lack of competition in the new superannuation system "arising from members having no choice of fund either in relation to contributions or [to] accumulated balances".[7] They noted that the Commonwealth Government announced a policy of choice of fund in 1996 and introduced a detailed proposal in the 1997 Budget. However, the relevant Bill was defeated in the Senate in August 2001. A subsequent bill was referred to the Senate Select Committee on Superannuation on August 21, but not subsequently enacted.[8]

Parliamentary Joint Committee 2007

In 2007, the *Parliamentary Joint Committee on Corporations and Financial Services* (PJCCFS) carried out an inquiry into the structure and operation of the superannuation industry.[9] This focused on reporting requirements, including disclosure issues, and on the security of superannuation funds, including capital adequacy and compensation arrangements. It also considered portability, exit fees and 'lost' superannuation. A particular issue examined was the use of member funds for promotional expenditure, for which "industry support . . . . was widespread", but on which the Committee could see a "potential application of *Australian Accounting Standards Board* (AASB) standards to the superannuation industry".[10] The Committee also expressed concern to ensure that on "payments to third party service providers . . . members are getting a reasonable deal on these transactions, they are conducted at arm's length and overpricing is not occurring".[11] Concern was also expressed over the "inadequacy of current regulatory arrangements for the provision of basic, limited advice on superannuation".[12]

6 Ibid. 11. These duties include that the trustee shall consider (a) The trust funds as a whole, the nature, composition and purposes of the trust and its anticipated duration; (b) The needs and circumstances of the beneficiaries; (c) The suitability of the investments held and of investments proposed; (d) The need for diversification of investments; (e) The administrative costs, including commission, fees, charges and duties payable, of making or varying any investment; (f) The taxation consequences of making or varying any investment; (g) The possible impact of inflation or deflation; Further explanation of the legal basis of these duties is given in Ford, Harold and W.A. Lee (1990) *Principles of the Law of Trusts* (Law Book Company) and Lee, W.A. (1989) (ed.), *Model Trustee Code for Australian States and Territories* (Working Party); The definition of a Trust under Australian law is given in Meagher, R.P. and W.M.C. Gummow (1986) *Jacobs' Law of Trusts in Australia* (Butterworths, 5th ed.) 7.

7 Drew and Stanford, above n 5, 13. These issues are discussed further in Drew, Michael E. and Jon D. Stanford (2003) 'Principal and Agent Problems in Superannuation Funds' 36(1) *Australian Economic Review* 98.

8 Select Committee on Superannuation, *Provisions of the Superannuation Legislation Amendment (Choice of Superannuation Funds) Bill 2002 (Cth)* (2002). The committee reported in November 2002, raising issues which needed improvement before successful implementation would be possible.

9 Parliamentary Joint Committee on Corporations and Financial Services (2007) *Inquiry into the Structure and Operation of the Superannuation Industry* (Parliament of Australia).

10 Ibid. xiv.

11 Ibid. xv.

12 Ibid. xviii.

A particular focus of PJCCFS attention was legislative barriers to cost-effective financial advice,[13] the ways advisers were remunerated, and conflicts of interest related to commission-based remuneration models.[14] Concerns were reported over the relationship between advisers and superannuation product providers:

> Although consumers are aware of the sales motivations of the supplier's representative when visiting a car dealership, in the financial planning sector the incentives may not be as apparent to consumers where a financial services company integrates product supply and sales through its team of financial planners.[15]

The PJCCFS accepted that "commission-based remuneration generates conflicts of interest for advisers that can lead to inappropriate advice", but rejected the prohibition of commissions on superannuation products,[16] and instead focused on shelf fees.[17] Disclosure of conflicts of interest "needs to be more effective to ensure consumers are better able to measure their likely effect on the quality of advice they receive".[18] The report also discussed reasons for the growth in SMSFs.[19] The Committee made thirty-one recommendations for the improvement of the Australian superannuation system, including that exit fees in excess of the actual transaction costs of exiting the member be prohibited prospectively.[20]

Ripoll Inquiry 2009

The newly elected Labor government initiated an inquiry in 2009 into the corporate collapses in the Australian financial services sector, especially the problems at Storm Financial and Opes Prime.[21] This highlighted particularly the role of financial advisers, and the way they were remunerated. It made eleven recommendations, including that a fiduciary duty should be imposed on licensed financial advisers to place their clients' interests ahead of their own; that the government

13 Ibid. 99.

14 Ibid. 137.

15 Ibid. 150.

16 Ibid. xix. Prohibition of commissions was rejected because 'many consumers cannot afford . . . up-front fee-for-service advice'. The Committee view is elaborated at ibid. 158.

17 Recommending that the industry move towards a more competitive method of meeting the cost of product listings, and ultimately moving towards fees-for-advice.

18 Parliamentary Joint Committee on Corporations and Financial Services, *Inquiry into the Structure and Operation of the Superannuation Industry* (Parliament of Australia), xx.

19 Ibid. 179, ch. 8. At the time the report was written, SMSFs accounted for 99% of all funds and 23% of total superannuation savings: at xxi.

20 Ibid. xxiii, xxvi; Parliament of Australia (2009) *Review into the Governance, Efficiency, Structure and Operation of Australia's Superannuation System, Phase 2: Operation and Efficiency Issues Paper*, 26.

21 Parliamentary Joint Committee on Corporations and Financial Services (2009) Parliament of Australia, *Inquiry into Financial Products and Services in Australia: Final Report* (Cth).

should find the most appropriate way to abolish product commissions; and that ASIC be given increased resources and legislative powers to suspend or cancel licences where licensees were not complying with their obligations. It also suggested more regular 'shadow shopping' by ASIC, a new independent standards board, and the development of a statutory last resort compensation fund.[22]

The *Ripoll Inquiry* led to the *Future of Financial Advice* (FOFA) reforms announced in April 2010.[23] These included the banning of 'conflicted remuneration structures', including commissions, and a call for the expansion of low-cost 'simple advice'. However, the ban on conflicted remuneration structures does not apply to general insurance, basic banking products, product advice to wholesale clients or advice where the client pays the benefit to the provider (as in fee-for-service arrangements). FOFA also includes opt-in arrangements, in that advice providers are obliged to renew their client's agreement to ongoing fees every two years.[24] Compliance was mandatory from 1st July 2013.

The FOFA reforms have led to intense lobbying from the financial services industry, and particularly by the *Financial Planning Association* (FPA) and the *Association of Financial Advisers* (AFA). Financial planners argued that forcing them to see clients once every two years would create an onerous administrative burden.[25] The *Finance Industry Council of Australia* (FICA) sought to reopen discussions, including about the selling of products in bank branches, and has accused the Labor government of favouring the Industry Funds.[26] This lobbying was effective in persuading the incoming Coalition government to make changes to the FOFA arrangements which had the effect of diluting them.

Super System Review 2010

In 2009, the Minister for Financial Services, Superannuation and Corporate Law[27] commissioned a Committee chaired by Jeremy Cooper to examine the Australian superannuation system.[28] The *Super System Review* examined and

22 Shadow shopping involves ASIC staff acting as clients to explore the terms that are offered.

23 Enacted in the *Corporations Amendment (Future of Financial Advice) Act (No. 67) 2012* (Cth). An overview of the reforms is provided at Australian Securities and Investments Commission, *Future of Financial Advice* www.asic.gov.au/asic/ASIC.NSF/byHeadline/Future%20of%20financial%20advice.

24 However, ASIC has the ability to exempt advisers from this requirement if they are satisfied that the adviser is signed up to a suitable professional code. ASIC issued a revised version of *Regulatory Guide 98 – Licensing: Administrative Action against Financial Services Providers (RG 98)* on 28 June 2012.

25 St Anne, Christine (2012) *A Super History: How Australia's $1 Trillion+ Superannuation Industry Was Made* (Major Street),, 248.

26 Ibid. 238.

27 The Hon Chris Bowen MP.

28 The Terms of Reference of the *Super System Review* are to be found at Australian Government, *Terms of Reference* www.supersystemreview.gov.au/content/terms_of_reference.aspx. The *Review* was required to 'comprehensively examine and analyse the governance, efficiency, structure and operation of Australia's superannuation system, including both compulsory and voluntary aspects'.

analysed the governance, efficiency, structure and operation of Australia's superannuation system, including both compulsory and voluntary aspects, and reported in July 2010. This review involved extensive submissions from interested parties and discussions with most participants in the Australian superannuation industry.

The *Super System Review* highlighted a number of further issues, including that members' interests were not always treated as paramount, that the efficiency of the system was not regulated, that the system was too complex and opaque, that disclosure to members had failed to achieve its objectives, and that there was ambiguity about the role of trustees. Past performance data had been given too much prominence, there were inadequate accounting and financial reporting standards, fees were too high, and the frequency of changes to rules could undermine confidence in the system.[29] The review also identified that in some cases, "trustee self-interest has hindered rationalisations that are clearly in members' interests".[30] The review also proposed changes to the regulatory system, described below.[31] Recently, concern has been expressed that APRA and ASIC are under-resourced for the task of regulating effectively what is now a large and complex industry effectively.[32]

The reasons for the problems identified by the review included that members often cannot choose the fund to which they belong; that there is a lack of price awareness; that members have a lack of interest in their super; that there are limited incentives for agency vigilance over prices, and that the system is so complex that many consumers lack confidence to make decisions. Lack of information and transparency about fees and performance was found to lead to a lack of comparability between funds. Paperwork and 'frictions' in changing funds were said to be substantial.

29 Parliament of Australia (2010) *Review into the Governance, Efficiency, Structure and Operation of Australia's Superannuation System, Final Report.*

30 Ibid. 7.

31 Details of these recommendations are summarised in ibid. [5.10], 17–8.

32 Boyd, Tony (2012) 'Regulators Face Harsh Reality' *Australian Financial Review* (Sydney, 9 May 2012); APRA highlights the potential inadequacy of trustees' financial, technical and human resources in Australian Prudential Regulation Authority, 'Prudential Practice Guide: SPG 221 — Adequacy of Resources' (November 2013); Super System Review Panel (2010) *Review into the Governance, Efficiency, Structure and Operation of Australia's Superannuation System: Final Report ('Super System Review'), Part Two: Recommendation Packages*, 9.6.1, ch. 10 identifies both needs for increased resources and authorities, and the scope for regulator efficiencies; the potential risks of under-resourced regulators were discussed in Stanford, Jon D. (2003) 'Is Superannuation Safe? The Background and the Issues' 36 *Australian Economic Review* 1, 79; Grant, Richard (2005) 'Australia's Corporate Regulators — the ACCC, ASIC and APRA' (Research Brief No. 16, Parliamentary Library, Parliament of Australia) discussed the challenges of co-ordination between regulators and the difficulties of ensuring participation of stakeholders in the regulatory process.

The Committee developed ten recommendation packages,[33] with the two major recommendations of the Review described as:

> The **MySuper** concept is aimed at lowering overall costs while maintaining a competitive market-based, private sector infrastructure for super. The concept draws on and enhances an existing and well-known product (the default investment option). MySuper takes this product, simplifies it, adds scale, transparency and comparability, all aimed at achieving better member outcomes.[34]
>
> **SuperStream** is a package of measures designed to bring the back-office of superannuation into the twenty-first century. Its key components are the increased use of technology, uniform data standards, use of the tax file number as a key identifier and the straight-through processing of superannuation transactions.[35]

The Review reported Treasury estimates of short-term annual system savings of about $1.55 billion and long-term annual system savings of around $2.7 billion as a result of MySuper and SuperStream.[36] In the long run, a cut of around 40% in fees for the average member was expected, lifting their final superannuation balance by around $40,000 or 7% after 37 years in the work force.[37]

The Review also recommended an increased mandate for APRA, as well as measures to ensure that service providers, auditors and regulators support the self-managed superannuation fund ('SMSF') sector effectively. A new code of trustee governance was proposed, and industry fund boards were recommended to include independent members.[38] To assist members to make meaningful

33 These recommendation packages are provided in Parliament of Australia, above n 29, pt 2.

34 Detail of this recommendation is provided in Chapter 1, summarised in Parliament of Australia, above n 29 [5.1], 10–2.

35 Detail of this recommendation is provided in Chapter 9, summarised in Parliament of Australia, above n 29 [5.9], 17.

36 Modelling for the Review was carried out by the Australian Treasury, using assumptions as defined in Parliament of Australia, above n 29, Appendix C, 72. This modelling provided forecasts of the size and structure of the superannuation system in 2035. However, although the forecasts do assume implementation of the 'MySuper' proposals, and subsequent switching from existing funds, there was little empirical investigation of fees and charges in existing funds, or of the possible evolution of such fees and charges. Estimation of the reduction in operating costs (of up to $1 billion) which might be generated by the SuperStream proposals was based on submissions provided to the review, and this figure was used in the Treasury forecasts. However the '[T]reasury has not independently verified these cost reduction estimates': at 74, which also provides a listing of the submissions which provided such estimates.

37 Parliament of Australia, above n 29, 3.

38 Detail of this recommendation is provided in Chapter 2 (Trustee Governance) and Chapter 3 (Investment Governance), summarised in ibid. [5.2], 12–3.

choices standard product 'dashboards' and standardised investment performance reporting were also proposed.[39] Enhanced disclosure rules requiring each fund to provide free of charge on its website, detailed financial and operational information about the fund (including its portfolio holdings) and the fund's management were also recommended. The Committee envisaged that in future trustees would have a duty to address longevity, inflation and investment risks for retirement phase members in developing their strategies.[40]

The *Super System Review* 'Operation and Efficiency Issues' paper identified "much greater scope to improve system efficiency overall by refining and streamlining operational processes and reducing costs and leakages (including agency costs)"[41] and that these efficiencies may be achieved either by reducing costs or through lower profit margins.[42] The paper noted that "achieving efficiencies by this method is appropriate if there is evidence that competition between service providers is less than optimal",[43] and cited a recent survey in the United States which "found that fund sponsors were not fully aware of the fee revenues they sustained for fund managers, generally perceiving that managers earn between 10 per cent and 20 per cent less than they actually do".[44] The Issues Paper also identified that "inactive accounts in different default funds can expose members

Table A1 Super system review forecasts of growth in the Australian superannuation idustry

	1996	*June 2009*	*2035 (nominal)*	*2035 (current)*
Overall industry scale	**$245b**	**$1.1t**	**$6.1t**	**$3.2t**
Ratio of accumulation to post-retirement assets		4:1	3:1	3:1
Biggest fund		$41.5b	$350b	$187b
Number of large APRA funds (excluding ERFs)	4734	447	74	74
Average large APRA fund size	$40m	$1.5b	$53b	$28b
Average accumulation member balance	$15,000	$70,000	$335,000	$180,000
Total super assets – proportion of GDP	**47%**	**90%**	**130%**	**130%**

Source: Super System Review Panel, Review into the Governance, Efficiency, Structure and Operation of Australia's Superannuation System: Final Report (2010).

39 Detail of this recommendation is provided in Chapter 4, summarised in ibid. [5.4], 13–4.

40 Ibid. 1–2.

41 Ibid. 4.

42 Ibid. 5.

43 Ibid.

44 Callan Associates (2009) '2009 Investment Management Fee Survey' (September 2009), cited in ibid. 5.

to duplicated fees and charges".[45] A further issue is the amount of funds that are 'lost' and hence placed in eligible rollover funds (ERFs).[46]

The Super System Review Final Report provided the following forecasts for the Australian superannuation industry in 2035, including an expectation that assets would grow to $6.1 trillion in nominal terms or 130% of GDP.

Issues for the future raised by the Review included that the average fund will be much larger in real terms, with implications for fund governance, for investment strategy and for prudential regulation. The size of member account balances will put pressure on member transfer and remediation processes across the system and will increase concerns around identity theft and fraud and trustee accountability to members. Local funds will increasingly find themselves competing with large global funds.[47]

Financial System Inquiry 2014 (FSI)

A further inquiry into the financial system was commissioned by the Abbott government, under the chairmanship of David Murray.[48] The terms of reference were published on 20 December 2013.[49] First-round submissions were received by 31 March 2014, an interim report was published in July 2014, and second round submissions were received by 26 August 2014.[50]

The FSI interim report cited numerous reasons why competition had not exerted sufficient downward pressure on fees, including failure to exercise choice, lack of price awareness, agency and structural issues, complexity and 'frictions' in changing funds.[51]

The FSI took the view that

> There is little evidence of strong fee-based competition in the superannuation sector, and operating costs and fees appear high by international standards. This indicates there is scope for greater efficiencies in the superannuation system.[52]

The FSI also noted that the decline in fees over the past decade had been modest, given the economies of scale that the sector had achieved, citing in particular a

45 Parliament of Australia, above n 29, 8.

46 Ibid. [6.4.1] provides estimates that at 30 June 2008 some $12.9 billion of assets were in the Lost Member Register, across 6.4 million accounts.

47 Ibid. 6.

48 Previously Chief Executive Officer of Commonwealth Bank of Australia.

49 See http://fsi.gov.au/terms-of-reference/.

50 Over 280 first round submissions and 6,300 second round submissions were received (of which over 5,000 were on the issue of credit card surcharges and around 700 on the issue of "too big to fail' or "bail in", see http://fsi.gov.au/consultation/.

51 Commonwealth, above n 32, *Part One, Overview and Recommendations*, 7.

52 Commonwealth (2014) *Financial System Inquiry: Interim Report* (July 2014), xxiii.

submission from Industry Super Australia,[53] and expressed concern that long-term confidence and trust in the system was damaged by lack of stability in policy settings.[54] The FSI interim report noted that "views on the likely effectiveness of these [MySuper and SuperStream] reforms to reduce costs and fees are mixed".[55] The FSI sought views on whether the use of trust law as the basis for superannuation governance was appropriate, and noted that several submissions highlighted active investment strategies as a major contributor to costs and fees.[56] However, the FSI did not suggest radical reform of the 'way government intervenes in or regulates the financial system'.[57]

The subsequent (second round) submissions took issue with some FSI interim report conclusions, and included many suggestions for continued reform.[58] ANZ, for example, highlighted the different regulatory focus of the various agencies involved in superannuation (and argued for reconciliation of these differences and an increased role for self-regulation), the need for improvement to APRA and RBA data, and also difficulties created by limited financial literacy.[59] The SMSF Professionals Association of Australia does not believe that there are any problems over operating expenses for SMSFs, or that there is a need to establish minimum balance restrictions.[60]

The Centre for Law, Markets and Regulation (CLMR) recommended the creation of a 'Standing Regulatory Conference', and changes to the financial licensing regime, to improve market conduct.[61] Westpac recommended the creation of an independent statutory body to provide oversight and policy advice

53 Ibid. 2–102; Industry Super Australia (2014) 'First round submission to the Financial System Inquiry', 140. The FSI comments that fees have remained high partly because of a shift towards investing in higher cost asset classes, growth in member engagement services and investment in administration platforms.

54 Parliament of Australia, above n 52, 1–9.

55 Ibid. 2–106.

56 Ibid. 2–107. FSI provides Rice Warner estimates of fee differences of 45 basis points between MySuper funds which are predominately actively managed and those which are predominately actively managed, Ibid. 2–109.

57 Ibid. 1–3.

58 Although some submissions, for example that of Commonwealth Bank, regarded the status quo, including the extensive use of active management, as broadly acceptable: Commonwealth Bank (2014) 'Wellbeing, Resilience and Prosperity for Australia: Financial System Inquiry Final Submission' (August 2014). National Australia Bank (NAB) did not support the proposed default auction process: NAB (2014) 'NAB's Response to the Financial System Inquiry's Interim Report' (August 2014) 3. REST Industry Super argued the merits of active management and provided evidence of its own superior returns using the strategy: REST (2014) 'Financial System Inquiry (FSI) (August 2014).

59 ANZ (2014) 'Attachment to Response to the Interim Report of the Financial System Inquiry' (26 August 2014) 39 [Xxxvii, 3–121]; 10 [xx1, 2–68]; 33 [3–87].

60 SMSF Professionals Association of Australia (2014) 'Financial System Inquiry: SPAA Response to the FSI Interim Report' (August 2014) 4.

61 O'Brien, Justin and George Gilligan (2014) 'Submission to the Final Report process of the Financial System Inquiry' (CLMR, 20 August 2014), 6; 12.

on superannuation.[62] ASIC regards it as "timely to review fees and costs and the operation of fee-based competition for superannuation",[63] highlighting barriers to fee reduction caused by complexity and lack of transparency,[64] and also recommended further regulation of the financial reporting and audit of large superannuation funds.[65] The RBA supported continued focus on the cost and efficiency of the superannuation system, and measures to optimise liquidity management and limit leverage.[66] APRA argued that "overlap with other Australian regulators is minimal and respective roles are clearly delineated", citing the investigation carried out by the Regulation Taskforce in 2006.[67]

Unisuper focussed on the need for improved retirement products, and also recommended that the FSI focus on the Netherlands, Denmark and Canada as countries with well-functioning systems.[68]The AMP second-round submission to the FSI included an annex commissioned from advisory firm Towers Watson that explored, inter alia, fees, costs and the role of active management in Australian superannuation.[69] Towers Watson noted that there are many reasons why the headline costs reported, for example, in the Grattan Institute and OECD reports cited above may not be comparable with international experience. These include that reported administrative costs in Australia include some investment management costs, the existence of multiple accounts, benefit design differences, and regulatory and compliance costs.[70]

62 Westpac (2014) 'Second Submission to the Financial System Inquiry' (August 2014), 5.

63 ASIC (2014) 'Financial System Inquiry interim report: Submission by the Australian Securities and Investments Commission' (August 2014) 7 [25].

64 Ibid. 52 [212]. ASIC provide a long list of inconsistent fee disclosure practices, based on research reported in ASIC, Fee and cost disclosure: Superannuation and managed investment products (REP 398, 2014).

65 Ibid. 12 [53].

66 RBA (2014) 'Supplementary Submission to the Financial System Inquiry' (August 2014), 1, 2, 19.

67 APRA (2014) 'Financial System Inquiry: Response to the Interim Report' (26 August 2014), 60.

68 UniSuper (2014) 'Comments on the Financial System Inquiry's Interim Report' (26 August 2014), 4.

69 Towers Watson (2014) 'Information for Financial System Inquiry Submission' (26 August 2014, Annex to AMP, 'Financial System Inquiry: Comments on Interim Report').

70 Ibid. 19.

Annex C

The APRA database

APRA collect data on all superannuation funds they regulate through formal annual returns. Funds with greater than four members are analysed in APRA's 'Annual Superannuation Bulletin'. The latest version for the financial year ending June 2016 was published in February 2017.[1]

Detailed data, including asset value, income and expenses, for a subset of these superannuation funds is published annually. Some superannuation funds are listed in the APRA database but the data is 'blanked out' citing reasons of privacy and confidentiality.[2]

For the superannuation funds for which data is provided, the following data is provided at fund level:

Net assets at beginning of period	Investment management fees
Net operating performance after tax	Custodian fees
Net assets at end of period	Property maintenance costs
Total assets at end of period	Asset consultant fees
Total liabilities at end of period	Other investment expenses
	Total investment expenses
Employer contributions	Net investment income
Personal member contributions	Interest expense
Other contributions	Management fees
Total contributions	Administration fees
Contributions tax and surcharge	Actuary fees
Inward rollovers	Director/trustee fees and expenses
Outward rollovers	Total fees paid to audit firm

(continued)

1 Australian Prudential Regulatory Authority (2014) *Statistics: Superannuation Bulletin 2012* (Revised ed., 5 February 2014).

2 APRA has provided detail of the rules whereby data is withheld, which refers to the relevant funds being small, and also that confidentiality is required in some other cases because of recent or pending corporate activity.

(continued)

Net rollovers	Other operating expenses
Repatriation to employer sponsor	Total operating expenses
Lump sum benefit payments	
Pension benefit payments	
Total benefit payments	Other income
Net contribution flows	Fees and commissions
Total proceeds on insurance policies	Other income + Fees and commissions
Net cost of member benefit insurance	Reconciling item
Insurance policy proceeds – net cost of insurance	
Interest	
Dividends	Net earnings
Rent	Tax expense on earnings
Trust distributions	Net earnings after tax
Doubtful debts/bad debt expense	Cash flow adjusted net assets
	Rate of return (%)
Investment income/dist after doubtful debt expense	
Other investment income	
Investment income/dist after doubtful debt expense + Other investment income	
Total foreign exchange gains/losses (realised and unrealised)	
Total unrealised gains/losses on investments	
Total realised gains/losses on investments	
Total gains/losses on investments	
Total investment income	

Annex D

The synthetic benchmark model

The synthetic benchmark model is based upon data from various years' APRA 'Annual Superannuation Bulletin'.

In each year, i, net growth in actual fund assets, ag_i, is computed as:

$$ag_i = c_i + t_i - b_i + ar_i - o_i - ins_i + lo_i - e_i$$

where c = contributions net of tax and surcharge, t = net benefit transfers and rollover, b = benefit payments, ar = actual net investment return after tax, o = total reported operating expenses, ins = net insurance flows and other charges, lo = change in the balance of life office statutory funds and e = balancing item (principally unreported costs and other adjustments).

End year actual fund assets, af_i, are then computed as:

$$af_i = af_{i-1} + ag_i$$

The resulting f_i in each year is validated against relevant starting fund assets reported in the APRA statistics for the next year.

The benchmark growth, bg, for year i against which this growth is compared is calculated by

$$bg_i = c_i + t_i - b_i + br_i - FUM_i{*}0.01 - CF_i{*}0.005 - tax_{i-1}$$

where br_i is benchmark return, FUM_i is average funds under management in year i, CF is cash inflow for investment in year I and tax_i is estimated tax liability in the previous year. Operating and investment management costs are assumed to be 100 bps and commission on inflow of invested funds are assumed to be 50 bps.

The classes of assets used in the model are Australian equities, international equities, property, infrastructure, cash returns, fixed interest returns and private equity returns. The model permits portfolio allocation to be set as parameters by the user.

Benchmark return on invested funds is computed by summing estimated returns r across j asset classes as follows:

$$br_i = \Sigma_j h_j r_j FUM_i$$

where h_j = share of asset class in portfolio and r_j = change in accumulation index for asset class j during the year.

Taxation in year i, is computed as:

$$tax_i = br_j * t_j - fc_i$$

where t_j is the assumed tax rate on asset class j and fc_i are franking credits for year i. Assumed tax rates, t, are 5% for property, infrastructure and private equity (because these are assumed to be suitably optimised for tax), and 15% for international equities, cash and fixed interest, throughout the period.

Franking credits, fc_i, are calculated as $FUM_{Australian\ Equities} * ct_i * fp_i$, where ct is the corporate tax rate (30% throughout the period) and fp is the franking proportion (assumed to be 80%).

The rebate to be offset against other earnings, contributions tax and surcharge, fc = fp*ct. This is carried forward if not offset in year t.

End year benchmark fund assets, bf_i, are then computed as:

$$bf_i = bf_{i-1} + ag_i$$

Shortfall in year i, sf_i, which is the difference between the growth in assets under the benchmark scenario and actual growth in assets, is computed as:

$$sf_i = bg_i - ag_i$$

Overall shortfall over the twenty-year period is

$$\Sigma^1{}_{20}\ sf_i$$

It follows that final assets in year 20 under the benchmark scenario, bf_{20}, will be:

$$bf_{20} = af_{20} + \Sigma^1{}_{20}\ sf_i$$

Internal rates of return for both the actual and benchmark outcome, across time periods and types of fund, were calculated using Excel's XIRR function. This uses as inputs the initial overall assets at the beginning of the period, net cash flows (contributions and rollover less benefits) during the period, and the final assets at the end of the period.

Formally, XIRR may be specified as the IRR that satisfies the following equation over period n:

$$(-f1 + \Sigma^1{}_n\ ncf_j + f_n)/((1+IRR)^{((dj-d1)/365)}) = 0$$

where f_1 is the starting assets, ncf_j are net cash flows in each sub-period j, d_j is the mid-point date for each sub-period and d_1 is start date, and f_n is final assets.

Annex E

Variables available in the Rotman CEM data

The Rotman CEM data contains the following variables for each fund, on an annual basis:

Total fund size (millions) 31 Dec

Average total fund size

Total cost bp

Oversight of the fund bp

Trustee and custodial bp

Custody – foreign bp

Custody – domestic bp

Consulting and performance measurement bp

Audit bp

Other bp

Total overlay cost bp

Gross return

Policy return

Gross value added

Net value added

% sec. lending kept by custodian – domestic

% sec. lending kept by custodian – foreign

net sec. lending income – domestic

net sec. lending income – foreign

net sec. lending income – total

Members – active

Members – retired

Members – other

Members – other no accrual

Play type

Contractual inflation protection of benefits

Ad hoc inflation protection of benefits

Cap on inflation indexation/other notes

Percentage of liability associated with retired members

Liability discount rate

Salary progression rate

Expected rate of return

Average assets held in various types of stock, passive and active (including associated costs and returns)

Average assets held in various types of fixed income, passive and active (including associated costs and returns)

Average assets held in cash, TAA, Commodities, Infrastructure (fee paid and nav basis), limited partnership, fund of funds, REITs, Natural Resources, Real Estate, other real assets, hedge funds, private equity, venture capital, LBO (including associated costs and returns)

Notional value of derivatives/overlays, internal and external – currency hedge, discretionary currency, passive beta, duration, global TAA, policy tilt TAA, commodity futures, long/short, (including associated costs and profit/loss)

Investment costs for each type of asset (as listed above)

Benchmark stock indicators for each type of asset

External managers stock holdings, all types of asset

Annex F

Undisclosed costs in APRA data

The following summarises the data that is available at fund level, and the procedure that has been followed to identify remaining undisclosed costs. This is the residual between the movement in assets and the total change in assets implied by all recorded inflows to and outflows from the fund.

Note that this is only the costs directly incurred by the fund. Investment costs incurred by external managers are reflected in lower reported investment earnings and so are external to this computation.

Calculation of undisclosed costs	*In APRA spreadsheets*	*APRA codes*							
Change in net assets during year	A = K4 – I4	**Net assets at beginning of period ($'000)**		**Net assets at end of period ($'000)**					
		SRF 200.0 Item 22		**Item 12 SRF 210.0**					
Inflows: contributions and inward rollovers, fees and commissions	B = Q4 + S4 + BG4	**Total contributions ($'000)**		Inward rollovers ($'000)		Fees and commissions ($'000)			
		SRF 200.0 0 Item 1.5		**SRF 200.0 Item 2.1**		**SRF 200.0 Item 13.4**			
Investment income, proceeds on insurance policies, interest, dividends, rent, trust distributions, other income	C = AJ4 + AO4 + SUM (AD4:AG4) + AA4 + BF4	Other investment income ($'000)	**Total gains/ losses on investments inc. foreign exchange ($'000)**	Interest ($'000)	Dividends ($'000)	Rent ($'000)	Trust Distributions ($'000)	**Total proceeds on insurance p olic ies ($' 000)**	Other income ($'000)
		SRF 200.0 Item 14.1	**SRF 200.0 Item 11.3 & 12.11**	**SRF 200.0 Item 10.1**	**SRF 200.0 Item 10.2**	**SRF 200.0 Item 10.3**	**SRF 200.0 Item 10.4**	**SRF 200.0 Item 6.3**	**SRF 200.0 Item 15.1**

Outflows: lump sum, pensions, outward rollovers, contributions tax, surcharge, tax on investment income, insurance costs, repatriation, bad debts	D = −(T4 + V4 + W4 + X4 + R4 + BK4 + AB4 + AH4)	Outward rollovers ($'000) **SRF 200.0 Item 2.2**	**Repatriation to employer sponsor ($'000)** **SRF 200.0 Item 3**	Lump sum benefit payments ($'000) **SRF 200.0 Item 5.1 to 5.9**	Pension benefit payments ($'000) **SRF 200.0 Item 5.10**	**Contributions tax and surcharge ($'000)** **SRF 200.0 Item 4.3**	**Tax expense on earnings ($'000)** **SRF 200.0 Item 20**	**Net cost of member benefit insurance ($'000)** **SRF 200.0 Item 9**	Doubtful debts/ bad debt expense ($'000) **SRF 200.0 Item 10.6**
Reported Investment and Operating Expenses	E = −(AV4 + BE4)	**Total investment expenses ($'000)** **SRF 200. Item 17.6**				**Total operating expenses ($'000)** **SRF 200. Item 18.8**			
Unexplained shortfall (undeclared expenses?)	F = A − (B + C + D + E)								

Annex G

Data considerations and adjustments

The APRA database covers all larger APRA-regulated superannuation funds in Australia, while the CEM database is a selection of pension funds from the US, Canada and Europe. The selection process employed by CEM includes possible self-selection bias, as the funds are those that are willing to reveal a reasonably full set of data about costs and asset allocation.

Although the CEM database contains data for 6,129 fund-years, it only contains a full set of data for the period 2004 to 2012 for 114 pension funds, and these were the funds used for the calculations reported in Chapter 3.[1] So the final database used for international benchmarking consisted of 142 APRA superannuation funds and 114 pension CEM funds, a total of 256 funds.

A further difference between the APRA and CEM data is that the CEM data reports all costs, including the costs of investment management, while the APRA data only reports costs that are disclosed to APRA for regulatory purposes. These latter are the costs that are incurred internally by the superannuation funds, and do not include the costs of investment management or other activities when management of the assets is outsourced to a third party (including companies within the same group as the corporate trustee).[2] To make the data more comparable, it is necessary to estimate a proxy for the undisclosed investment costs of investment managers to whom the Australian superannuation funds delegate.

These costs form what Ellis, Tobin and Tracy term a 'drag' between gross and net returns.[3] They estimated the aggregate 'drag' to be 1.7% in the period 2001 to 2006, observing that the net return in their sample of large funds was 6% per annum, some 1.7% per annum below the pre-tax, pre-expenses benchmark return. On average, they assumed, funds' managers should at least match the benchmark on a gross basis, and hence the difference between benchmark return and that actually achieved provides a lower bound to the investment management and

1 Ten of the 114 CEM funds do not contain data on number of members. These funds were used for the DEA stage of the analysis, but were excluded from second-stage regression analysis which required this information.

2 As set out in Annex F.

3 Ellis K., A. Tobin and B. Tracey (2008) 'Investment Performance, Asset Allocation, and Expenses of Large Superannuation Funds' (APRA Working Paper, October 2008, and 3 *Insight* 2).

other costs incurred externally. However, although this procedure improves the estimate of investment costs somewhat, it still substantially under-estimates investment costs for those who achieve returns close to or in excess of the benchmark.

Cummings followed a similar procedure in his more recent exploration of economies of scale in 280 superannuation funds for the period 2004 to 2010, providing an estimate of average 'drag' of 1.96% per annum.[4] He disaggregated the drag estimate into both types and size of fund, noting that medium-sized funds have higher drag than the larger or smaller funds,[5] and that retail funds have higher drag (2.53%) than not-for-profit funds (1.42%).

In order to derive a proxy measure of total cost for the Australian superannuation funds, including investment management costs incurred by organisations to which the funds outsource, Ellis et al. and Cummings were followed, by deriving a measure of this additional 'drag' between net and gross returns by estimating, year-by-year, the benchmark return that could have been expected on the asset mix implied by the fund's policy settings in that year.[6] This was then compared with the actual return and the difference was interpreted as a proxy for the undisclosed investment costs, which are described as 'drag' in the literature. The average annual estimated 'drag' for the 142 Australian superannuation funds in our sample over the eight-year period (2004–2012) was 1.09%, a number lower than that estimated in the previous work.[7] It is, however, probable these costs are still underestimated, despite operating costs[8] being recorded as higher in the APRA data, as high charges levied by third parties are not fully reflected in the 'drag' estimates.

APRA data provides for each superannuation fund the average asset allocation of the default option in each year, for the classes of asset specified in A2 below. The table also shows the accumulation index (return plus dividends where relevant) that has been used for this class of asset. Most of these indices are readily available in the public domain. However, it was necessary to construct a combined Australian Residential and Commercial Property Index from ABS property price data[9] and rental yield data.

4 Cummings, James Richard (2012) 'The Effect of Fund Size on the Performance of Australian Superannuation Funds' (Working Paper, Australian Prudential Regulation Authority, March 2012). Cummings' analysis is restricted to accumulation-phase superannuation funds and hybrid superannuation funds. Funds with all members having defined benefits are excluded. The data cover superannuation funds with total assets of at least $50 million at the end of their most recent year of income.

5 Ibid. Table 4. The estimated drag for the fourth quintile by fund size was 2.11%.

6 For Australian funds the portfolio allocation of the default fund was used, and for CEM funds the policy settings as specified in the CEM database were maintained.

7 This difference may be attributable to the fact that the larger and more established funds were used in the analysis, many of which have more established in-house resources. 0.3% funds management costs were deducted from the benchmark estimates in order to reflect typical costs incurred by passively managed funds.

8 'Administration costs' were deducted from the total operating costs used for this purpose, as these include member administration costs, not covered in the CEM data.

9 Price Index of Established Houses; Weighted Average of 8 Capital Cities, from ABS Series A2333590K after 2005 and A2333613R prior to 2005.

Table A2 Asset classes and benchmark indexes used

Australian Equities	S&P/ASX All Ordinaries Accumulation index
International Equities	MSCI World ex-Australia Net Total Return
Listed Property	S&P/ASX Listed Property Trust Accumulation Index
Unlisted Property	Combined residential and commercial property overall yield (ABS, constructed)
Australian Fixed Interest	UBS Warburg Australia Corporate Bond Accumulation Index
International Fixed Interest	Barclays Capital Global Treasury Index ($ Hedged)
Cash	UBS Warburg Australia Bank Bill Accumulation Index
Other	As Australian Fixed Interest

The weighted average estimated 'drag' for the 142 'APRA' superannuation funds over the full period was calculated by estimating, year-by-year, the return that could have been expected on the asset mix employed by the fund in that year. This was then compared with the actual return and the difference was interpreted as in the work of Ellis et al. and Cummings. The average annual estimated 'drag' for the 146 funds over the eight-year period was 1.57%, a number consistent with that estimated in the previous work, albeit lower than either previous estimate.[10]

A further problem exhibited by the data for the 'APRA' superannuation funds is internal inconsistency. In 46 of the 142 funds, there is a discrepancy between the change in assets implied by the sum of all income and expenses, and the recorded movement in total assets. These entries were reconciled and an estimate of the remaining costs (which are not individually disclosed but which are reflected in the movement in fund assets) was created. The residual was added to administrative costs for comparison purposes.

Although the new method for estimating investment and other unreported costs is an improvement, it is probable that the process still underestimates these costs for APRA data. Nevertheless, the proxy estimated for investment costs is necessary given the current state of disclosure and data collection in Australia.

10 This difference may be attributable to the fact that the larger and more established funds were selected for analysis, many of which have more established in-house resources, and also that 0.3% fund management costs were deducted from the benchmark estimates.

Annex H

Different styles and types of regulation

This annex sets out the various ways in which regulation has been used, in various countries, to seek to control the principal-agent, conflict of interest and rent-seeking behaviour discussed in this book.

Principles-based regulation

Principles-based regulation seeks to use the regulatory framework to establish trust and responsibility.[1] Regulators define a framework of goals and expectations through the definition of principles. The regulated institutions are then responsible for ensuring that they develop the processes and practices to ensure that these goals are achieved. Often these processes involve a formalised risk management approach. Supervision relies on the institutions adopting appropriate governance arrangements, and requires firms to take responsibility for how they meet their regulatory responsibilities.[2] Senior management and boards remain responsible for assessing risk and making decisions about the balance between risk and return.[3] Thus supervision is mostly limited to evaluating whether internal systems and processes can in principle deliver the required outcomes, rather than assessing technical skills, encouraging efficiency and challenging risk models.[4]

The advantages of a principles-based approach are said to include greater flexibility and effectiveness, so that it is more adaptable to a changing environment. As firms are given the flexibility they need to run their businesses it minimises compliance costs.[5] In addition, regulatory principles are likely to be more accessible to senior management than thousands of complex rules.

1 Black, Julia (2008) 'Forms and Paradoxes of Principles Based Regulation' (Working Paper No. 13/2008, London School of Economics), 8.
2 Financial Services Authority, 'Principles-based Regulation: Focusing on the Outcomes that Matter' (FSA Report, April 2007), 12.
3 Financial Services Authority (2009) The Turner Review: a Regulatory Response to the Global Banking Crisis (FSA Report, March 2009), 87.
4 Ibid.
5 Black, above n 11, 7.

Thus principles-based regulation enables greater focus on the goals instead of diverting attention to detailed rules and adherence to the letter rather than the purpose of regulations.[6]

Principles-based regimes have been criticised for the ineffectiveness of governance arrangements, allowing firms to provide only minimal compliance, and for providing inadequate protection to customers.[7] The key question regarding the effectiveness of principles-based regulation, however, relate to ethics and to the trustworthiness of those who have responsibility for ensuring the principles are not breached. As was highlighted by Hector Sants (then CEO of the FSA), principles-based regulation relies on the presence of professional integrity and trust.

> . . . a principles-based approach does not work with people who have no principles.[8]

Rules based regulation

Rules based regulation involves the specification of detailed requirements, against which compliance is enforced. It is sometimes characterised as 'tick box regulation'. Rules-based regulation is strong on enforcement, and typically involves high regulatory and compliance costs. Rules-based regulation tends to be least effective where the products and services being provided are complex and lack transparency, because of the difficulty faced by regulators in defining appropriate rules and in identifying meaningful measures of whether requirements have been satisfied.

One issue with rules-based regulation is that the regulatory process can itself effectively 'kill ethics', if compliance is undertaken mainly through process management. This is because such regulation focuses on processes and not judgements, and turns compliance into a mechanical exercise. In addition, process management serves to make non-compliance an option to be considered, so that decisions depend on the likelihood and consequences of getting caught.[9] Therefore the fundamental question is how to embed the ethics required for a regulatory system to work effectively. History has shown both rules-based and principles-based systems have so far proved incapable of delivering the ethical restraint required for effective market integrity.[10]

6 Financial Services Authority, above n 12, 6.

7 Ibid. 3.

8 Sants, Hector (2009) 'Delivering Intensive Supervision and Credible Deterrence' (Speech delivered at the Reuters Newsmaker Event, London, 12 March 2009).

9 Black, above n 11, 34.

10 O'Brien, Justin (2011) 'The Price of Sophistication: Wholesale Investor Protection in the Aftermath of the Global Financial Crisis' (Paper presented at the Duty of Care in Finance Study Group, Balliol College, 15 June 2011), 3.

Outcomes-based regulation

Outcomes-based regulation involves measuring specific output measures and enforcing compliance with target levels. The outputs can be price- or quality-oriented. In traditional monopoly services, such as water supply or electricity distribution, the ability to make monopoly rents is limited by the application of price controls. However, such mechanisms rely on the quality of the service being provided being of a uniform standard and capable of clear definition. In financial services, the absence of the ability to measure or even define risk in a robust manner makes such an approach impractical. Instead, reliance is often placed on competition and disclosure to ensure the integrity of capital markets.

However, if sophisticated participants are unable to price risk, then disclosure is of limited usefulness.[11] As the *Turner Review* suggested for the UK, some form of direct product regulation may also be required to protect both retail and wholesale customers.[12]

For regulation to be effective, it is important for regulatory policy and institutions to have credibility. Further, this credibility needs to be maintained in periods of stability. It is sometimes suggested that regulators can use key performance indicators to 'inoculate' themselves against political pressures, using measures such as the balanced scorecard approach.[13] However, simplistic performance indicators can be misleading and/or self-seeking, and performance indicators can lead to skewed policy directions and ineffectiveness if used inappropriately. Indicators also need to be specific and objective in measuring progress.

However, the introduction of such regulation continues to meet with resistance. In the UK, the Sandler Report recommendations for simplified financial products were not implemented (even though the accompanying recommendation for simplified regulation was adopted). In the wake of the financial crisis, the concern to not inhibit financial innovation remains prevalent:

> . . . any undue hampering of the ability of bank boards to be innovative and to take risks would itself bring material costs. It would check the contribution of the banks to wider economic recovery and delay restoration of investor confidence in banking capable of generating reasonable returns for shareholders.[14]

Codes of conduct

Codes of conduct can be used to set the ethical standards of professional behaviour, and often form the basis of self-regulation. They cover the basic requirements

11 Ibid. 1.

12 Financial Services Authority, above n 13, 110.

13 O'Brien, Justin (2009) *Engineering a Financial Bloodbath* (Imperial College Press) 147.

14 Walker, Stan (Chair) (2009) *A Review of Corporate Governance in UK Banks and Other Financial Industry Entities* (Final Recommendations)., 6.

for establishing trust in a professional relationship, as for example in the legal and medical professions. Codes of conduct can be self-regulatory, or enforced by an external regulator. Cressey and Moore note that most of the codes that underpin self-regulatory activity in the US were written in the 1970s following the Watergate scandal and the departure of President Richard Nixon.[15] At the time, large public companies were keen to emphasise their social responsibility.[16] Business leaders feared that unless they took steps to 'put their own house in order', the public might demand restrictive regulation. The Cohen Commission emphasised the need for corporate executives to recognise the ethical standards, traditions, and concerns of society as well as company profits in order to reduce the 'substantial gap . . . between some corporate behaviour and society's view of appropriate corporate conduct'.[17]

Light-handed regulation

Experience of the last twenty years in Australia, combined with the revelations following the Lehman, Trio and Optus Prime scandals, suggests that light-handed, principles-based, regulation may not work well in this environment. It seems clear that more intrusive intervention, not least to ensure effective disclosure, is necessary in the shorter-term, with a single regulatory agency charged with improving efficiency and competition. In the medium-to-longer term, hopefully the role and competence of trustees can be developed, members can become more engaged, competition can be enhanced, and reputation be made more important to suppliers and agents. In this world, it may be possible to rely more on self-regulation and on the trustworthiness of those in the industry. Effective disclosure and robust governance systems will inevitably be required. The following Sections elaborate on what can be learned from the literature and recent experience to help guide appropriate regulatory design.

In the US, the Securities and Exchange Commission (SEC) and the Commodities and Futures Trading Commission (CFTC) followed a 'rules-based' approach to regulation, while until the GFC the UK's Financial Services Authority (FSA) followed a 'principles-based' one. The latter emphasised trust and responsibility, leaving it to financial services organisations to implement regulatory goals set by the regulator. As noted above, both approaches have been severely criticised – the former for its 'box ticking' and lack of flexibility; and the latter for trusting unprincipled and incompetent firms.

15 Cressey, Donald R. and Charles A. Moore (1983) 'Managerial Values and Corporate Codes of Ethics' 25(4) *California Management Review* 53. Their paper provides a useful survey of the motivations of those who established the codes of ethics at the time.

16 Fred T. Allen, a senior executive, was quoted in the *Wall Street Journal* (19 October 1975) as saying that "corporate officials were beginning to be perceived as 'little more than manicured hoodlums'".

17 Cohen, Manuel F. 'The Work of the Commission on Auditors Responsibilities' (Speech delivered at the Emanuel Saxe Distinguished Lectures in Accounting, City University of New York, 8 March 1977) http://newman.baruch.cuny.edu/digital/saxe/saxe_1976/cohen_77.htm.

A financial crisis usually leads to reform but as the following period of stability lengthens, public unease dissipates and arguments in support of the efficiency of markets become widespread. Concern about regulatory over-reach, judicial criticism and political pressure prompted by continued lobbying then weaken the restrictions imposed by regulation until the next crisis occurs.[18] In the UK, progressive de-regulation during the 1980s reflected belief in the power of markets and by 2007 the political environmental was unfavourable to any measures that tightened financial conditions.[19]

The prevailing view was that:

> The best guarantee of financial stability was that market participants had the interests of their investors and shareholders at heart, and those interests were far more powerful than any regulatory intervention.[20]

and in a speech in May 2005, UK Prime Minister Tony Blair characterised the FSA as:

> ..hugely inhibiting of efficient business by perfectly respectable companies that have never defrauded anyone.[21]

The Turner review in the UK accepted that, in the run-up to the GFC, the FSA:

> focused on individual institutions rather than the whole system; on systems and processes rather than the underlying risks in business models; on oversight of the probity of 'approved persons' rather than their competence; and on business rather than prudential regulation.[22]

Following the GFC, regulators on both sides of the Atlantic have signalled an intention to move towards a 'risk-based, outcomes focused' approach. However, this only works if both the risks that need to be avoided and the outcomes that are desired are defined adequately. As noted above, there are also dangers that a regulatory system based on outcomes can itself effectively kill ethics, if compliance is mostly undertaken through complex risk management and other models.

The direct control of principal-agent and conflict of interest problems by external regulators is difficult in a complex environment such as investment management. Even with adequate disclosure, it will always be the case that those directly involved in the management of a specific superannuation fund will know more about its intricacies than even a skilled and well-resourced regulator can. Trustees will also often struggle to have enough expertise and knowledge to

18 O'Brien, *Engineering a Financial Bloodbath*, above n 23, 109.
19 Davies, Howard (2010) *The Financial Crisis: Who is to Blame?* (Polity Press), 216.
20 Ibid.
21 Quoted in a letter by Callum McCarthy, Chairman of the FSA, to Tony Blair dated 31 May 2005.
22 FSA (Turner Review), above n 13.

outwit a determined rent-seeker. As a result it is worth exploring whether some form of self-regulation can be made to work in the longer term for Australian superannuation.

Self-regulation

Self-regulation is defined by David Garvin, in a seminal work on the subject, as occurring "when industry members jointly pursue regulatory or standard-setting activities in the absence of explicit legal requirements" and as relating to "the disclosure of product information, the policing of deceptive practices, the establishment of minimum standards of safety and quality, the grading of products, and the creation of industry codes of conduct".[23]

Self-regulation as a means of controlling principal-agent and conflict of interest problems has a long history in other countries. It has been estimated[24] that by the early 1990s 43% of industry associations in the US had codes of conduct.[25] Self-regulatory bodies in the UK include the London Stock Exchange (LSE)[26] and Committee of Advertising Practice (CAP);[27] and in the US the New York Stock Exchange (NYSE),[28] Financial Industry Regulatory Authority (FINRA), the International Securities Exchange (ISE), the Municipal Securities Regulatory Board (MSRB) and the American Arbitration Association (AAA). Historically, and in some countries today, self-regulatory bodies were the only forum for the resolution of some disputes. Canada, for example, has several national self-regulatory bodies for the securities market and does not have a national government-run securities regulator.[29] Rules resolving disputes

23 Garvin, David A. (1983) 'Can Industry Self-Regulation Work?' 25(4) *California Management Review* 37.

24 Hemphill, Thomas A. (1992) 'Self-Regulating Industry Behavior: Antitrust Limitations and Trade Association Codes of Conduct' 11 *Journal of Business Ethics* 917.

25 Nearly half of which were backed by some form of enforcement mechanism.

26 The Stock Exchange was established in London in the early 1800s with specific rules to prevent 'disorderly action' and thereby improve the reputation of its members. The first rulebook was issued in 1812, enforced by fines on members and the barring from its premises of anyone who was not a member. For current Stock Exchange rules see London Stock Exchange (2014) *Rules and Regulations*, available at www.londonstockexchange.com/traders-and-brokers/rules-regulations/rules-regulations.htm.

27 See Committee of Advertising Practice (2014) *Sanctions and Compliance*, available at www.cap.org.uk/Compliance.aspx for details of compliance processes and sanctions. The CAP uses the Office of Fair Trading (OFT) as a 'legal backstop' for cases that cannot be resolved through industry mechanisms. CAP provides codes of practice for both print and media advertising by the financial services industry. Previously, the UK had numerous self-regulatory bodies in the financial services sector, but most of these were absorbed into the FSA.

28 By 1920 the NYSE had a detailed set of rules for members as well as numerous by-laws.

29 The agencies are the Investment Dealers Association, Mutual Fund Dealers Association, Market Regulation Services and the Montreal Exchange; see ISCA (2006) 'Self-Regulation in Financial Markets: An Exploratory Survey' (ISCA, September 2006), 6. Policy development is carried out by provincial regulatory authorities.

between members at The Stock Exchange in London and at the New York Stock and Exchange Board were important in the nineteenth century since they provided the only dispute resolution mechanisms available for the enforcement of such transactions.[30]

Self-regulatory market practices have mostly emerged in the United Kingdom (and by extension, the Commonwealth) and the United States. In Continental European countries, legal systems generally demonstrate a preference for 'written law'. Tacit or overt delegation of authority or 'sharing' of regulatory responsibility with a government regulatory body is less common in modern Continental European legal culture.[31]

The UK has a long history of encouraging and utilising self-regulatory organisations (SROs) for financial services, and some UK legislation and institutional arrangements still require this. The White Paper that preceded the *Financial Services Act 1986* said that "self-regulation has a continuing and crucial contribution to make. It means commitment by practitioners to the maintenance of high standards as a matter of integrity and principle, not because they are imposed from outside."[32] Under Section 124 of the *Fair Trading Act*, the Director General of Fair Trading has a duty to 'encourage' trade associations to draw up and adopt codes that will safeguard and promote the interests of consumers.[33] The Association of British Insurers (ABI) has a code for the selling of general insurance that is monitored by an independent committee.[34]

Avner Greif suggests that self-regulation will only work when it includes explicit penalties and sanctions to prevent firms from free riding off others' efforts.[35] However, other commentators argue that the need for such sanctions can be reduced by informal means of coercion, the transferral of norms, and the diffusion of best practice.[36] In a more recent survey, King and Toffel observe that

30 See Banner, Stuart (1998) *Anglo-American Securities Regulation: Cultural and Political Roots, 1690–1860* (Cambridge University Press).

31 For further discussion, see Drezner, Daniel W. (2002) *Who Rules? The Regulation of Globalization*, available at www.danieldrezner.com/research/whorules.pdf; Jordan, Brook Cally (2005) 'The Conundrum of Corporate Governance' 983 *Journal of International Law* 1009.

32 This was published in January 1985 as a response to the Gower Report. The Gower Report was commissioned by the UK Government in 1981 to consider new legislation related to investor protection, investment advice and management, and consumer protection. Many of Gower's proposals were incorporated into the subsequent Financial Services Act 1986. Gower, Jim (1984) *A Report on the Protection of Investors* (UK Govt, 1984).

33 Office of Fair Trading (OFT) (1998) *Raising Standards of Consumer Care: Progressing beyond Codes of Practice*.

34 See National Consumer Council (2000) 'Models of Self-Regulation: an Overview of Models in Business and the Professions' (NCC, November 2000), 28.

35 Greif, Avner (1997) 'Microtheory and Recent Developments in the Study of Economic Institutions through Economic History', in D. Kreps and K. Wallis (eds), *Advances in Economic Theory and Econometrics (Volume II)* (Cambridge University Press) 79–113.

36 Nash, Jennifer and John Ehrenfeld (1997) 'Codes of Environmental Management Practice: Assessing Their Potential as a Tool for Change' 22 *Annual Review of Energy and Environment* 487.

firms are increasingly turning to self-regulatory institutions to solve environmental problems.[37]

Numerous other commentators emphasise the need for effective enforcement of self-regulatory rules.[38] In emerging industries, which still need to convince consumers about the value of their products, self-regulation can be quite popular, as unethical behaviour by one player can cause severe damage to others.[39] In such industries self-regulation can provide more accurate and reliable information on quality and reliability which can help to overcome buyer resistance.

37 King, Andrew and Michael W. Toffel (2007) 'Self-regulatory Institutions for Solving Environmental Problems: Perspectives and Contributions from the Management Literature' (Working Paper No. 07-089, Harvard Business School, July 2007).

38 See, e.g., de Jong, Abe, Douglas V. DeJong, Gerard Mertens and Charles E. Wasley (2004) 'The Role of Self-Regulation in Corporate Governance: Evidence and Implications from The Netherlands' (Working Paper No. FR 00-20, Simon School of Business).

39 For example information technology, telecoms and the media. The Software Business Practices Council in the US advanced this reason for its formation, see Santoro, Michael A. (1995) 'US Antitrust Laws' (Working Paper No. 9-395-215, Harvard Business School).

Index

For Product Safety Concerns and Information please contact our EU representative GPSR@taylorandfrancis.com
Taylor & Francis Verlag GmbH, Kaufingerstraße 24, 80331 München, Germany

www.ingramcontent.com/pod-product-compliance
Ingram Content Group UK Ltd.
Pitfield, Milton Keynes, MK11 3LW, UK
UKHW011010180926
475701UK00004B/656
* 9 7 8 0 3 6 7 5 9 1 8 3 0 *